T0300240

ROUTLEDGE LIBRARY EDITIONS:
ACCOUNTING

Volume 13

CORPORATE FINANCIAL REPORTING AND ANALYSIS IN THE EARLY 1900s

CORPORATE FINANCIAL REPORTING AND ANALYSIS IN THE EARLY 1900s

Edited by
RICHARD P. BRIEF

Routledge
Taylor & Francis Group

LONDON AND NEW YORK

First published in 1986

This edition first published in 2014
by Routledge
2 Park Square, Milton Park, Abingdon, Oxon, OX14 4RN

and by Routledge
711 Third Avenue, New York, NY 10017

Routledge is an imprint of the Taylor & Francis Group, an informa business

© 1986 Richard P. Brief

British Library Cataloguing in Publication Data
A catalogue record for this book is available from the British Library

ISBN: 978-0-415-53081-1 (Set)
eISBN: 978-1-315-88628-2 (Set)
ISBN: 978-0-415-87028-3 (Volume 13)
eISBN: 978-1-315-88646-6 (Volume 13)

Publisher's Note
The publisher has gone to great lengths to ensure the quality of this reprint but points out that some imperfections in the original copies may be apparent.

Disclaimer
The publisher has made every effort to trace copyright holders and would welcome correspondence from those they have been unable to trace.

CORPORATE FINANCIAL REPORTING AND ANALYSIS IN THE EARLY 1900s

Richard P. Brief, editor

Garland Publishing, Inc.
New York and London

For a complete list of Garland's publications in accounting,
please see the final pages of this volume.

Library of Congress Cataloging-in-Publication Data

Corporate financial reporting and analysis in the
early 1900s.

(Accounting thought and practice through the years)
Reprint of works originally published 1902–1911.
Bibliography: p.
1. Corporations—Accounting. 2. Corporation
reports. 3. Financial statements. I. Brief, Richard P.,
1933–   II. Series.
HF5686.C7C655 1986   657 s   [657'.3]   86-9897
ISBN 0-8240-7856-X

Design by Bonnie Goldsmith
The volumes in this series are printed on
acid-free, 250-year-life paper.
Printed in the United States of America

CONTENTS

INTRODUCTION

The early 1900s was a period in which accounting thought and the professional practice of accounting were rapidly developing in the United States. Many of the major accounting firms were organized, academic programs in accounting were initiated at some leading universities, and classic books by Montgomery, Sprague, Cole, and Hatfield were published. Many of these developments were influenced by British accountants, whose roots can be traced directly to the mid-nineteenth century, if not earlier.[1]

The turn of the century in the United States was marked by the formation of large trusts. Critics of these corporations called for greater publicity in corporate financial reporting to check their power. One of the first recommendations for improved financial reporting in the United States was made by Thomas W. Phillips, a member of the U.S. Industrial Commission, in its *Final Report*, reprinted in this volume.

Phillips not only called for detailed disclosure of a company's activities but also recommended a system of "public" auditing:

> First, each corporation should be required to make periodical reports of its business, supplemented by other reports upon official demand, all verified by the oaths of certain of its officers. Second, official examiners should also be maintained, who should, at irregular periods and without notice, appear at the offices of each corporation and make rigid examination of its affairs, using its books in the first instance but verifying the correctness thereof by every practicable method.

While many companies at this time did not issue detailed financial statements, there were some notable exceptions; early annual reports of several of these are reprinted here, including the 1902 annual report of the United States Steel Corporation, the 1909 annual report of the International Harvester Company, the 1910 annual report of the American Telephone & Telegraph Company, and the 1911 annual report of Westinghouse Electric & Manufacturing Company. This sample is not intended to be representative of the reporting practices of all large

American companies, but it does suggest that at least some companies (and there were others) believed that it was in their best interest to present detailed reports to their stockholders.

Why some companies were more advanced in their ideas of accountability is an interesting question and merits further study. Perhaps companies like U.S. Steel issued detailed annual reports in the belief that this information would reduce the perceived risk of creditors and shareholders and lower the cost of capital. Another explanation is that improved disclosure would satisfy demands for reporting by critics of big business and reduce political costs.

It should be emphasized that there is no special rationale for reprinting these particular annual reports other than the fact that each has several points of interest. Since few accountants are familiar with the evolution of financial reporting, it seemed like a good idea to make a few of these early reports more readily available.

U.S. Steel's annual reports have been the subject of several articles and books,[2] and its first annual report is a milestone in the history of financial reporting. The other annual reports also provide a glimpse into the state-of-the-art at this time. International Harvester's report is similar in format to that of U.S. Steel, but since both companies were under the influence of J. P. Morgan & Co., the similarity is not surprising.

The 1910 annual report of American Telephone & Telegraph is different from the rest. Unquestionably a public relations document, it contains some interesting material about depreciation, the nature of regulation and competition, and the early history of "Ma Bell."

The last item in this section is the 1911 annual report of Westinghouse Company, which Dewing described this way:[3]

> This annual report of March 31, 1911, is worthy of permanent preservation for its fulness, frankness, and the willingness of Mr. Mather to express opinions of the "worth" of the inventoried investments. It was his last report and shows clearly the foundation of a policy, the good results of which were just beginning to bear fruit. In its detailed completeness, the present writer knows not its equal among corporation reports. He has used it in his classes in "Corporation Finance" and "Accounting" as a model of this kind.

These remarks are in striking contrast to those of Ripley, a colleague of Dewing's at Harvard who was a well-known critic of the trust movement. He conveyed a much different impression when he wrote more than a decade later that "other striking examples of sealed situations of this period are the Westinghouse Company, which seems to have held no annual meeting for almost a decade prior to 1906 (1897–1905)."[4]

Even though the financial reports of many industrial companies were below these standards of reporting, the fact remains that many large corporations did publish financial statements at this time. The question that naturally arises, therefore, is how did analysts use them?

Thomas Warner Mitchell, one of the first to write on the subject of financial statement analysis, wrote a monthly column on the subject in *The Journal of Accountancy* from October 1906 until September 1907. The October 1906 column was not attributed to Mitchell but the others were. He also published a financial analysis of the regional railroads in the northeastern United States in the February 1909 issue of *The Journal of Accountancy*. Mitchell, who taught at the University of Pennsylvania, was the author of several articles dealing with corporate financial problems published in the *Quarterly Journal of Economics*.

Four of Mitchell's monthly columns, called "Reviews of Corporation Reports," and his article on railroads are reprinted in this volume as is the editorial in the October 1906 issue of *The Journal of Accountancy* that introduced the series. At the time, the editors of the journal were Joseph French Johnson and Edward Sherwood Meade, both honorary members of the American Association of Public Accountants. Since Meade wrote extensively on issues in corporate finance and also taught at the University of Pennsylvania, it is likely that he commissioned Mitchell to write these columns. Mitchell was a perceptive analyst, and his use of the funds statement to analyze a company's financial condition was clearly ahead of his time. According to Kafer and Zimmerman,[5] Mitchell was "probably the first to use the expression 'sources of funds' {which} did not, interestingly enough, come from practice but was the result of his financial statement analysis study." The study they refer to is Mitchell's first column on the Chicago and Northwestern Railway Company in October 1906.

Although this book is not a systematic study of corporate financial reporting and analysis in the early 1900s, it does provide some interesting anecdotal evidence on a subject that many accountants have not had the opportunity to review, and it may stimulate further research into the area.

NOTES

1. For further discussion of this episode in American accounting history, see Gary John Previts and Barbara Dubis Merino, *A History of*

Accounting in America (New York: John Wiley & Sons, 1979).

2. The latest book published on U.S. Steel's annual reports is Richard Vangermeersch, *Financial Accounting Milestones in the Annual Reports of United States Steel Corporation—The First Seven Decades* (New York: Garland Publishing, 1986). Vangermeersch's introduction briefly reviews these other studies.

3. Arthur Stone Dewing, *Corporate Promotions and Reorganizations* (Cambridge, Mass.: Oxford University Press, 1914), p. 200.

4. William Z. Ripley. *Main Street and Wall Street* (Lawrence, Kansas: Scholars Book Co., 1972). First published in 1927.

5. Karl Kafer and V. K. Zimmerman, "Notes on the Evolution of the Statement of Sources and Application of Funds," *The International Journal of Accounting* (Spring 1967), pp. 89–121. Reprinted in T. A. Lee and R. H. Parker, eds., *The Evolution of Corporate Financial Reporting* (Sunbury-on-Thames: Thomas Nelson and Sons, 1979). Reprint edition (New York: Garland Publishing, 1984).

An Early Proposal for
Corporate Financial Reporting

COMBINATIONS: STATEMENT OF MR. PHILLIPS

Recommendation As To Publicity

Many intolerable evils arising from the operations of corporations can be cured only when the public have full information concerning all their doings. This is imperatively demanded, and legislation should be enacted, both by Congress, for interstate commerce and under the general welfare clause, and by the several States, providing, for those coporations within their control, a rigid system of public accounting.

While the recommendations of the Commission on this subject are fully indorsed, they should be developed in greater detail in order to make them effective. For this reason the following amplification is submitted to serve as a guide in legislative enactment:

To be efficient a system of public accouting must adopt two separate methods. First, each corporation should be required to make periodical reports of its business, supplemented by other reports upon official demand, all verified by the oaths of certain of its officers. Second, offfical examiners should also be maintained, who should, at irregular periods and without notice, appear at the offices of each corporation and make rigid examination of its affairs, using its books in the first instance but verifying the correctness thereof by every practicable method. The reports of this offical should be made to a supervising official, and by him duly made public.

Systems of this kind are already in successful operation under the internal-revenue laws and the national-bank acts of the United States. Men who resort to questionable practices in corporation finance are held to a strict line of conduct when they engage in banking or when they manufacture those articles on which the Government levies internal taxes. If the Government protects itself by rigid supervision in such important matters, why should it not protect the people against the wrongdoing of corporations controlling vast industries. The Government grants privileges to corporations and should protect against their abuse. No business whose management is secret is entitled to the privileges of incorporation. The lines of supervision, inspection, and regulation already laid down in the internal-revenue laws and the national-bank act may well furnish models for adoption, whenever practicable, in the inspection of industrial corporations. A system of inspection outlined in the following recommendations will not only make discriminations and other unlawful methods more difficult and less probable, but will also facilitate other methods of regulation, should they be necessary.

The legislation proposed should embody the following details:

As to reports. - 1. Every corporation governed by the act should make annual reports to an officer provided for in the act, who is hereinafter designated as an auditor.

2. The report shall in all cases include -

(a) Capital authorized and issued, the amount paid up in cash or otherwise, with a statement of the method of payment, where it is not in cash.

(b) Debts, including details as to amount thereof, and the security given therefor, if any.

(c) Obligations due from officers should be separately stated.

(d) A statement of the method of valuing assets, whether at cost price, by appraisal, or otherwise, and of the allowance made for depreciation.

(e) Gross earnings for the period covered by the report, all deductions necessary for interest, taxes and expenses of all sorts, the surplus available for dividends, and dividends actually declared.

(f) The increase in assets since the last statement, with a showing in what way such increase has been secured.

(g) The names and addresses of stockholders, with the number of shares held by each at the date of the report.

(h) The amount of property taken for stock at any time previously and sold since the date of the last report, with all facts necessary to show the result of the transaction.

(i) A statement showing that the corporation in question has not, during the period covered by said report, received any rebates, drawbacks, special rates or other discriminations, advantages or preferences, by money payments or otherwise from any railroad, pipe line, water carrier, or other transportation company. Or if any such have been received or given, stating when, from whom, on what account, and in what manner they were so received, with all other details necessary to a full understanding of the transaction or transactions.

(j) The names and addresses of all offices, location of transfer or registry offices, wherever located.

(k) A statement that the corporation has not fixed prices or done any other act with a view of restricting trade or driving any competitor out of business.

(1) A statement of the proportion of goods going into interstate commerce.

3. The auditor shall prescribe the form of the reports and the matters to be covered thereby, in addition to those stated under No. 2 above. He may, in his discretion, require additional reports at any time when he may see fit on reasonable notice. But his determination shall be prima facie proof that the notice given is reasonable.

4. He may also require supplemental reports whenever, in his judgement, the report rendered is, in any particular or particulars, insufficient, evasive, or ambiguous.

5. In case of assets, small items of personal property included in a plant or organization may be described by the term "sundries" or like general term. The auditor may prescribe rules so as to avoid undue detail in making lists, yet prevent the abuse of this provision.

6. No detail of the business of the corporation shall be considered private so as to be exempt from the examination of the auditor, whenever he may demand report thereon.

7. The auditor shall make public in his reports, which shall be issued annually, all the information contained in the reports so made to him. When a report has been made, and, with

all supplemental and additional reports required by the auditor, shall have been approved by him, the corporation making such reports shall publish them in some newspaper or newspapers, after the usual custom in such cases, with the auditor's minute of approval, and shall file with the auditor proof of such publication by the publisher's certificate.

8. If any corporation shall fail to make a report when required, either by the terms of this act or when required by the auditor, as hereinafter provided, said corporation shall be fined not less than [amount left blank] dollars for each offense. Every day of failure after a written demand has been made by the auditor shall constitute a separate and distinct offense. In case of failure, also, each of the directors of the said corporation shall be ineligible, for the year succeeding the next annual meeting, to hold either directorship or any other office in the said corporation. But any director shall be exempt from said penalty upon making a showing that he had individually made such report as he was able from the facts at his disposal.

9. If such report is false in any material respect, the corporation shall be fined not less than [amount left blank] dollars and not more than [amount left blank] dollars, and each false statement in any material matter shall constitute a separate offense.

As to examinations. - 1. Expert accountants shall be provided for, to whom shall be paid a salary and necessary expenses. These shall be under the direction of the auditor, and may be sent by him to make examination of any corporation.

2. Any of said examiners presenting his official credentials shall be furnished by the officers of the corporation every facility for complete and full examination, not only of the books, but of all the property, records, or papers of the corporation, which may be necessary, in the judgement of the examiner, for a complete knowledge of the affairs of the concern.

9

3. Such examinations shall not be at fixed periods, but shall be at such times as the auditor shall fix and without notice.

4. Examiners shall have the power to examine under oath all officers or employees of a corporation, or any other persons having any knowledge of its affairs, and to send for, demand, and inspect books, papers, and any other matter of evidence whatever which is in the possession or control of the said corporation. The act shall provide for a process by attachment in some appropriate court to enforce the authority of the examiner.

5. The auditor shall likewise have all the authority of an examiner in any case wherein he chooses himself to act.

6. No examiner shall be assigned to examine any corporation who is himself interested in the business thereof, or of any competing concern, or who has relatives who are so interested.

7. Any blackmailing or receiving of bribes by any examiner or by the auditor shall be duly punished.

8. It shall be unlawful for an examiner to divulge private business except by his report to the auditor. But such report, or the substance thereof, shall be open to public inspection.

10()

9. Each examiner shall follow the rules, regulations, and directions which the auditor may, from time to time, lay down or communicate to him as to the method of examination, the form of report, the matters to be covered by the said examination, and all other matters pertaining to his duties.

10. Said examination and reports shall always cover, among others, the following questions:

(a) Has the said corporation, during the period covered by the examination and report, received any rebates, drawbacks, special rates, or other discriminations, advantages, or preferences, by money payments or other, from any railroad, pipe line, water carrier, or other transportation company?

(b) If there have been such preferences, when were they received, from whom, on what account, and in what manner, giving all details necessary to a full understanding of the transactions?

(c) Is the said corporation a member of any combination having or intending to secure a monopoly of any commodity other than such monopolies as are legally granted by patent or otherwise?

(d) Has the said corporation any such monopoly, or does it use methods tending and intending to secure such monopoly?

(e) Has it made any contracts or agreements tending to secure any such monopoly to itself or any other concern, whether owned by an individual or individuals, a corporation, or some combination of individuals and corporations?

11. Said reports of examiners shall be prima facie true and may be introduced in evidence in all courts to prove the facts therein set forth. Copies certified by the auditor shall be admissible with like effect and under the same circumstances as the original.

12. Reports to be made to [left blank] and full authority to be given to enforce by appropriate provisions the foregoing requirements.

Some Notable Corporation Reports

FIRST ANNUAL REPORT

OF THE

United States Steel Corporation

FOR THE FISCAL YEAR ENDED

DECEMBER 31, 1902

DIRECTORS

16

FIRST ANNUAL REPORT

TO STOCKHOLDERS OF

United States Steel Corporation

OFFICE OF UNITED STATES STEEL CORPORATION,
51 Newark Street, Hoboken, New Jersey.
April 6, 1903.

To the Stockholders:

The Board of Directors submits herewith a combined report of the operations and affairs of the United States Steel Corporation and its Subsidiary Companies for the fiscal year which ended December 31st, 1902, together with the condition of the finances and property at the close of that year.

INCOME ACCOUNT FOR THE YEAR.

The total net earnings of all properties after deducting expenditures for ordinary repairs and maintenance (approximately $21,000,000*), also interest on Bonds and fixed charges of the subsidiary companies, amounted to.. .... $133,308,763.72

Less, Appropriations for the following purposes, viz.:

Sinking Funds on Bonds of Subsidiary Companies.........................	$624,064.43	
Depreciation and Extinguishment Funds (regular provisions for the year)....	4,834,710.28	
Extraordinary Replacement Funds (regular provisions for the year)..........	9,315,614.76	
Special Fund for Depreciation and Improvements.........................	10,000,000.00	
		24,774,389.47
Balance of Net Earnings for the year.............		$108,534,374.25

* The actual expenditures for ordinary repairs and maintenance, as see table on page 7, were $21,230,218 13   It cannot be stated, however, that this specific sum was taken out of the net earnings for the year because in the manufacturing and producing properties the expenses for repairs and maintenance enter into and form a part of production cost. And as the net earnings of such properties are stated on the basis of gross receipts for product shipped less the production cost thereof, the income for the year is charged with outlays for repairs and maintenance only to the extent that the production during such period was actually shipped But as the shipments in 1902 equaled practically the year's production, approximately the entire amount of the expenditures in question has been deducted before stating the net earnings as above.

Balance of Net Earnings for the year, brought forward $108,534,374.25

Deduct.

Interest on U. S Steel Corporation Bonds for the year $15,187,850.00

Sinking Fund on U S Steel Corporation Bonds for the year 3,040,000.00
                                                                      ———————
                                                                      18,227,850.00

Balance $90,306,524.25

18

Dividends for the year on U S Steel Corporation Stocks, viz.:

Preferred, 7 per cent $35,720,177 30

Common, 4 per cent 20,332,690 00
                                                         ———————
                                                         56,052 867 30

Undivided Profits or Surplus for the year $34,253,656 75

UNDIVIDED SURPLUS OF U. S. STEEL CORPORATION AND ITS
SUBSIDIARY COMPANIES.

(Since Organization of U. S. Steel Corporation, April 1, 1901.)

Surplus or Working Capital provided at organization.. .. . . $25,000,000.00

The Surplus arising from operations for the nine months ended December 31, 1901,

as reported was .   .   . $19,828,827 14

Add, Profits during this period of properties owned but not heretofore included   375,627 86
                                                                      ———————
                                                                      $20,204,455 00

Less, Written off in 1902 to Cost of Property and for adjustment of sundry contracts

and accounts 1,583,514 70
                                                         ———————
                                                         18,620,940.30

Surplus for the year 1902, as above 34,253,656.75

Total Surplus, December 31, 1902   . ... $77,874,597 05

6

NET PROFITS AND SURPLUS OF UNITED STATES STEEL CORPORATION AND SUBSIDIARY COMPANIES AT CLOSE OF EACH OF THE QUARTERS NAMED.

(INCLUDES ONLY SURPLUS RECEIVED OR EARNED ON OR SUBSEQUENT TO APRIL 1ST, 1901.)

Quarter Ending	Net Profits for Quarter Available for Dividends	Surplus at Close of Quarter before Declaration of Dividends *	Dividends on U S Steel Corporation Stock for Respective Quarters.	Balance of Surplus
June 30th 1901	$19,907,277 28	$44,907,277 28	$13,957,028 25	$30,950,249.03
September 30th 1901	20,066,626 25	51,013,875 28	14 010,277 75	37,003,597 53
December 31st, 1901	20,629,205 52	57,632 803 05	14,011,862 75	43,620,940 30
March 31st, 1902	16,760,221 26	60,321,161 56	14 013,434 23	46,307,727 31
June 30th, 1902	26 742 277 86	73,050,005 17	14,013 542 75	59,036 462 42
September 30th, 1902	25 849,817 58	84,896,280 00	14,012 946 25	70,873,333 75
December 31st, 1902	21,014,207 35	91 887,541 30	14,012,944 25	77 874 597 05

* Includes Capital Surplus of $25 000 00, provided at date of organization.

NOTE.—Special Depreciation and Improvement Fund of $10 000,000, set aside from 1902 Net Earnings, is distributed in above table, $2,500,000 to each quarter of 1902.

MAINTENANCE, RENEWALS AND EXTRAORDINARY REPLACEMENTS.

The physical condition of the properties has been fully maintained during the year, the cost of which has been charged to current operations. The amount expended by all properties during the year for maintenance, renewals and extraordinary replacements aggregated $29,157,010.73

This total is apportioned as follows:

Expended on	Ordinary Maintenance and Repairs *	Extraordinary Replacements †	Total.
Manufacturing Properties	$16,099,217.94	$6,978,230.48	$23,077,448.42
Coal and Coke Properties	881,804.77	94,664 39	976,469.16
Iron Ore Properties	355,220.12	....	355,220.12
Transportation Properties:			
Railroads	3,544,654.27	607,967.88	4,152,622.15
Steamships and Docks	313,801.37	102,317.80	506,119.17
Miscellaneous Properties	35,519 66	53,612.05	89,131.71
Total	$21 230,218 13	$7,926,792.60	$29,157,010 73

* See explanatory footnote on page 5
† These expenditures were paid from funds provided from earnings to cover requirements of the character included herein, as more fully explained on page 8

7

SINKING, DEPRECIATION AND EXTRAORDINARY
REPLACEMENT FUNDS.

Provisional charges are made monthly to operations for Bond Sinking Funds and to establish funds for Depreciation, and for reserves for Extraordinary Replacements. The purposes for which these funds are particularly designed are as follows:

BOND SINKING FUNDS.—These are the funds required by the respective mortgages to be set aside annually for retirement of the bonds issued thereunder.

DEPRECIATION AND EXTINGUISHMENT FUNDS.—The appropriations for these purposes have been made with the idea that thus aided the bond sinking funds will liquidate the capital investment in the properties at the expiration of their life These moneys are used not for current operating expenses, but to offset consumption and depreciation by the provision of new property or of reserve funds.

EXTRAORDINARY REPLACEMENT FUNDS.—These are designed to be used to improve, modernize and strengthen the properties. They are not used for ordinary maintenance, repairs and renewals (such expenses are included in current operating costs), but for the substitution of improved and modern machinery, plants, facilities, equipment, etc.

During the year ended December 31, 1902, the appropriations made for the foregoing funds, together with the payments therefrom, and the balances in the funds at the close of the year, were as follows:

FUNDS	CREDITS TO FUNDS.			PAYMENTS FROM AND CHARGES TO FUNDS.		Balances to Credit of Funds Dec 31, 1902.
	Balance December 31, 1901.	Set Aside from Earnings during 1902	Total.	Payments to Trustees of Sinking Funds	Other Payments and Charges.	
Sinking Fund on United States Steel Corporation Bonds	$1,773,333 33	$3,040,000 00	$4,813,333 33	$3,040,000 00	......	$1,773,333,33
Sinking Funds on Bonds of Subsidiary Companies	157,344 36	624,064 43	781,408 79	564 064 43	......	217,344,36
Total Bond Sinking Funds	$1,930,677 69	$3 664,064 43	$5,594,742 12	$3,604,064 43	...	$1,990,677,69
Depreciation and Extinguishment	8,884,756.84	4,834,710 28	13,719,467 12	...	$12,011,856.33 (a)	1,707,610.39
Extraordinary Replacement	5,052,388 74	9,315,614 76	14,368,003.50	......	7,801,812 60 (b)	6,566,190.90
Special Depreciation and Improvement	......	10,000,000 00	10,000,000 00	......	......	10,000,000.00
Total.	$15,867,823.27	$27,814,389.47	$43,682,212 74	$3,604,064 43	$19,813,669 13	$20,264,479.18

(a) Construction Expenditures charged off to Depreciation and Extinguishment Funds.
(b) Expended for Extraordinary Replacements $7,926,702 60
    Less Miscellaneous Receipts credited to Extraordinary Replacement Fund 124,930 00

Net $7,801,862.60

8

The balances to the credit of the several funds on December 31, 1902, per the preceding table, are included in the current assets of the organization, viz.:

In General Cash $1,773,333.33
In Current Assets—Cash, Marketable Securities, Inventories, etc. 18,491,145.85

Total $20,264,479.18

TRUSTEES OF BOND SINKING FUNDS.

FUNDS.	Cash on Hand Dec 31, 1901	Instalments Received in 1902	Interest Accretions Received in 1902	Total.	BONDS REDEEMED		Cash on Hand Dec. 31, 1902.
					Par Value of Bonds	Premium Paid on Same	
U S Steel Corporation Bonds.	......	$3,040,000.00	$39,645.65	$3,079,645.65	$2,698,000	$373,498.61	$8,147.04
Subsidiary Companies' Bonds	$245,319.38	564,064.43	58,715.29	868,099.10	417,000	......	451,099.10
Total	$245,319.38	$3,604,064.43	$98,360.94	$3,947,744.75	$3,115,000	$373,498.61	$459,246.14

Total redeemed bonds, at par, held by Trustees on December 31, 1901 .... $907,000
Redeemed in 1902 as above 3,115,000

Total December 31, 1902 .... $4,022,000

BALANCE SHEET.

The Balance Sheet included in this report, page 24, exhibits the combined assets and liabilities of the United States Steel Corporation and of the Subsidiary Companies, based on the valuation at which the stocks and bonds of the Subsidiary Companies were taken over by the Steel Corporation, liabilities from one company to another company being omitted.

The accounts of the Steel Corporation and the Subsidiary Companies for the year 1902 have been audited by Price, Waterhouse & Company, the chartered accountants selected for this purpose by the stockholders at the annual meeting, February 17, 1902. The certificate of the chartered accountants is printed in full on page 24.

VOLUME OF BUSINESS.

The volume of business done by all companies during the year, including sales between the companies, and the gross receipts of transportation and miscellaneous properties, aggregated the total sum of $560,510,479.39.

PRODUCTION.

The production of the several properties for the year 1902 was as follows:

IRON ORE MINED:

		Tons.	Tons.
From Marquette Range...		1,487,370	
From Menominee Range		2,675,754	
From Gogebic Range		2,064,492	
From Vermilion Range		2,057,537	
From Mesaba Range		7,778,026	
			16,063,17

COKE MANUFACTURED.. 9,521,56

COAL MINED, not including that used in making coke....... 709,36

BLAST FURNACE PRODUCTS:

Pig Iron	7,802,812	
Spiegel	128,265	
Ferro-Manganese and Silicon	44,453	
		7,975,53

STEEL INGOT PRODUCTION:

Bessemer Ingots	6,759,210	
Open Hearth Ingots	2,984,708	
		9,743,91

ROLLED AND OTHER FINISHED PRODUCTS FOR SALE.

	Tons.
Steel Rails	1,920,786
Blooms, Billets, Slabs, Sheet and Tin Plate Bars	782,637
Plates	649,541
Merchant Steel, Skelp, Shapes, Hoops, Bands and Cotton Ties	1,254,560
Tubing and Pipe	744,062
Rods	109,330
Wire and Products of Wire	1,122,809
Sheets—Black, Galvanized and Tin Plates	783,576
Finished Structural Work	481,020
Angle and Splice Bars and Joints	139,954
Spikes, Bolts, Nuts and Rivets	42,984
Axles	136,787
Sundry Iron and Steel Products	29,177
Total	8,197,232
Spelter	23,982
Copperas	14,224
	Bbls.
Cement	486,357

INVENTORIES.

The aggregate inventories of all properties on December 31, 1902, equaled the total sum of $104,390,844. About one-third of this sum is represented by the value of iron ore on hahd. It is necessary to accumulate large tonnages of ore during the summer and fall months for conversion during the period extending from December 1 to April 15 when, owing to the close of navigation on the Great Lakes, the mining of ore is reduced and shipment from the mines entirely stopped.

The quantities of partly finished materials (Blooms, Billets, Bars, etc.), also of finished products, are somewhat above the normal average, owing largely to the railroad congestion at principal producing centres, which prevented prompt deliveries from the mills.

Inventories are taken on basis of actual cost of the materials and products at the several departments of the companies holding the same.

The following is a general classification of the inventories on December 31:

Ores	$34,072,939
Pig Iron, Scrap, Spiegel and Ferro......................................	6,294,358
Coal and Coke...	858,820
Pig Tin, Lead and Spelter..	1,362,466
Limestone, Fluxes and Refractories.....................................	969,203
Rolls and Molds and Stools..	2,359,505
Manufacturing Supplies, Stores and Miscellaneous items not otherwise classified..............	10,299,689
Ingots, Blooms, Billets, Sheet and Tin Plate Bars, Skelp, Rods, etc........................	12,824,909
Finished Products...	18,968,396
Mining Supplies and Stores..	1,866,125
Railroad Supplies and Stores..	1,165,374
Material, labor and expense locked up in bridge and structural contracts, including estimated profit thereon.. $27,443,409	
Less bills rendered on account.. 17,447,810	
	9,995,599
Material in transit and on consignment	3,353,461
Total	**$104,390,844**

CAPITAL STOCK.

The outstanding capital stock of the United States Steel Corporation was increased during the year by the issues of the following amounts for the acquisition of additional shares of capital stock of the subsidiary companies surrendered for exchange, viz.:

Common Stock issued... $75,200

Preferred Stock issued... 75,500

The total capital stock of the United States Steel Corporation issued and outstanding on December 31, 1902, was as follows:

Common Stock.............................. ....……….....… $508,302,500

Preferred Stock....... 510,281,100

BONDED, DEBENTURE AND MORTGAGE DEBT.

At the beginning of the year the bonded and mortgage debt of the United States Steel Corporation and Subsidiary Companies in the hands of the public was............................. $366,097,697.82

Issues were made during the year by the several companies, as follows, viz.:

Bessemer & Lake Erie R R. Co., Erie Equipment Trust Bonds............. $1,220,000.00

Pittsburg, Bessemer & Lake Erie R.R. Co. Debenture Gold Bonds, total issue

$500,000 (Carnegie Company proportion)............................... 260,895.00

Elgin, Joliet & Eastern Ry. Co. First Mortgage Bonds 648,000.00

Duluth, Missabe & Northern Ry Co. Con. Second Mortgage Bonds......... 75,000.00

Sundry Real Estate Mortgages assumed by Coke Companies 166,443.35

2,370,338.35

$368,468,036.17

Less, retired or acquired during the year, viz.:

The Johnson Co (of Pa.) First Mortgage Bonds........................... $95,000.00

National Steel Co.'s issues:

Ohio Steel Co., First Mortgage Bonds................................ 80,000.00

Junction Iron & Steel Co, Mortgage Bonds........................... 35,000.00

Shenango Valley Steel Co. Mortgage Bonds........................... 150,000.00

Raney & Berger Iron Co., Mortgage Bonds........................... 80,000.00

American Tin Plate Co. issues:

U. S. Iron & Tin Plate Mfg. Co., Mortgage Bonds.....................	$55,000.00
American Bridge Co., Purchase Money Mortgage Bonds....................	100,000.00
South-West Connellsville Coke Co., Mortgage Bonds........................	36,000.00
Continental Coke Co., Purchase Money Mortgage Bonds...................	37,000.00
H. C. Frick Coke Co., First Mortgage Bonds.............................	91,000.00
H. C. Frick Coke Co., Purchase Money Mortgage Bonds...................	150,000.00
Hostetter-Connellsville Coke Co., Purchase Money Mortgage Bonds (H. C. Frick Coke Co proportion)......................................	12,500.00

Pittsburg, Bessemer & Lake Erie R. R. Co. Bonds (Carnegie Company proportion):

Car Trust Warrants...	17,639.40
Conneaut Equipment Trust..	26,089.50
Bessemer Equipment Trust..	39,134.25
Illinois Steel Co , Debenture Scrip..............................	1,418.55
Sundry real estate mortgages of various companies...................	691,795.63
Total Bonds and Mortgages paid and canceled....................	$1,697,577.33

Bonds purchased by Trustees of Sinking Funds for investment therein, viz.:

U. S. Steel Corporation, 50 Year Gold Bonds......	$2,698,000.00	
Duluth, Missabe & Northern Ry. Con. First Mortgage.........	83,000.00	
Duluth, Missabe & Northern Ry. Con. Second Mortgage.......	151,000.00	
American Steamship Co., First Mortgage....................	183,000.00	
		3,115,000.00
		4,812,577.33

Bonded, Debenture and Mortgage Debt in hands of Public, December 31, 1902......... $363,655,458.84

Net Decrease during the year... $2,442,238.98

In addition to the foregoing transactions in bonds there were surrendered for exchange $207,000 of

13

The Carnegie Company Collateral Trust Bonds, and in lieu of which an equal amount of United States Steel Corporation 5 per cent. Fifty Year Gold Bonds was issued.

The amount of bonds and mortgages retired, $4,812,577.33, was paid from sinking and depreciation fund provisions and surplus earnings. Since the organization of the United States Steel Corporation, April 1, 1901, to January 1, 1903, the amount of bonds and mortgages paid and retired by all properties, including bonds purchased for sinking funds, was $6,384,758 75. There were issued during this same period bonds and mortgages for new property acquired to the amount of $3,456,659 76, a net decrease of $2,928,098 99.

A detailed schedule of the bonds of the several properties issued and outstanding in hands of public on December 31, 1902, will be found on page 27.

PURCHASE MONEY OBLIGATIONS, BILLS PAYABLE AND SPECIAL DEPOSITS.

The unsecured liabilities of the Subsidiary Companies of the above character were reduced during the fiscal year of 1902, and also during the period from April 1, 1901 (date of organization of U. S. Steel Corporation), to December 31, 1902, by the following respective amounts, viz.:

	Paid Off Between April 1, 1901, and December 31, 1901.	Paid Off During Year of 1902	Total Reduction, April 1, 1901, to December 31, 1902
Purchase Money Obligations and Bills Payable...........	$8,678,836 01	$12,884,558 85	$21,563,394.86
Special Deposits.	2,369,134 56	767,809 09	3,136,943.65
Total	$11,047,970 57	$13,652,367 94	$24,700,338.51

The funds for the payment of the above liabilities were provided entirely from the surplus net earnings of the organization—no new capital or bonded or other liability has been created in lieu thereof, although practically all of such payments might properly be funded, as the liabilities were those of the Subsidiary Companies prior to or at the time of organization of U. S. Steel Corporation for the acquirement of additional property or for moneys borrowed, which were in turn used for purchase of property and construction expenditures.

As shown by the General Balance Sheet, the amount of these liabilities outstanding on December 31, 1902, is as follows:

Purchase Money Obligations...	$6,689,418.53
Bills Payable	6,202,502.44
Special Deposits....	4,485,546.58
Total	$17,377,467.55

14

PROPERTY ACCOUNT.

The expenditures made during the year by all the properties and charged to Property Account equaled, less credits for property sold, the total sum of $16,586,531.77. These outlays were made for the completion of construction work at manufacturing properties under way when the U. S. Steel Corporation was organized, also for necessary additions and extensions authorized since its organization, for the acquirement of additional ore and coal property, the opening and development of new mines and plants, for additional equipment and facilities demanded by the growing requirements of the business of the transportation properties, to secure material reduction in cost of manufacture, transportation of raw and unfinished materials, and distribution of finished products, etc. As stated in the certificate of the chartered accountants (see page 24), "during the year only actual additions and extensions have been charged Property Account." The outlays as above are classified by properties as follows:

Expended by

United States Steel Corporation, on account of acquirement of stocks of subsidiary companies..	$258,473.31
Manufacturing Properties..	9,743,125.78
Ore Properties..	1,071,547.08
Coal and Coke Properties..	2,043,168.51
Transportation Properties..	2,741,652.51
Miscellaneous Properties... Cr.	171,430.52
Total	$16,586,531.77

Some of the principal additions to the properties of the subsidiary companies on account of which the above expenditures were made during the year are as follows:

MANUFACTURING PROPERTIES.

	Expenditures in 1902.
CARNEGIE STEEL CO.:	
Two New Blast Furnaces, Edgar Thomson Works...................................	$793,041
Fourteen inch Billet and ten inch and thirteen inch Bar Mills, Duquesne Works....	186,489
Two New O. H. Furnaces, Duquesne Works......................................	249,794
Additional Blowing Engines, Duquesne Works...................................	84,015
Extension Armor Plate Plant, Homestead Works.................................	1,102,41
Two New O. H. Furnaces, Homestead Works....................................	162,371
One New Blast Furnace, Carrie Plant..	375,158
ILLINOIS STEEL CO.:	
Two New Blast Furnaces and Ore Unloading Equipment, South Works..........	245,818
Addition to Cement Plant, South Works..	70,843
Ingot Heating Furnace, Slab Mill, South Works.................................	79,999

15

AMERICAN STEEL AND WIRE CO.:

	Expenditures in 1902
Oxide Plant, Worcester..	$87,062
Rail Bond Drop Forging Plant, Worcester...	60,518
Extension of three track Steel Trestle, Central Furnaces.................................	87,223
New Mixer and Blooming Mill, Newburgh Works...	120,604
New Tinning Department, Newburgh Works..	29,041
New Copperas Plant, Rockdale Works..	22,432
Real Estate, New Works, Equipment and Warehouse, Pacific Works, San Francisco............	242,687

NATIONAL TUBE CO.:

New Blast Furnace, Riverside Department...	414,542
Real Estate, McKeesport..	90,288

NATIONAL STEEL CO.:

Eighteen inch Continuous Mill, Mingo Works..	210,277
New Shear Building, Mingo Works...	22,971
Enlargement Blooming Mill, Mingo Works..	22,293
New Blast Furnaces and Condenser Plant, Mingo Works	53,887
Addition to Converting Works, New Castle Works..	145,835
Additional Blowing Engines, Furnaces, New Castle Works	64,839
Additional Real Estate, Ohio Works...	21,000

AMERICAN STEEL HOOP CO.:

Enlargement and Improvement of Blast Furnaces, Isabella Furnaces........................	915,236
Sixteen inch Mill and Equipment, McCutcheon Mills.......................................	39,688

AMERICAN TIN PLATE CO.:

Eight Additional Tin Mills, Extension to Specialty Tin House, Additional Warehouse and other Additions at Laughlin Works...	54,783
Construction of New Works and Sundry Additions at Chester Works.........................	67,177
Twelve Additional Tin Mills at Monessen Works...	518,099
Continuous Mill and Sundry Additions at Monongahela Works...............................	155,041

AMERICAN SHEET STEEL CO.:

New Jobbing Mill, Aetna Works	$53,179
Sixteen Annealing Furnaces, Aetna Works	55,506
Extension to Boiler Plant, Machine and Roll Shop, Aetna Works	28,064
Eight New Sheet Mills, Vandergrift Works	131,827
Two New O. H. Furnaces, Vandergrift Works	81,157
Extension of Natural Gas Line, Vandergrift Works	130,714
Five Annealing Furnaces, Dover Works	33,348
Electrical Equipment, Houk Mine, Dover Works	13,905
Additions to Plant, Wellsville Works	193,008
Two Jump Mills and other Additions at Scottdale Works	36,921
Four Annealing Furnaces, Struthers Works	43,854
Two Cold Mills, Struthers Works	11,625
New Thirty Ton Electric Crane, Struthers Works	25,332
Additions to Sheet Mill and two Additional Boilers, Struthers Works	34,601
Two New Sheet Mills, Wood Works	41,986
Extension to Buildings, Wood Works	28,431

AMERICAN BRIDGE CO.:

New Plant at Economy, Pa., Ambridge Plant	683,494
Additions to the Trenton Plant	154,861
Additions to the Toledo Plant	43,970
Additions to the Brooklyn Plant	110,864
New Machine Shop and accessory Buildings and Machinery, Pencoyd Plant	158,710

ORE PROPERTIES.

Additional Fee properties, leases, etc., acquired	$985,322
Purchase of Additional Real Estate, and Timber Lands to provide Mining Timber	565,659
For construction at Savoy and Sibley mines of two new Steel Shaft Houses, new Engine, Power and Hoisting Plant, Compressors, Equipment, etc.	162,119
Additional Equipment and Additions to the Mining Plants at Fayal, Stephens and Adams mines	145,813
General Additions to Mining Plants and Equipment at various mines of a total expenditure, less credits for property sold and transferred, to amount of	112,629

COAL AND COKE PROPERTIES.	*Expenditures in 1902.*

Additional coking and steam coal lands... $258,480

Development of new coking coal properties in the Connellsville and Lower Connellsville districts, viz.:

    Development and opening of mines... $498,854

    Coke ovens... 284,596

    Mine and oven equipment... 146,704

    Dwellings 101,473

                                            1,031,627

Development of coking coal property in the Pocahontas district in West Virginia..................... 585,885

    This is the property referred to in the preliminary report to stockholders submitted at the annual meeting, February 17, 1902. Fifty thousand acres of coking coal are held under lease on a royalty basis, and on terms favorable for production and transportation.

Development of steam coal property in Washington and Allegheny counties, Pa..................... 198,058

TRANSPORTATION PROPERTIES.

Additional Equipment—16 Locomotives, 1,050 Steel Gondola and Hopper cars, 400 Steel Coal cars, 150 Box cars, 8 Caboose and 5 Passenger cars.. $1,763,158

Union R R.—Construction retaining wall along Monongahela River.... 151,202

Bessemer and Lake Erie RR.:

    New line, Kremis to Osgood... 196,367

    New Shops and Office Building at Greenville................................... 72,472

    New Hotel, Exposition Park... 25,575

General Construction by all railroads, including additional right of way, buildings, mine and logging spurs, sidings, etc........ 532,878

MISCELLANEOUS PROPERTIES.

Carnegie Natural Gas Co.—New gas lines and pumping station..................................... $293,698

Carnegie Land Co—Credit for property sold, less cost of additional land and improvements acquired..Cr. 582,155

Additional property, real estate and improvements acquired by sundry Water and Supply Companies.... 117,027

PROPERTY ACCOUNT EXPENDITURES SINCE ORGANIZATION U. S. STEEL CORPORATION.

    The total amount of expenditures for property account by all properties, from April 1, 1901, to December 31, 1902, was as follows:

    During the nine months ending December 31, 1901..................................... $16,956,868.63

    During the fiscal year ending December 31, 1902, as hereinbefore shown.... .... 16,586,531.77

    Total $33,543,400.40

    On account of the expenditures as above, funds have been provided by issue of bonds and mortgages by the Subsidiary Companies (chiefly securities of railroads) to amount of....... 3,456,659.76

    Balance of outlays for Property Account from April 1, 1901, to December 31, 1902, paid in Cash from depreciation accounts and surplus earnings................................. $30,086,740.64

SUMMARY OF CASH PAYMENTS FOR PROPERTY ACCOUNT AND REDUCTION OF PURCHASE MONEY OBLIGATIONS, BILLS PAYABLE, BONDS, MORTGAGES, ETC., SINCE ORGANIZATION OF THE UNITED STATES STEEL CORPORATION.

Amount paid in Cash from depreciation accounts and surplus earnings, for Property Account from April 1, 1901, to December 31, 1902, per preceding page $30,086,740.64

Paid from surplus during the above period to reduce Purchase Money Obligations, Bills Payable and Special Deposits of Subsidiary Companies, as heretofore shown (Page 14)................. 24,700,338.51

Amount of Bonds and Mortgages discharged during the same period (exclusive of bonds redeemed with sinking fund moneys) and paid out of surplus earnings 3,091,758.75

Making a grand total paid in Cash from April 1, 1901, to December 31, 1902, from depreciation accounts and surplus, for Property Account and reduction of various liabilities outstanding at time Corporation was organized..... .... $57,878,837.90

UNION-SHARON PURCHASE.

In December, 1902, the Corporation acquired the entire issue of Capital Stock of the Union Steel Company, which latter company had absorbed the Sharon Steel Company and had acquired the entire issues of Capital Stock of the Sharon Ore Company, the Sharon Coke Company, the Sharon Sheet Steel Company, the Donora Mining Company, the Republic Coke Company, the River Coal Company, and a controlling interest in the Capital Stock of the Sharon Tin Plate Company and the Sharon Coal and Limestone Company. Such acquisition was effected by direct negotiation with the owners, on the basis of actual cost of the properties to the vendors, except as to certain ore and coal property and other lands, and as to them on a basis not exceeding actual present value.

In consideration of the transfer of the Union Steel Company's stock the Steel Corporation guaranteed the principal and interest of the Union Steel Company's Fifty Year First Mortgage and Collateral Trust Five per Cent. Gold Bonds issued and to be issued to the aggregate principal sum of $45,000,000. The amount of these bonds which were outstanding at the time the stock was formally turned over to the Steel Corporation was............... $29,114,000

The balance of the issue of the above bonds is reserved for the following purposes:

Sold for cash at par to be taken in monthly instalments during 1903 by the vendors of Union Steel Company stock, in accordance with agreement with them.................................... 8,512,000

> The cash received from the sale of these bonds is to be used for completing furnaces, mills, additions and extensions to the property under way on December 1, 1902, and to provide working capital.

Reserved to retire outstanding bonds of the Sharon Steel properties at their maturity................. 3,500,000

Reserved for future use for additions, construction and improvements............................ 3,874,000

Total authorized issue....................... .... $45,000,000

The property acquired through the capital stock of the Union Steel Company, completed and under construction, is as follows:

Manufacturing Plants at Donora and Sharon, Pa.—5 Blast Furnaces, 24 O. H. Furnaces, 2 Blooming, Slabbing and Sheet Bar Mills, 4 Rod Mills, 2 Wire and Nail Mills, 1 Skelp Works, 1 Tube Works, 1 Plate Mill, 1 Tin Plate Plant, 1 Sheet Plant, By-Product Coke Plant, 212 ovens.

Coking coal property in Lower Connellsville district, 4,740 acres of coal and 810 acres of surface.

Steam coal property on Monongahela River, 1,524 acres of coal and 179 acres of surface.

The Sharon and Penobscot mines (in fee) and Donora and Sweeny mines (leases) on the Mesaba Range, containing approximately 40,000,000 tons of iron ore.

Two modern steel ore steamers.

The negotiations preliminary to the transfer of the above properties were completed and the properties formally turned over to this organization after January 1, 1903. Therefore the earnings of such properties for December, 1902, and the assets, liabilities and bonded debt thereof at the close of the year are not included in the statements and balance sheet embraced in this report.

It is believed the earnings of the above properties will be sufficient to provide at least the interest on the bonds and a sinking fund which will eventually pay and retire the bonds.

PURCHASE OF TROY STEEL PRODUCTS COMPANY.

The American Steel and Wire Company acquired as of January 1, 1903, the entire issues of Capital Stock and First Mortgage Bonds of the Troy Steel Products Company, at the price of $1,100,000.

The property owned by above company is situated on Breaker Island, in the Hudson River, at Troy, N. Y., together with property and accessory works on the east side of the river. The property consists of three Blast Furnaces, Steel Works and Rolling Mill.

EMPLOYES AND PAY ROLLS.

The average number of employés in the service of all properties during the entire year was....... 168,127
The aggregate amount paid during the year for salaries and wages of employés was........... $120,528,343
The following shows the classification of the number of employés between the several departments named:

Employés of	Number.
Manufacturing Properties....................................	125,326
Coal and Coke Properties.......	16,519
Iron Mining Properties.................................... ..	13,465
Transportation Properties....................................	11,160
Miscellaneous Properties..........	1,657
Total.	168,127

EMPLOYES' SUBSCRIPTIONS TO PREFERRED STOCK.

On December 31, 1902, the Board of Directors submitted to the employés of the Corporation and its Subsidiary Companies a plan whereby every employé was granted the opportunity to participate in the profits of the organization through the purchase of Preferred Stock of the Corporation. Copy of the circular setting forth the plan in detail was sent to each stockholder of record.

The plan was most favorably received by the employés, the subscriptions exceeding by about one hundred per cent the amount it was anticipated would be taken. Allotments of stock were made to subscribers on the following basis:

To Class "A" employés, 50 per cent. of their subscription.
To Class "B" employés, 60 per cent. of their subscription.
To Class "C" employés, 70 per cent. of their subscription.
To Class "D" employés, 80 per cent. of their subscription.

To Class "E" employés, 90 per cent. of their subscription.

To Class "F" employés, 100 per cent. of their subscription.

The total number of employés who subscribed for stock was 27,379 and the number of shares allotted them 48,983.

As indicated in the circular above referred to it is the intention of the Corporation, if the plan meets with continued success, to annually make a similar offer to employés, excepting, of course, that the price at which the stock then will be offered cannot now be determined. At the date of submitting this report every indication points to the complete success of the plan.

To provide for the offer for sale of Preferred Stock to employés under the above plan, the Corporation purchased the necessary shares of its Preferred Stock. The investment in this stock is included in the General Balance Sheet, in the item of "Sundry Marketable Stocks and Bonds." The amount paid for purchase of this stock will be collected in cash from employés in monthly instalments during 1903 and subsequent years, together with 5 per cent. interest on the deferred payments.

NUMBER OF STOCKHOLDERS.

The following shows the number of stockholders in the United States Steel Corporation in March, 1903, in comparison with the number at corresponding date in preceding year:

	1902.	1903.	Increase.
Preferred	25,296	31,799	6,503
Common	17,723	26,830	9,107
Total	43,019	58,629	15,610

The foregoing does not include the subscriptions for preferred stock by the 27,379 employés referred to in the preceding section.

ORDERS ON HAND.

The tonnage of unfilled orders on the books at the close of 1902 equaled 5,347,253 tons of all kinds of manufactured products. At the corresponding date in preceding year the orders booked equaled 4,407,749 tons. In many of the classes of heavier products, like rails, plates and structural material, practically the entire capacity of the mills is sold up until nearly the end of the year 1903.

ORGANIZATION.

In the Preliminary Report submitted to stockholders at the first annual meeting, February 17, 1902, reference was made to what had been accomplished to that time in bringing into harmonious co-operation the various companies and departments within the organization. During the year further advances have been made in this direction and the beneficial results anticipated therefrom, as was indicated in the report above referred to, have been fully realized.

The policy and business of this Corporation, and the companies in which it is interested, are to a large extent considered and determined by the regular committees, or their sub-committees, or special committees consisting of the presidents or other officers of subsidiary companies or some of them, thus deriving the benefit which necessarily results from deliberate and combined action of all.

. Direct control and active management of the subsidiary companies are in charge of their respective offic Each company has a complete organization, consisting of a president, vice-president, general manager, superintende etc., etc. The presidents of the subsidiary companies are as follows:

W. E. Corey	{ Carnegie Steel Company, { National Steel Company, { American Steel Hoop Company.
James H. Reed	{ Bessemer & Lake Erie Railroad Company, { Union Railroad Company.
Thomas Lynch	H. C. Frick Coke Company, and other Coal and C Companies.
Thomas F Cole	{ Minnesota Iron Company, { Oliver Iron Mining Company, and other Mining Co panies.
D. M Clemson	Pittsburg Steamship Company.
William P. Palmer	American Steel and Wire Company.
William B. Schiller	{ National Tube Company, { Shelby Steel Tube Company.
W. T. Graham	American Tin Plate Company.
E. J. Buffington	Illinois Steel Company.
George G. McMurtry	American Sheet Steel Company.
Alfred J. Major	American Bridge Company.
Joshua A. Hatfield	American Bridge Company of New York.
Daniel Coolidge	Lorain Steel Company.
A. F. Banks	{ Elgin, Joliet & Eastern Railway Company, { Chicago, Lake Shore & Eastern Railway Company.
F. E House	Duluth & Iron Range Railroad Company.
W J Olcott	Duluth, Missabe & Northern Railway Company.

Each subsidiary company is fully equipped for success independently of any other company or corporation, but the association and connection with the officers of other companies in which this Corporation is interested, and with the officers and committees of this Corporation, results in great benefit to each subsidiary company, and to this Corporation. It is believed the officials of subsidiary companies represent the very best talent that can be secured.

These presidents are in constant communication with each other, and with the officials and members of the committees of this Corporation The officers and committees of this Corporation are also in daily communication with each other. The Executive Committee and the Finance Committee of this Corporation meet regularly each week, and frequently in special session; and sub-committees for special work are appointed from time to time.

As an illustration of the method of transacting business, suppose one of the subsidiary companies is desirous of making a substantial expenditure for improvements, or of entering into a contract of sale or purchase involving a large sum of money, or of making some important change in policy, the superintendent or manager who first suggests the proposed action will make recommendation to his superior officer, giving reasons in detail. This will reach the president of the particular company, and be considered by him and his committee. After decision the subject is submitted to the president, or other officer, of this Corporation, and is brought before the Executive Committee of this Corporation for consideration. As the presidents of subsidiary companies meet monthly for consultation, many, if not most, important questions are also considered at these meetings, and recommendations then made for consideration by the officials and committees of this Corporation. After the question has been considered by the Executive Committee of this Corporation, if a question of money is involved (and frequently if a question of policy is involved) the subject is then considered by the Finance Committee.

35

The Board takes pleasure in acknowledging the loyal and efficient services of the officers and employés of the Corporation and the several Subsidiary Companies.

By order of the Board of Directors.

CHARLES M. SCHWAB,
President.

NEW YORK, March 12, 1903.

To the Stockholders of the United States Steel Corporation:

We have examined the books of the U. S. Steel Corporation and its Subsidiary Companies for the year ending December 31, 1902, and certify that the Balance Sheet at that date and the Relative Income Account are correctly prepared therefrom.

We have satisfied ourselves that during the year only actual additions and extensions have been charged to Property Account; that ample provision has been made for Depreciation and Extinguishment, and that the item of "Deferred Charges" represents expenditures reasonably and properly carried forward to operations of subsequent years.

We are satisfied that the valuations of the inventories of stocks on hand as certified by the responsible officials have been carefully and accurately made at approximate cost; also that the cost of material and labor on contracts in progress has been carefully ascertained, and that the profit taken on these contracts is fair and reasonable.

Full provision has been made for bad and doubtful accounts receivable and for all ascertainable liabilities.

We have verified the cash and securities by actual inspection or by certificates from the Depositories, and are of opinion that the Stocks and Bonds are fully worth the value at which they are stated in the Balance Sheet.

And we certify that in our opinion the Balance Sheet is properly drawn up so as to show the true financial position of the Corporation and its Subsidiary Companies, and that the Relative Income Account is a fair and correct statement of the net earnings for the fiscal year ending at that date.

PRICE, WATERHOUSE & Co.

UNITED STATES STEEL CORPORATION AND SUBSIDIARY COMPANIES.

SUMMARY OF FINANCIAL OPERATIONS OF ALL PROPERTIES.

Year Ending December 31, 1902.

Showing the Net Resources for the Year and Disposition Thereof.

RESOURCES.

Profit and Loss Surplus for the year, per Income Account, page 6..............		$34,253,656 75
Net Receipts appropriated from: Earnings for Bond Sinking, Depreciation and		
Improvement Funds (See Income Account, page 8).....................	$27,814,389.47	
Less, Payments therefrom to Trustees of Bond Sinking		
Funds $3,604 064 43		
Expended for Extraordinary Replacements......... 7,926,792 60		
	11,530,857.03	
	$16,283,532.44	
Net Receipts account Insurance and Contingent Funds during the year..	804,319 35	
Balance of Receipts for Year included in Fund accounts		17,087,851.79
Bonds and Mortgages issued..		2,370,338 35
Sundry Miscellaneous Receipts		5,920.98
Total Net Resources.		$53,717,767.87

PAYMENTS MADE FROM ABOVE.

Expended for Additional Property and Construction, per page 15..............	$16,586,531.77	
Bonds and Mortgages paid (not including bonds redeemed with sinking funds) .	1,697,577 33	
Purchase Money Obligations, Bills Payable and Special Deposits paid off	13,652,367.94	
		31,936,477.04
Balance of Net Resources for the year, accounted for as below........................		$21,781,290.83

INCREASE IN CURRENT ASSETS, VIZ.:

In Sundry Securities and Investments................................	$3,193,604.83	
In Accounts and Bills Receivable in excess of increase in Accounts Payable.	9,595,635.15	
In Inventories and Miscellaneous Accounts.............................	12,625,946.02	
	$25,415,186.00	
Less, Decrease in Cash on hand December 31, 1902, as compared with pre-		
ceding year...	3,633,895.17	
Balance as above..................	$21,781,290.83	

CONDENSED GENERAL BALANCE SHEET, DECEMBER 31, 1902.

ASSETS.

PROPERTY ACCOUNT.

Properties owned and operated by the several companies	$1,453,635,551.37	
Less Surplus of Subsidiary Companies at date of acquirement of their Stocks by U. S. Steel Corporation April 1, 1901	$116,356,111.41	
Charged off to Depreciation and Extinguishment Funds	12,011,856.53	
	128,367,967.94	
		$1,325,267,583.43

DEFERRED CHARGES TO OPERATIONS

Expenditures for Improvements, Explorations, Stripping and Development at Mines, and for Advanced Mining Royalties, chargeable to future operations of the properties. 3,178,759.67

TRUSTEES OF SINKING FUNDS

Cash held by Trustees on account of Bond Sinking Funds. 459,246.14
($4,022,000 par value of Redeemed bonds held by Trustees not treated as an asset.)

INVESTMENTS

Outside Real Estate and Other Property.	$1,874,872.39	
Insurance Fund Assets	929,615.84	
		2,804,488.23

CURRENT ASSETS

Inventories	$104,300,844.74	
Accounts Receivable	48,944,180.68	
Bills Receivable	4,153,204.13	
Agents' Balances	1,091,318.99	
Sundry Marketable Stocks and Bonds	6,091,340.16	
Cash	50,163,172.48	
		214,834,157.18

		$1,546,544,234.65

LIABILITIES.

CAPITAL STOCK OF U. S. STEEL CORPORATION:

Common	$508,302,500.00	
Preferred	510,281,100.00	
		$1,018,583,600.00

CAPITAL STOCKS OF SUBSIDIARY COMPANIES NOT HELD BY U. S. STEEL CORPORATION (Par Value):

Common Stocks	$44,400.00	
Preferred Stocks	72,800.00	
Lake Superior Consolidated Iron Mines, Subsidiary Companies	98,714.38	
		215,914.38

BONDED AND DEBENTURE DEBT:

United States Steel Corporation Bonds	$303,757,000.00	
Less, Redeemed and held by Trustee of Sinking Fund	2,698,000.00	
Balance held by the Public	$301,059,000.00	
Subsidiary Companies Bonds	$60,978,000.75	
Less, Redeemed and held by Trustees of Sinking Funds	1,324,000.00	
Balance held by the Public	59,654,000.75	
Debenture Scrip, Illinois Steel Company	40,426.02	
		360,754,326.77

MORTGAGES AND PURCHASE MONEY OBLIGATIONS OF SUBSIDIARY COMPANIES

Mortgages	$2,901,132.07	
Purchase Money Obligations	6,689,418.53	
		9,590,550.60

CURRENT LIABILITIES:

Current Accounts Payable and Pay Rolls	$18,675,080.13	
Bills and Loans Payable	6,202,502.44	
Special Deposits due Employes and others	4,483,546.98	
Accrued Taxes not yet due	1,051,605.42	
Accrued Interest and Unpresented Coupons	5,398,572.06	
Preferred Stock Dividend No 7, payable February 16, 1903	8,929,919.75	
Common Stock Dividend No 7, payable March 30, 1903	3,085,025.00	
Total Capital and Current Liabilities		$1,438,970,643.53
		49,826,251.78

SINKING AND RESERVE FUNDS:

Sinking Fund on U S Steel Corporation Bonds	$1,773,333.33	
Sinking Funds on Bonds of Subsidiary Companies	217,344.36	
Depreciation and Extinguishment Funds	1,702,610.59	
Improvement and Replacement Funds	16,566,190.90	
Contingent and Miscellaneous Operating Funds	3,413,783.50	
Insurance Fund	1,539,485.25	
		25,217,747.93

BOND SINKING FUNDS WITH ACCRETIONS 4,481,246.14
Represented by Cash, and by redeemed bonds not treated as assets (see contra).

UNDIVIDED SURPLUS OF U. S. STEEL CORPORATION AND SUBSIDIARY COMPANIES:

Capital Surplus provided in organization of U. S. Steel Corporation	$25,000,000.00	
Surplus accumulated by all companies since organization of U. S. Steel Corporation	52,874,597.05	
		77,874,597.05*

		$1,546,544,234.65

*NOTE—In preliminary Report submitted to stockholders at the First Annual Meeting, February 17, 1902, the accumulated surplus of all subsidiary companies to November 30, 1901, was shown as $170,340,793.32. This total, however, included the surplus of the subsidiary companies at time of the original acquisition of their stocks by United States Steel Corporation in 1901, which surplus in this balance sheet is stated in diminution of Property Account.

BONDED AND DEBENTURE DEBT OUTSTANDING, DECEMBER 31, 1902.

39

	Total Bonds.	Held by Trustees Skg. Funds.	Balance in Hands of Public.	Maturity.	INTEREST. Rate.	INTEREST. Payable.
U. S. Steel Corporation 50 Year Gold Bonds	$303,757,000 00	$2,698,000 00	$301,059,000 00	April 1, 1951.	5	1/12 Monthly
The Carnegie Co., Collateral Trust.........	243,000 00	....	243,000 00	April 1, 2000.	5	
Illinois Steel Co., Conv. Debentures......	2,872,000 00	....	2,872,000 00	January 1, 1910.	5	Jan. and July
Illinois Steel Co., Non-Conv. Debentures .	6,000,000 00	....	6,000,000 00	April 1, 1913	5	April and Oct
The Johnson Co. (now Lorain Steel Co.), 1st Mortgage......	1,208,000 00		1,208,000 00	$100,000 each Sept. 1.	6	Mar. and Sept.
Am. S. & W. Co , Allegheny Furnace Mtge.	78,000.00	....	78,000 00	August 1, 1911.	5	Feb and Aug
National Steel Co. Bonus, viz..						
Ohio Steel Co , 1st Mortgage.	845,000.00	.	845,000.00	Various amts. on June 1, to 1908.	6	June and Dec
Bellaire Steel Co., 1st Mortgage........	301,000 00	.	301,000 00	March 2, 1906	6	Mar. and Sept.
Rosena Furnace Co , 1st Mortgage....	250,000 00	.	250,000 00	December 1, 1912	5	June and Dec
Buhl Steel Co , 1st Mortgage	200,000 00	.	200,000 00	November 1, 1903.	6	May and Nov.
King, Gilbert & Warner, 1st Mortgage.	100,000 00	.	100,000 00	May 1, 1905.	6	May and Nov.
American Tin Plate Co. Bonds, viz :						
New Castle Steel and Tin Plate Co	75,000 00	....	75,000 00	March 1, 1906.	6	Mar. and Sept.
American Sheet Steel Co Bonds, viz .						
W. Dewees Wood Co., 1st Mortgage....	2,000,000 00	......	2,000,000 00	May 1, 1910.	5	May and Nov.
Total...........................	....	....	$316,131,000 00			
COAL AND COKE COMPANIES.						
H C Frick Coke Co , 1st Mortgage	1,600,000 00	.	$1,600,000 00	$100,000 each July 1.	5	Jan. and July
H. C Frick Coke Co , Pur Money Mtge	300,000 00		300,000 00	$50,000 each Jan 1.	5	Jan. and July
Host.-Conn. Co e Co., Pur Money Mtge	1,000,000 00	.	*1,000,000 00	February 1, 1942.	5	Feb. and Aug
Hostetter Coke Co., 1st Mortgage	175,000 00	.	*175,000 00	$25,000 each August 1.	6	Feb and Aug
Continental Coke Co., Pur. Money Mtge	900,000 00		900,000 00	$100,000 each Feb 1	5	Feb and Aug
Continental Coke Co , Pur Money Mtge	629,000 00	....	629,000 00	$37,000 each April 27.	4 1/2	April 27
*Less, half of these bonds outstanding account stock of Host -Conn. Co. not owned by Frick Coke Co			4,604,000 00			
			587,500 00			
Balance of Coal & Coke Co 's Bonds	...	....	$4,016,500 00			
TRANSPORTATION COMPANIES.						
Union Railroad Co , 1st Mortgage...	2,000,000 00	.	$2,000,000 00	September 1, 1946.	5	Mar and Sept.
*Pitts., Bess & Lake Erie R R Co. Bonds:						
1st Mortgage Consolidated	6,342,000 00	.	6,342,000 00	January 1, 1947.	5	Jan and July
Debenture Gold Bonds	2,000,000 00	.	2,000,000 00	June 1, 1919.	5	June and Dec
Pittsburg, Shenango & Lake Erie Ry :						
1st Mortgage ..	3,000,000 00	.	3,000,000 00	October 1, 1940.	5	April and Oct
1st Mortgage Consolidated	655,000 00	....	655,000 00	July 1, 1943	5	Jan and July
Bessemer Equipment Trust	300,000 00		300,000 00	$75,000 each July 1.	6	Jan. and July
Conneaut Equipment Trust	350,000 00		350,000 00	See Note " A "	6	Mar and Sept.
Shenango Equipment Trust..........	725,000 00		725,000 00	See Note " B "	5	April and Oct.
Greenville Equipment Trust....	1,000,000 00		1,000,000 00	See Note " C "	5	May and Nov
Butler Equipment Trust.............	2,050,000 00	.....	2,050,000 00	April 1, 1921.	5	April and Oct
Note " A." $50,000 1903 and $60,000 each March 1 thereafter. Note "B " $72,000 April 1, 1904 to 1908, $73,000 each April 1 thereafter. Note "C." $100,000 May 1, 1911 to 1920.						
Bessemer & Lake Erie R. R. Co Erie Equipment Trust	1,220,000 00	....	1,220,000 00	March. 1, 1922.	5	Mar. and Sept
Elgin, Jol & East Ry. Co , 1st Mortgage	8,500,000 00	....	8,500,000 00	May 1, 1941.	5	May and Nov
Duluth & Iron Range R. R. Co. Bonds.						
1st Mortgage............	6,732,000 00	....	6,732,000 00	Oct. 1, 1937.	5	April and Oct
2d Mortgage	1,000,000 00	....	1,000,000.00	Jan. 1, 1916.	6	Jan and July
Duluth, Missabe & No. Ry Co. Bonds						
First Division, 1st Mortgage	1,174,000 00	......	1,174,000 00	Jan. 1, 1922.	6	Jan. and July
Consolidated, 1st Mortgage	2,326,000 00	555,000 00	1,771,000 00	Jan. 1, 1923.	6	Jan. and July
Consolidated, 2d Mortgage	2,621,000 00	408,000 00	2,213,000 00	Jan. 1, 1918.	5	Jan and July
Pittsburg Steamship Co. Bonds:						
1st Mortgage (P S. S)	2,437,000 00		2,437,000 00	Jan. 1, 1915.	5	Jan. and July
No. Lakes S S. Co., Mortgage	60,000 00		60,000 00	$10,000 each Sept. 1.	5	Mar. and Sept
American S S Co , 1st Mortgage	5,250,000 00	361,000 00	4,889,000 00	Nov 1, 1920.	5	May and Nov.
*Less, proportion of P., B & L E R R Bonds outstanding account stock not owned by Carnegie Co			$48,421,000 00			
	...	. ...	7,854,599 25			
			$40,566,400 75			
Total Bonds	....	....	$360,713,900 75			
Debenture Scrip, Illinois Steel Co (Payable April 1, 1913)	40,426 02	....	40,426 02			
Grand Total	.....		$360,754,326 77			

United States Steel Corporation and Subsidiary Companies.

Monthly Earnings from April 1, 1901, to December 31, 1902.

40

	1901.	1902.
January	....	$8,901,015 72
February	....	7,678,583. 47
March	....	10,135,858.40
April	$7,356,744.32	12,320,765 87
May	9,612,349.23	13,120,930.23
June	9,394,747.72	12,220,361.97
July	9,580,151.46	12,041,913.53
August	9,810,880.60	12,972,728.87
September	9,272,811.38	11,930,846.47
October	12,205,773.73	12,652,706.97
November	9,795,840.34	10,686,905.74
December	7,758,297 73	8,646,146 48
Total Nine Months 1901	$84,787,596.51	....
Total Year 1902	....	$133,308,763.72

Total Nine Months 1901.. ...$84,787,596 51

Total for same period 1902.. 106,593,306.13

28

SUMMARY OF MANUFACTURING-PLANTS
OWNED BY SUBSIDIARY COMPANIES OF
UNITED STATES STEEL CORPORATION

Name of Operating Company	Number of Blast Furnaces	Bessemer Steel Works (No. of Works)	Bessemer Steel Works (No. of Converters)	Open Hearth Steel Works (No. of Works)	Open Hearth Steel Works (No. of Furnaces)	Blooming, Slabbing, Billet and Sheet Bar Mills (No. of Works)	Blooming etc. (No. of Mills in Works)	Number of Rail Mills	Plate Mills (No. of Works)	Plate Mills (No. of Mills in Works)	Puddling Mills (No. of Works)	Puddling Mills (No. of Puddling Furnaces)	Puddling Mills (No. of Knobling Fires)	Strip Mills (No. of Works)	Strip Mills (No. of Mills in Works)	Merchant, Bar, Hoop and Cotton Tie Mills (No. of Works)	Merchant etc. (No. of Mills in Works)	Structural Shape Mills (No. of Mills in Works)	Structural Shape Mills (No. of Mills)	Rod Mills (No. of Works)	Rod Mills (No. of Mills in Works)	Wire Mills (No. of Works)	Wire Mills (Galvanizing Depts.)	Wire Mills (Tinning Depts.)	Sheet, Black Plate and Tin Plate Mills (No. of Works)	Sheet etc. (No. of Mills in Works)	Sheet etc. (Depts. for Tinning)	Sheet etc. (Depts. for Galvanizing)	Number of Tube Mills	Number of Bridge and Structural Plants	Number of Foundries	Miscellaneous Works
Carnegie Steel Co.	21	8	8	4	60	8	11	2	3	7	8	161	8			8	6	2	8												2	1 Axle Works, 1 Armor Plant, 2 Bolt and Rivet Depts.
National Steel Co.	17	5	10	1	6	6	14	1				161				11	12			1										1		1
Am. Steel Hoop Co.	3	2				2	6	2	1	2	8		8			2	8													1		2 Cement Plants, 1 Spike Bolt and Nut Factory
Illinois Steel Co.	19	1	5	1	10	4	21	1	1		4	121	5			3	8			1	2									1		1
Lorain Steel Co.	21	8	6	3	15	2	6	2	1	3																					5	1 Frog and Switch Works
Am. Steel & Wire Co.	12	2	4			5	2				1		5	5	5					13	21	22	17	6	2	2						4	2 Zinc Smelting Works
National Tube Co.	5			2										22											2	161	21	5	16		1	2 Cut Nail Mills, 1 Galvanizing Works
Shelby Steel Tube Co.														19															7			
Am. Sheet Steel Co.				2	10	5	12				1		1	1	1										20	164	21				1	
Am. Tin Plate Co.				1	11	1	1					19													33	32					1	
American Bridge Co.																			3											26	3	1 Axle Works
Union Steel Co.	5			2	7	2	5		1	1	1		1	3	1			1		2	4	2	2		1	2	30	1	1				
Grand Total	**84**	**16**	**35**	**11**	**136**	**31**	**60**	**6**	**6**	**13**	**13**	**301**	**11**	**12**	**13**	**19**	**61**	**3**	**11**	**10**	**27**	**24**	**19**	**6**	**17**	**116**	**22**	**6**	**24**	**27**	**22**	(13) Miscellaneous

MANUFACTURING PLANTS OWNED
BY SUBSIDIARY COMPANIES OF
UNITED STATES STEEL CORPORATION

Operating Company and Name of Works	Location of Works		Miscellaneous Works
Carnegie Steel Co.			
Edgar Thomson Works	Bessemer	Penn	
Duquesne	Cochran	"	
Homestead	Munhall	"	
Lower Union	29th St., Pittsburg	"	
Upper Union	33rd St., Pittsburg	"	1 Bolt & Rivet Dept. / 1 Armor Plant
Carrie Furnaces	Rankin	"	
Lucy	51st St., Pittsburg	"	1 Bolt & Rivet Dept.
Howard Axle Works	Homestead	"	1 Axle Works
Total Carnegie Steel Co.			4 Works
National Steel Co.			
Columbus Works	Columbus	Ohio	
Zanesville	Zanesville	"	
Niles	Niles	"	
Ohio	Youngstown	"	
Mingo	Mingo Junction	"	
Bellaire	Bellaire	"	
New Castle	New Castle	Penn	
Sharon	Sharon	"	
Total National Steel Co.			
American Sheet & Hoop Co.			
Warren Mills	Warren	Ohio	
Girard	Girard	"	
Upper Union	Youngstown	"	
Lower Union	Youngstown	"	
Mingo	Mingo Junction	"	
Greenville	Greenville	Penn	
McCutcheon	"	"	

Porter "	S. Side, Pittsburg		
Clark "	35th St., Pittsburg		
Isabella Furnaces	Etna		
Monessen ___ Mills	Monessen		
Duncansville ___	Duncansville		

TOTAL AMERICAN STEEL HOOP CO.

AMERICAN STEEL & WIRE CO.

Granite City ___ Works	Granite City ___ Ill	
Waukegan "	Waukegan ___ "	
DeKalb "	DeKalb ___ "	
Bluff Street "	Joliet ___	
Meeker Avenue "	Joliet ___	
Rockdale "	Joliet ___	
Scott Street "	Joliet ___	
Anderson "	Anderson ___ Ind	
American "	Cleveland ___ Ohio	Die Foundry
Consolidated "	Cleveland ___ "	
Central Furnaces	Cleveland ___ "	
Emma Furnace	Cleveland ___ "	
Newburg ___ Works	Cleveland ___	Die Foundry
H P "	Cleveland ___	
Salem "	Salem ___ "	
New Castle "	New Castle ___ Pa	
Beaver Falls "	Beaver Falls ___	
Neville Island "	Neville Island ___	
Allegheny Furnaces	Allegheny ___ "	
Bloomsburg ___ Works	Pittsburg ___ "	
26th Street "	Pittsburg ___ "	
South Side "	South Side Pittsburg ___ "	
Rankin "	Rankin ___ "	
Braddock "	Braddock ___	
Allentown "	Allentown ___	
North "	Worcester ___ Mass	
Central "	Worcester ___	
South "	Worcester ___	
Troy "	Breaker Island ___ N Y	Die Foundry
Pacific "	San Francisco ___ Cal	Zinc Smelters 500 Retorts
Cherryvale "	Cherryvale ___ Kan	" " 2000 "
Carondelet "	Carondelet ___ Mo.	2 Works

TOTAL AMERICAN STEEL & WIRE CO.

44

MANUFACTURING PLANTS OWNED – CONTINUED

Operating Company and Name of Works	Location of Works	Miscellaneous Works
ILLINOIS STEEL CO.		
North _____ Works	Chicago _____ Ill	1 Cement Plant
Union "	Chicago "	
South "	Chicago "	1 Cement Plant
Joliet "	Joliet "	1 Spike Bolt and Nut Factory
Milwaukee "	Milwaukee _____ Wis	
TOTAL ILLINOIS STEEL CO.		3 Works
LORAIN STEEL CO.		
Lorain _____ Works	Lorain _____ Ohio	
Johnstown "	Johnstown _____ Penn	1 Frog and Switch Works
TOTAL LORAIN STEEL CO.		1 Works
UNION STEEL CO.		
Sharon _____ Works	Sharon _____ Penn	
Donora "	Donora "	
TOTAL UNION STEEL CO.		
AMERICAN SHEET STEEL CO		
Midland _____ Works	Muncie _____ Ind	
Piqua "	Piqua _____ Ohio	
Dresden "	Dresden "	
Cambridge "	Cambridge "	
Dennison "	Dennison "	
New Philadelphia "	New Philadelphia "	
Dover "	Canal Dover "	
Canton "	Canton "	
Falcon "	Niles "	
Struthers "	Struthers "	

	Wellsville	"
Wellsville	"	Penn.
Astra Standard	McKeesport	
Wood	Scottdale	"
Scottdale	Old Meadows	"
Old Meadows	Saltsburg	"
Saltsburg	Apollo	"
Apollo	Vandergrift	"
Vandergrift	Hyde Park	"
Hyde Park	Leechburg	"
Kirkpatrick		

TOTAL AMERICAN SHEET STEEL CO.

AMERICAN TIN PLATE CO.		
Great Western—Works	Joliet	Ill.
Champion	Muskegon	Mich.
American	Elwood	Ind.
Anderson	Anderson	"
Morewood	Gas City	"
Irondale	Middletown	"
Cambridge	Cambridge	Ohio
Crescent	Cleveland	"
Falcon	Niles	"
Beaver	Lisbon	"
Laughlin	Martins Ferry	"
LaBelle	Wheeling	W. Va
Chester	Chester	"
New Castle	New Castle	Penn.
Shenango	New Castle	"
Ellwood	Ellwood City	"
Star	Pitsburg	"
Monongahela	Pitsburg	"
United States	Demmler	"
Pitsburg	New Kensington	"
Pennsylvania	New Kensington	"
National	Monessen	"
Humbert	So. Connellsville	"

TOTAL AMERICAN TIN PLATE CO.

46

MANUFACTURING PLANTS OWNED — CONTINUED

Operating Company and Name of Works	Location of Works		Miscellaneous Works
NATIONAL TUBE CO.			
Warren Works	Warren	Ohio	
Youngstown "	Youngstown	"	
Steubenville "	Steubenville	"	
Riverside Nail Mill	Wheeling	W. Va.	2 Cut Nail Mills
Riverside Works	Benwood	"	
Pennsylvania "	Pittsburg	Penn.	
Pittsburg "	Pittsburg	"	
Republic "	So. Side, Pittsburg	"	
Continental "	Pittsburg	"	
Boston I. & Steel "	McKeesport	"	
National Dept.	McKeesport	"	1 Galvanized and Kalamein Pipe Works
U.S. Seamless Dept.	Christy Park	"	
National Galv. Works	Versailles	"	
Stand. Seamless "	Ellwood City	"	
Oil City "	Oil City	"	
American "	Middletown	"	
Allison "	Philadelphia	"	
Chester "	Chester	"	
Morris Tasker "	New Castle	Del	
Cohoes "	Cohoes	N.Y.	
Syracuse "	Syracuse	"	
TOTAL NATIONAL TUBE CO.			2 Works
SHELBY STEEL TUBE CO.			
Albany Works	Albany	Ind.	
Toledo "	Toledo	Ohio	

		1 Axle Works	Structural and Bridge Plant under Construction	1 Works

Greenville ———— Penn.				
Ellwood ———— "	Ellwood City ———— "			
Auburn ———— "	Auburn ———— "			
Hartford ———— "	Hartford ———— Conn.			

Total Shelby Steel Tube Co.

American Bridge Co.

Minneapolis — Plant	Minneapolis ———— Minn			
Milwaukee ———— "	Milwaukee ———— Wis.			
American ———— "	Chicago ———— Ill			
Lassig ———— "	Chicago ———— "			
Lafayette ———— "	Lafayette ———— Ind			
Detroit ———— "	Detroit ———— Mich			
Toledo ———— "	Toledo ———— Ohio			
Columbus ———— "	Columbus ———— "			
Canton ———— "	Canton ———— "			
Youngstown ———— "	Youngstown ———— "			
Ambridge ———— "	Economy ———— Penn.			
Schultz ———— "	McKees Rocks ———— "			
Pittsburg ———— "	Pittsburg ———— "			
Shiffler ———— "	Pittsburg ———— "			
Keystone ———— "	Athens ———— "			
Athens ———— "	Pencoyd ———— "			
Pencoyd ———— "	Edge Moor ———— Del.			
Edge Moor ———— "	Trenton ———— N J.			
Trenton ———— "	Greenpoint, L.I. ———— N Y			
Brooklyn ———— "	East Berlin ———— Conn.			
Berlin ———— "	North Albany ———— N Y			
Albany ———— "	Rochester ———— "			
Rochester ———— "	Buffalo ———— "			
Buffalo ———— "	Horseheads ———— "			
Horseheads ———— "	Elmira ———— "			
Elmira, North Shop	Elmira ———— "			
Elmira, South Shop				

Total American Bridge Co.

* These are used only for producing blanks for Seamless Tubing.

IRON ORE MINES.—LIST OF ACTIVE IRON ORE MINES OWNED BY SUBSIDIARY COMPANIES IN THE LAKE SUPERIOR ORE DISTRICT.

Located on Marquette Range:

Bessie Mine.

Hartford Mine.

Queen Mine (¾ Interest).

Section 16 Mine (¾ Interest).

Section 21 Mine (¾ Interest).

Hard Ore Mine (¾ Interest)

Hematite Ore Mine (¾ Interest).

Moore Mine.

Negaunee Mine.

Stegmiller Mine

Winthrop Mine.

Volunteer Mine

Located on Menominee Range

Columbia Mine.

Forest Mine.

Hope Mine.

Mansfield Mine.

Michigan Mine.

Riverton Mine.

Cuff Mine.

Hilltop Mine.

Chapin Mine.

Located on Menominee Range:

Aragon Mine.

Cundy Mine.

Iron Ridge Mine.

Pewabic Mine (½ Interest).

Located on Gogebic Range:

Norrie Mine.

Aurora Mine.

Chicago Mine.

Tilden Mine.

Atlantic Mine.

Located on Vermillion Range:

Pioneer Mine.

Savoy Mine.

Sibley Mine.

Zenith Mine.

Chandler Mine (½ Interest).

Soudan Mine.

Located on Mesaba Range:

Mountain Iron Mine.

Stephens Mine

Virginia Mine.

Fayal Mine.

Located on Mesaba Range:

Auburn Mine.

Genoa Mine.

Chisholm Mine.

Sauntry Mine.

Clark Mine.

Adams Mine.

Burt Mine.

Day Mine.

Duluth Mine.

Glen Mine.

Hull Mine.

Pillsbury Mine.

Rust Mine.

St. Clair Mine.

Sellers Mine.

Spruce Mine.

Donora Mine.

Sharon Mine.

Penobscot Mine.

Sweeny Mine.

Union Mine (½ Interest).

Biwabik Mine (½ Interest).

Mahoning Mine (1-5 Interest).

In addition to the foregoing active mines, the subsidiary companies own on the ranges named extensive acreages of land, much of which contain large quantities of ore yet unopened, and on which there are also great quantities of standing timber designed for future use in mining operations.

COKING COAL PROPERTIES OWNED BY SUBSIDIARY COMPANIES.

In the Connellsville and Lower Connellsville Districts in Westmoreland and Fayette Counties, Pa.:

Acreage of Coal.. 59,740 acres.

Acreage of Surface... 18,273 "

Number of Coking Coal Plants (Bee-hive Ovens)....................................... 60

Number of Bee-hive Ovens... 16,661

In the Pocahontas District, McDowell County, W. Va.:

Lease of 50,000 acres of coking coal.

On this property there are to be constructed coking coal plants which will have in all 3,000 Bee-hive ovens. Work is now in progress on the first 1,000 ovens.

By-Product Coke Ovens, located at Benwood, W. Va., at Sharon, Pa., and South Sharon, Pa., in all.. 357 ovens

49

STEAM COAL PROPERTIES OWNED BY SUBSIDIARY COMPANIES,

In Washington, Allegheny, Somerset, Green and Fayette Counties, Pa., an acreage of steam
and gas coal is owned to the amount of... 24,375

Sundry tracts of steam coal located at or near furnaces and mill plants of the Subsidiary Companies in Pennsylvania, West Virginia, Ohio and Indiana, and in Williamson County,
Illinois, of an acreage of about... 6,500

Total Steam Coal.. 30,875 acres

MISCELLANEOUS PROPERTIES OWNED BY SUBSIDIARY COMPANIES.

WATER SUPPLY PLANTS:

In the Connellsville Coke regions various water supply plants having eight large reservoirs and seven pumping stations and extensive pipe lines. Water is supplied from these plants for use in manufacturing coke, and is also furnished for general purposes.

NATURAL GAS PROPERTY:

Carnegie Natural Gas Company owns in Pennsylvania, Ohio and West Virginia extensive natural gas territory, either owning or having under lease about 120,000 acres; also owns 1,134 miles of pipe lines and two pumping stations.

Extensive natural gas territory and pipe lines are also owned by the American Sheet Steel Company in Pennsylvania, the gas therefrom being used at its Vandergrift plants; also by American Tin Plate Company adjacent to its plants in the Gas Belt district in Indiana.

ORE DOCKS:

Large forwarding ore docks situated on Lake Superior are owned as follows:

At Two Harbors, Minn., owned by Duluth & Iron Range RR. Company, 5 Docks.

At Duluth, Minn., owned by Duluth, Missabe & Northern Ry. Company, 3 docks.

Receiving ore docks are owned at the furnace plants at Chicago, Ill.; Milwaukee, Wis.; Lorain, Ohio, and Cleveland, Ohio.

Receiving and forwarding docks are owned at Lake Erie ports as follows:

At Conneaut, Ohio, by Pittsburg and Conneaut Dock Company.

At Ashtabula, Ohio, by Minnesota Dock Company and National Steel Company.

At Fairport, Ohio, by Pennsylvania and Lake Erie Dock Company.

At Buffalo, N. Y., by Minnesota Dock Company.

SUMMARY OF STANDARD GAUGE RAILROAD MILEAGE OWNED BY SUBSIDIARY COMPANIES, DECEMBER 31, 1902.

OWNED OR OPERATED BY	Line Owned.	Branches and Spurs.	Operated Under Trackage Rights.	Second Tracks.	Sidings.
Duluth & Iron Range R. R..					
Duluth to Ely, Minn	117 22	. . . .	80	. . . . . .	. . . .
Tower Junction to Tower, Minn	1 40	. . . .	. . . . . .	. . . . . .	. . . .
Allen Junction to Virginia, Minn.	25 31	. . . .	. . . . . .	. . . . . .	117 83
McKinley to Eveleth, Minn	8 63	. . . .	. . . . . .	. . . . . .	. . . . . .
Waldo to Drummond	8 50	. . . .	. . . . . .	. . . . . .	. . . . . .
Two Harbors to Wyman	. . . . . .	. . . .	. . . . . .	49 85	. . . . . .
Summit Switch to Eveleth Switch	. . . . . .	. . . .	. . . . . .	14 43	. . . . . .
Between South End of Allen Junction and West Switch at Wyman	. . . . . .	. . . .	. . . . . .	1 30	. . . . . .
Branches and Spurs to Mines, etc	. . . . . .	48 80	. . . . . .	. . . . . .	. . . . . .
Total D. & I R R R .	161 06	48 80	80	65.58	117 83
Duluth, Missabe & Northern Railway					
Stony Brook to Mount Iron	48 62	. . . .	. . . . . .	. . . . . .	. . . . . .
Missabe Junction to Columbia Junction	29 84	. . . .	. . . . . .	. . . . . .	. . . . . .
Iron Junction to Biwabik	15 54	. . . .	. . . . . .	. . . . . .	. . . . . .
Wolf to Hibbing	17 07	. . . .	. . . . . .	. . . . . .	54 36
Main Line Branches	18.57	. . . .	. . . . . .	. . . . . .	. . . . . .
Proctor to Ore Dock	. . . . . .	. . . .	. . . . . .	7 20	. . . . . .
Shaw to Wolf Switch	. . . . . .	. . . .	. . . . . .	6 00	. . . . . .
Second Track Branches	. . . . . .	. . . .	. . . . . .	10 89	. . . . . .
Branches and Spurs to Mines, etc	. . . . . .	31 28	. . . . . .	. . . . . .	4 18
Total D M & N Ry	129 14	31.28		24 09	58 54
Elgin, Joliet & Eastern Ry					
Waukegan Ill , to Porter, Ind .	129 01	. . . .	. . . . . .	. . . . . .	. . . . . .
Walker to Wilmington, Ill	33 80	. . . .	. . . . . .	. . . . . .	. . . . . .
Normantown to Aurora, Ill.	9 65	. . . .	. . . . . .	. . . . . .	107 53
E. Joliet to Joliet, Ill	1 79	. . . .	. . . . . .	. . . . . .	. . . . . .
State Line to Whiting, Ind.	7 08	. . . .	. . . . . .	. . . . . .	. . . . . .
Griffith to Clarke Junction, Ind	10 67	. . . .	. . . . . .	. . . . . .	. . . . . .
E. Joliet to Frankfort, Ill	. . . . . .	. . . .	. . . . . .	13 50	. . . . . .
Spurs to Coal Mines, Quarries, etc ..	. . . .	22 11	. . . .	. . . . . .	. . . . . .
State Line to 112th Street (C & W I Ry) .	. . . . . .	. . . .	4 80	. . . . . .	. . . . . .
112th Street to 98th Street (Belt Ry.) .	. . . . . .	. . . .	2 05	. . . .	. . . . . .
Total E, J & E Ry...	192 43	22 11	6 85	13 50	107 53
Chicago, Lake Shore & Eastern Ry					
So. Chicago, Ill , to Clarke Junction, Ind	9 31	. . . .	. . . .	9 31	. . . . .
At Brimson and at So Chicago .	. . . . . .	69 65	. . . .	. . . . . .	. . . . .
At Bridgeport (S & S Ry.) .	. . . . . .	9 93	. . . .	. . . . . .	. . . . .
At No Chicago (C & K Ry)	. . . . . .	5 08	. . . .	. . . . . .	. . . .
At Joliet (J & B I Ry)	. . . . . .	24 10	. . . .	. . . . . .	. . . .
At Milwaukee (M, B, V & C R. ,	. . . . . .	18 15	. . . .	. . . . . .	. . . . .
Chicago Heights to Westville, Ill (C. & E. I. R. R.)	. . . . . .	. . . .	111 20	. . . . . .	. . . . .
E Joliet, Ill., to Clarke Junction, Ind.(E J. & E Ry.)	. . . . . .	. . . .	44 27	. . . . . .	. . . . .
Total C., L. S & E Ry	9 31	125.91	155 47	9.31	. . . .

SUMMARY OF STANDARD GAUGE RAILROAD MILEAGE—CONTINUED.

OWNED OR OPERATED BY	Line Owned.	Branches and Spurs	Operated Under Trackage Rights.	Second Tracks	Sidings
Bessemer & Lake Erie R. R.					
Kremis to Osgood	8 87	. . .	. . . .	. .	87
North Bessemer to Conneaut Harbor	146 09	. . .	. . . .	. .	. .
No Bessemer to Bessemer (Leased to Union R R) . .	6 97	. . .	. . .	. . . .	. . .
Branchton to Hilliard	10 30	20 74	. . .	18 54	119 36
Conneaut Junction to Wallace Junction	8 71	. . . .	. . .	. . . .	. . . .
Main Line Branches	6 42	. . . .	. . .	. . .	. . .
Meadville to Linesville	20 54		. . .	. . .	. . .
Lynces Junction to Exposition Pk. (M C L & L R. R . .	1 20		. . .	. . .	. .
Meadville to Valonia	1 05		. . .	. . . .	. .
Cascade to Wallace Junction (N Y C & St. L. R R)	.		12 40	. . . .	. . . .
Pittsburg Junction to Butler (B. & O R. R)		.	.50	. . . .	. . .
Total B. & L. E. R. R.	210.75	20 74	12.90	18 54	120 23
Union Railroad :					
East Pittsburg to Streets Run, Pa., & Duquesne Jct. to Duquesne, Pa	5.64	10 43	. . . .	8.43	46.36
McKeesport Connecting Ry :					
McKeesport, Pa , to Port Perry	.58	. . .	. . . .	. . .	. . . .
Benwood & Wheeling Conn Ry.:					
Riverside Yards	7 82	.	.	. . . .	. . . .
Waukegan & Mississippi Val. Ry.					
Between E. J & E. & C N. W Rys at Waukegan .	4.41	. . .	. . .	. . . .	. . . .
Newburg & South Shore Ry :					
At Newburg and Cleveland	4 53	. . . .	. . . .	. . .	18 47
Pittsburg & Ohio Valley Ry.:					
At Allegheny, Braddock, Neville Island and Rankin Pa	12.58	. .	. . .	. . . .	. . . .
Northern Liberties Ry.					
At Pittsburg	.67	. . .	. . .	. . . .	. . . .
Johnstown & Stony Creek R. R					
Bedford Station to Stony Creek Bridge	2 44	. . . .	. . . .	. . .	. . . .
The Lake Terminal R. R :					
Lorain Steel Co s Plant to C. L. & W. R. R. . .	11 66	. . .	. .	. . . .	. . . .
Youghiogheny Northern Ry :					
Broad Ford to Summit, Pa	1 92	. . .	. .	. .	. . . .
Etna & Montrose R R					
Etna to Pine Creek, Pa	. . . .	. . . .	2 00	. . . .	. . . .
South West Connecting Ry :					
Marguerite Coke Wks to Sta 56 of Bess. C Co	2 20	. . . .	. . . .	. . .	.50
Mount Pleasant & Latrobe R R :					
Standard Coke Wks , Mt Pleasant. Pa., to S W Pa R. R.	1 06		. . . .	. . . .	. . . .
Elwood, Anderson & Lapelle Ry.:					
Elwood, Ind., to connections with L E. & W. & P. C. C & St L. Rys	1.20	. . . .	. . . .	. . . .	2 60
Masontown & New Salem R. R.:					
Buffington to Moser Run Junction (Leased to Pa. R. R.)	6 04	. . . .	. . . .	. . . .	. . .
Total Mileage	767 84	250 27	178.02	139.45	471.56

STANDARD GAUGE RAILROAD EQUIPMENT OWNED BY SUBSIDIARY COMPANIES, DECEMBER 31, 1902.

	Duluth and Iron R. R.	Duluth, Missabe & Nor Ky.	Elgin, Joliet & E. Ry.	Chicago, L. S. & E. Ry.	Bessemer & L. E. R. R.	Union R. R. & Subs.	All Other Railroads.	Steel and Coke Companies	Total.
Locomotives	70	40	54	62	86	75	52	32	471
Cars:									
Passenger	9	8	3	....	31	....	2	....	53
Combination (Passenger and Bagg.)	3	3	....	....	7	....	....	....	13
Combination (Bagg, Mail and Ex)	2	1	....	....	7	....	....	....	10
Officers'	2	2	....	....	3	....	....	....	7
Box, Freight	85	62	435	1,636	193	4	81	4	2,498
Flat	321	274	87	402	202	16	106	35	1,443
Pig Iron	....	....	....	25	....	....	....	....	25
Iron Ore	2,591	3,475	....	496	....	....	....	....	6,552
Iron Ore, Steel	350	5	....	....	3,585	100	24	300	4,364
Coal	15	....	2,018	212	....	....	....	....	2,245
Coke	....	....	....	976	....	....	....	2,746	3,722
Stock	2	2	....	4	19	....	....	....	27
Gondola, Steel	....	....	....	150	2,102	....	....	50	2,302
Gondola, Steel Hopper	....	....	....	125	....	....	80	10	215
Gondola, Wooden	....	....	....	....	1,749	....	140	133	2,022
Wire	....	....	....	21	....	....	....	....	21
Fence	....	....	....	....	....	....	....	8	8
Log	175	....	....	....	....	....	....	....	175
Refrigerator	2	9	....	....	....	....	....	....	21
Caboose	39	29	29	11	51	1	...	....	160
Boarding	8	4	....	....	....	....	....	....	12
Dump and Work	....	....	66	70	....	....	32	....	168
Steam Shovel and Tool	4	1	...	1	....	....	....	....	6
Pile Driver and Tool	2	....	...	....	1	....	....	....	3
Wrecking	4	1	....	1	11	1	....	....	18
Sundry Road	24	1	....	41	6	....	1	1	74
Total	3,638	3,877	2,636	4,171	7,967	122	466	3,287	26,164

MARINE EQUIPMENT.

Pittsburg Steamship Company:
Steamers 71
Barges 43

Total 114

During the season of 1902, extending from April 3. to December 15, 1902, this fleet carried 10,777,636 tons of Iron Ore and 179,217 tons of Miscellaneous Freight, total 10,956,853 tons. The gross earnings of the fleet were $9,059,099.94.

VIEWS OF REPRESENTATIVE PROPERTIES

OWNED BY

SUBSIDIARY COMPANIES OF

UNITED STATES STEEL CORPORATION.*

*Editor's Note: The final twenty-three pages of this report, which are not reprinted, contain "views of representative properties owned by subsidiary companies of United States Steel Corporation."

ANNUAL REPORT

OF THE

INTERNATIONAL HARVESTER COMPANY

DECEMBER 31 1909

INTERNATIONAL HARVESTER COMPANY

REPORT TO STOCKHOLDERS

OF

INTERNATIONAL HARVESTER COMPANY

To THE STOCKHOLDERS:

The Board of Directors submits the following report of the business of the International Harvester Company and affiliated companies for the fiscal year ending December 31, 1909, together with a statement of the financial condition at that date:

INCOME ACCOUNT FOR 1909

Total Earnings after deducting expenditures for ordinary repairs and maintenance ($2,244,404.47), and current experimental, development, and patent expenses ($474,515.12)		$19,225,329.74
Deduct:		
Appropriation for Fire Insurance Fund	$ 250,000.00	
Appropriation for Renewals and Minor Improvements	567,151.85	
Reserve for Pension Fund	250,000.00	
Reserves for Plant Depreciation and Ore Extinguishment	1,827,381.47	
Reserves for Contingent Losses and Collection Expenses on Receivables	880,000.00	$ 3,774,533.32
		$15,450,796.42
Deduct:		
Interest Paid on Purchase Money Obligations and Current Loans		558,056.21
Net Profit		$14,892,740.21

SURPLUS

Balance at December 31, 1908.   . . . . **$16,691,989.61**

ADD:

Net Profit for Season 1909. . . .   . **$14,892,740.21**

LESS:

Preferred Stock Dividends for Season 1909:

No. 9, 1¾%, paid June 1, 1909	**$1,050,000.00**	
No. 10, 1¾%, paid September 1, 1909	1,050,000.00	
No. 11, 1¾%, paid December 1, 1909	1,050,000.00	
No. 12, 1¾%, payable March 1, 1910	1,050,000.00	**4,200,000.00**

Undivided Profits for Season 1909 carried to Surplus. 10,692,740.21

Surplus at December 31, 1909, before distribution of $20,000,000 Stock Dividend on Common Stock. (See below) **$27,384,729.82**

The above Surplus is composed solely of the balance of net earnings of the business, after deducting dividend payments, the Board of Directors having charged off the surplus of $7,076,229 existing at organization, October 1, 1902, by reason of the excess of the appraised value of the physical properties (including inventories) then acquired ($67,076,229) over the par value of the capital stock issued therefor ($60,000,000). The remaining $60,000,000 Capital Stock was issued at par for cash.

On January 29, 1910, $20,000,000 additional Common Stock was issued as a stock dividend, and the sum of $20,000,000 was transferred from the Surplus and Undivided Net Profits arising from the business of the Company to the Capital of the Company. Thereby the above Surplus was reduced as follows:

Surplus at December 31, 1909, before distribution of Common Stock Dividend. **$27,384,729.82**

Deduct:

Common Stock Dividend to Common Stockholders of record February 3, 1910. . .   . .   20,000,000.00

Net Surplus after distribution of Common Stock Dividend .   . .   .   **$ 7,384,729.82**

4

RESERVES

RESERVES FOR PLANT DEPRECIATION AND EXTINGUISHMENT:

The annual appropriations from earnings for depreciation and extinguishment reserves constitute the necessary provision for the impairment and consumption of the plant assets utilized in the output of the product and should prove sufficient to reproduce the properties as their replacement becomes necessary. Amortization of ore is calculated at rates which will provide sinking funds sufficient to retire the whole of the Company's capital invested in mining properties before the extinguishment of the ore bodies. Timber depletion is figured at the market values of stumpage for the various kinds of timber cut. This stumpage provision will equal the original cost of the timber properties when the present standing timber is exhausted, after allowing a fair residual value for the lands either for reforestry or for agricultural purposes.

	Plant Depreciation	Ore and Timber Extinguishment	Total
Balance of Reserves for Plant Depreciation and Extinguishment at December 31, 1908	$4,370,788.94	$639,055 06	$5,009,844.00
Add:			
Provision for 1909	1,576,017.51	251,363.96	1,827,381.47
	$5,946,806.45	$890,419.02	$6,837,225.47
Deduct:			
Replacement Charges, etc.	326,550.71	. . . .	326,550.71
Balance at December 31, 1909	$5,620,255.74	$890,419.02	$6,510,674.76

REPAIRS RENEWALS AND MAINTENANCE

In accordance with the Company's policy, liberal expenditures were again made for repairs and renewals in order to maintain the properties in excellent condition and at their maximum of efficiency. All such expenditures are charged to operating expenses, and have been included in the cost of production. A comparison of these expenses for the last three seasons is:

	Season 1907	Season 1908	Season 1909
Harvester Works and Twine Mills	$1,599,116.13	$1,445,445.68	$1,666,597.85
Furnaces and Steel Mills	231,873.99	251,842.32	444,615.49
Miscellaneous Properties	142,687.87	142,556.40	133,191.13
	$1,973,677.99	$1,839,844.40	$2,244,404.47

RESERVES

SPECIAL MAINTENANCE:

These reserves provide for relining of blast furnaces, maintenance of docks and harbors, conversion of power systems, elevation of railroad tracks, and other renewal work of a current nature, the expenditure for which occurs at irregular intervals. To provide for such renewals when they become necessary, the future cost of the work is apportioned over current earnings.

Balance of Reserves for Special Maintenance at December 31, 1908		$ 469,653.14
Add:		
Operating Provision for 1909	148,278.11	
Special Provision for 1909	525,000.00	
		$1,142,931.25
Deduct:		
Relining, Renewal and other Charges during 1909	104,190.19	
Balance at December 31, 1909		$1,038,741.06

INSURANCE FUND:

The Company pursues the policy of carrying a reasonable portion of its own fire insurance. The risk is at present limited to plant and inventory valuations not exceeding $250,000 at any one location. In order that this policy may be more rapidly extended to cover larger risks, a special appropriation of $250,000 was again made to the Insurance Fund out of 1909 earnings, in addition to the regular credits through monthly insurance charges to operations.

Balance of Insurance Fund Reserves at December 31, 1908		$ 671,093.23
Add:		
Credit for 1909 from regular charges to operations	208,846.22	
Income from Insurance Fund Assets	43,673.52	
Special Appropriation from 1909 Earnings	250,000.00	
		$1,173,612.97
Deduct:		
Losses by Fire during 1909	80,151.24	
Balance at December 31, 1909		$1,093,461.73

At December 31, 1909, $1,070,862.50 of the Insurance Reserves was invested in income-bearing securities.

CONTINGENT:

Last year the reserve for deferred profits on forward sales amounted to $750,000, and was deducted from the receivables in the Balance Sheet, as explained in 1908 Annual Report. Assuming a continuance of present credit methods and the same proportion of forward sales, it is proposed to build up this reserve to a maximum of $2,500,000; and it has been decided to classify it with the other Reserves in the 1909 Balance Sheet under the heading Contingent. Theoretically and technically, a profit is earned when the sale is made; but when the actual realization of the profit on certain sales is deferred a considerable time beyond the close of the fiscal year, it is obviously a conservative and sensible policy to establish a contingent reserve to meet this condition inherent in the business. This policy prevents the misleading transfer of book earnings to surplus, where a long period of time elapses between the date of the sale and the realization of the profit in cash.

Balance of Contingent Reserve at December 31, 1908		$ 750,000.00
Add:		
Provision for 1909	500,000.00	
Balance at December 31, 1909		$1,250,000.00

RESERVES

CONTINGENT LOSSES ON RECEIVABLES:

The annual deductions from earnings to provide for losses which may ultimately be sustained in the realization of Bills and Accounts Receivable taken on each season's sales are based on long experience in this business and are considered sufficient to cover such contingencies. A systematic and careful investigation into the financial responsibility of prospective customers insures to the Company a high grade of notes and accounts; moreover, the greater portion of the receivables consist of farmers' notes or agents' acceptances, which have proved to be excellent credits. A recent compilation of bad debts incurred on the business of the seasons 1903 to 1907, inclusive, taking all accounts and notes already charged off in the books together with an estimate of the realization loss on balances still outstanding, the value of which can now be closely ascertained, proves that the reserves for bad debts provided out of earnings in those seasons are fully adequate.

The receivables are stated on the balance sheet as $46,212,035. This amount is arrived at after deducting $478,930, the provision for bad debts in the books of foreign companies; and also after deducting $300,000, the estimated amount of trade discounts and allowances, included in the receivables, which will be granted to customers at the time of collection. These deductions do not, therefore, form any part of the reserve for contingent losses shown on the balance sheet. The reserve for deferred profits on forward sales (which in the Balance Sheet of last year was deducted from the receivables) is included under Contingent Reserves on the Balance Sheet of December 31 1909, as explained on the preceding page.

Balance of Reserve for Contingent Losses on Receivables at December 31, 1908.	$2,224,829.91
Add:	
Provision for 1909	780,000.00
	$3,004,829.91
Deduct:	
Bad Debts charged off during 1909	360,204.11
Balance at December 31, 1909	$2,644,625.80

COLLECTION EXPENSES ON RECEIVABLES:

In most lines of business the time which elapses between the date of a sale and the collection of the proceeds in cash is comparatively short, and the need of a reserve to meet the future cost of collecting receivables outstanding at the date of the Balance Sheet would arise only in the event of liquidation. In the harvester business, where long credits in some lines are extended to the farming community, conservative management has adopted the principle of providing currently for such a reserve, which will be gradually built up to a reasonable amount, viz.: $1,000,000

Balance of Reserve for Collection Expenses on Receivables at December 31, 1908	$700,000.00
Add:	
Provision for 1909	100,000.00
Balance at December 31, 1909	$800,000.00

CAPITAL STOCK

The authorized Capital Stock of the International Harvester Company at December 31, 1909, all of which was issued and outstanding, was:

Preferred Stock, 7% Cumulative:
600,000 shares of $100 each, par value .... $ 60,000,000.00

Common Stock:
600,000 shares of $100 each, par value..... .... 60,000,000.00

$120,000,000.00

The $120,000,000 Capital Stock, as originally issued, consisted entirely of Common Stock and was all fully paid for when issued; $60,000,000 was paid for in cash at par, and the remaining $60,000,000 was issued for the Real Estate, Plants and Physical Inventories acquired at organization, which were conservatively valued by independent appraisers in excess of that amount, excluding any allowance for Goodwill or Patents.

On January 8, 1907, the original $120,000,000 Capital Stock was divided into $60,000,000 seven per cent cumulative Preferred Stock, and $60,000,000 Common Stock. Stockholders received one share of Preferred Stock and one share of Common Stock in exchange for every two shares of the original stock.

On January 28, 1910, the authorized Capital Stock of the Company was increased from $120,000,000 par value to $140,000,000 par value by increasing the amount of the authorized Common Stock from $60,000,000 to $80,000,000, such increase consisting of 200,000 additional shares of Common Stock par value $100 each, $20,000,000. This additional $20,000,000 Common Stock (fully paid by an equal amount of the accumulated earnings of the Company, which had not been available for the payment of cash dividends) was issued as a stock dividend to the holders of Common Stock of record on February 3, 1910; and the sum of $20,000,000 was transferred from the Surplus and Undivided Net Profits arising from the business of the Company to the Capital of the Company. The total authorized Capital Stock of the International Harvester Company thus becomes:

Preferred Stock, 7% Cumulative:
600,000 shares of $100 each, par value........... $ 60,000,000.00

Common Stock:
800,000 shares of $100 each, par value...... .. 80,000,000.00

$140,000,000.00

The Company has no bonded or other funded indebtedness, and its properties are free and unencumbered.

8

CURRENT LIABILITIES

	December 31 1908	December 31 1909
PURCHASE MONEY OBLIGATIONS:		
Obligations issued in part payment for new properties purchased in Europe during the year 1909	....	$2,250,000.00
BILLS PAYABLE:		
Loan maturing in 1912 and 1913	$6,000,000.00	$4,000,000.00
Loans maturing in January and February of following year...	680,884.95	....
Fiber drafts discounted at Manila, P. I. (since paid)	1,605,780.00	1,824,750.00
	$8,286,664.95	$5,824,750.00
ACCOUNTS PAYABLE:		
Audited Vouchers, etc., consisting almost entirely of current obligations of the Company for which vouchers were drawn in December and paid in January.............	$ 4,365,906.37	$ 4,488,258.40
Interest accrued	112,500.00	62,500.00
Taxes accrued:		
State, Municipal, etc., Taxes........................	250,981.21	343,371.62
Federal Corporation Tax	....	196,401.00
Preferred Stock Dividend for quarter ending February 15th in succeeding fiscal year	1,050,000.00	1,050,000.00
	$ 5,779,387.58	$ 6,140,531.02
Total Current Liabilities	$14,066,052.53	$14,215,281.02

PROPERTY ACCOUNT

A summary of the net value of the real estate and plant property acquired at organization, and the expenditures for capital additions and improvements from that date to December 31, 1909, chargeable to Property Account, is:

Net Appraisal Value of Real Estate and Plant Property at organization........ **$44,194,504.47**
Add:

Expenditures for capital additions and improvements and purchase of new properties from October 1, 1902 to December 31, 1909:

For Raw Material Facilities:

Equipment of iron ore mines, construction of new furnaces
and steel mills at South Chicago......................$5,770,285.52
Purchase of additional timber properties in Mississippi and
Missouri; construction of new saw mills, etc........... 527,569.22   6,297,854.74

For Manufacturing Facilities:

In United States.
Outlay for additional Real Estate, Buildings, Machinery
and Equipment for the manufacture of the increased
requirements of harvesting machines and tillage implements, and for the production of the Company's allied
lines of wagons, manure spreaders, gasoline engines,
cream separators, auto-buggies, tractors, American
flax twine, etc..... ... .$9,593,133.58

In Foreign Countries:
Outlay for Real Estate, Buildings, Machinery and Equipment for the manufacture of harvesting machines
and tillage implements in Canada, Sweden, France,
Germany and Russia 4,660,812.30   14,253,945.88

For Agency Warehouse and Transfer Properties:

Construction of new warehouses and additional storage and transfer
facilities on the territory..   1,183,921.52

For Railroads:

Track extension and additional rolling stock.............. ....   515,241.10
                                                                       $66,445,467.71
Deduct:
Miscellaneous Property Sales, etc.............................. ....   787,578.91

Add: **$65,657,888.80**
Expenditures for stripping and development at ore mines in advance of ore
extraction........ ....   874,720.06

Balance at December 31, 1909...... ....   **$66,532,608.86**

64

PROPERTY ACCOUNT

The principal Capital Expenditures for new property acquired or constructed and for additional equipment purchased during the fiscal year 1909, were as follows:

INTERNATIONAL HARVESTER COMPANY: Akron Works, Akron, Ohio: Installation of additional machinery and equipment for manufacturing auto-buggies and auto-wagons. Deering Works, Chicago, Ill.: Building and machinery for pulverizing coal. Keystone Works, Rock Falls, Ill.: New warehouse and equipment for manufacturing tillage implements. McCormick Works, Chicago, Ill.: New electric power sub-station. Milwaukee Works, Milwaukee, Wis.: New plant and equipment for additional gas engine capacity. Osborne Works, Auburn, N. Y.: Additional equipment for manufacturing tillage implements. Plano Works, West Pullman, Ill.: New plant and equipment for additional manure spreader capacity. Weber Works, Auburn Park, Ill.: New buildings and equipment for increased wagon output.

INTERNATIONAL HARVESTER COMPANY OF CANADA, LIMITED: Hamilton Works, Hamilton, Canada: Additional equipment to supply increasing demand for harvesting machinery and tillage implements in Canada.

AKTIEBOLAGET INTERNATIONAL HARVESTER COMPANY: Norrkoping Works, Norrkoping, Sweden: Additional mower and rake equipment.

COMPAGNIE INTERNATIONALE DES MACHINES AGRICOLES: Croix Works, Croix, France: Construction and equipment of plant for manufacturing French requirements of mowers, rakes, tedders, etc.

INTERNATIONAL HARVESTER COMPANY m. b. H.: Neuss Works, Neuss, Germany: Construction and equipment of plant for manufacturing German requirements of mowers, rakes, tedders, etc.

INTERNATIONAL HARVESTER COMPANY IN RUSSIA: Lubertzy Works, Lubertzy, Russia: Purchase of plant property at Lubertzy (near Moscow), Russia, equipped for manufacture of suction gas and crude oil engines.

WISCONSIN STEEL COMPANY: Completion of Merchant Mill No. 3 and installation of cold-drawing equipment; extensions to Merchant Mill No. 1 and Blooming Mill; new buildings and machine shops at ore mines.

WISCONSIN LUMBER COMPANY: New Saw Mill buildings; drainage ditch excavation.

RAILROAD COMPANIES: Sundry track extensions, new engine, 11 freight cars.

INTERNATIONAL HARVESTER COMPANY OF AMERICA: Construction of new general agency warehouses at Calgary, Alta., Detroit, Mich., Lincoln, Neb., Oklahoma City, Okla., Saskatoon, Sask. Additions to agency warehouses at Madison, Wis., Omaha, Neb., Watertown, S. D. Purchase of real estate for warehouse sites at Albany, N. Y., Bismarck, N. D., Minot, N. D., Sioux City, Ia., Sioux Falls, S. D.

Total amount of 1909 Capital Expenditures	$3,115,531.37
Deduct:	
Miscellaneous property sales and adjustments	398,947.06
Net Capital Additions during 1909 Fiscal Year	$2,716,584.31

PATENTS AND EXPERIMENTAL WORK

No capital stock was issued or cash paid for the patents, trademarks, shoprights, etc., which this Company received through the purchase of plants and properties at the time of organization. Those patents, trademarks, etc., were purchased, originated, or established at great cost by the former owners during long and successful terms of business, and are a valuable asset of the Company. The cost of all patents purchased since organization has been charged to Profit and Loss and all current patent expenses have been included in operating expenses as they were incurred.

The Company, in pursuance of its established policy, maintains a skilled force of inventors and designers for the purpose of producing new devices and improvements in type, design, or construction of its products. All experimental and development expenses, including money spent in developing new lines not yet profitably marketed have been charged to cost of operation.

The experimental, patent and development expenditures amounted to $474,515 for Season 1909, compared to $743,557 for Season 1908. The actual experimental expense for this season is somewhat larger than the previous season. A considerable saving has, however, been made in the cost of development work on the new lines, most of which are now becoming established as standard manufacturing propositions.

INVENTORIES

The character of the business of the International Harvester Company of America requires that large stocks of harvesting machinery and farm implements be carried at convenient locations throughout the world in order to meet the urgent local requirements of varying crop conditions. Therefore a large portion of the working capital is invested at the close of the fiscal year in manufactured products scattered over a wide territory. By this investment of capital and world-wide distribution of manufactured products the Company aims to meet the varying demands of a trade which is frequently unable to forecast its needs until the crops are assured and the harvest is at hand.

The inventories of finished products on the territory are taken at the close of the harvest season. The Works' inventories are taken as of September 1st, when the manufacturing season for the current year's requirements ends; and from that date material deliveries and manufacturing activities are devoted to the production for the succeeding fiscal year. This subdivision of inventories by periods and seasons has been preserved in the comparative inventory statement presented herewith.

The Raw Materials, Work in Process of Manufacture, and Finished Products on hand at the close of the season have been valued at cost, which is in all instances lower than the market values prevailing at December 31, 1909. A reasonable allowance for depreciation has been made on finished machines carried over on the territory and on repair parts not applicable to machines of current manufacture.

INVENTORIES

The principal classifications in the inventories at December 31, 1908 and 1909, are:

	Season 1908	Season 1909
At Harvester Works, Wagon Works, Twine Mills, etc., at close of manufacturing season, September 1st:		
Raw Materials and Supplies:		
Pig Iron and Scrap.................................. $ 313,028.00		$ 714,884.53
Steel... 1,075,901.71		1,140,538.02
Lumber... 5,507,011.30		6,380,130.28
Cotton Duck.................................... 130,304.78		230,237.52
Fiber and Flax Straw 2,312,571.12		2,238,998.52
Pipe and Tubing, Belting, Chain, Paint and Varnish, Nuts, Bolts, Rivets, etc 1,107,000.70		1,390,103.77
	$10,574,908.30	$12,109,892.04
Work in Process of Manufacture...................... 5,170,514.98		5,449,023.97
Finished Machines................................... 2,200,203.84		1,902,134.01
Repair Parts....................................... 827,103.78		870,380.58
Twine... 540,135.80		199,130.32
	$19,301,070.70	$20,530,570.52
Deduct:		
Manufacturing cost of shipments from Works after inventory-taking, September 1st, and prior to the close of the fiscal year December 31st, which were included in the season's sales............................. 3,103,337.64		4,102,022.22
	$10,287,739.12	$16,368,548.30
At Agency Warehouses, Transfer Points and on the Territory: Finished Machines, Repair Parts, Twine, etc., on hand at the close of the selling season:		
United States................................. $ 9,278,820.52		$ 7,916,920.08
Foreign Countries............................. 6,057,237.44		6,484,790.26
	$15,336,057.96	$14,401,710.94
At Ore Mines, Furnaces, and Steel Mills at December 31st:		
Iron Ores....................................... $ 1,023,451.10		$ 1,150,440.37
Pig Iron, Steel Billets, Bars, Scrap, etc.............. 251,827.20		291,571.31
Rolls, Moulds, Stools, etc........................... 148,896.10		139,412.04
Coal and Coke................................... 57,815.39		62,589.78
Stores and Supplies................................ 124,048.36		121,204.58
	$ 1,606,038.21	$ 1,765,218.68
At Saw Mills at December 31st:		
Lumber, Logs, Stores and Supplies.................... $ 109,696.10		$ 124,773.57
Advertising Supplies for the succeeding Season............... $ 230,616.87		$ 272,155.50
Stationery Stores, Paper Stock and Miscellaneous............ $ 284,784.62		$ 204,292.83
	$33,854,932.88	$33,136,705.82
Material Purchases and manufacture at Works subsequent to inventory-taking, September 1st, and prior to the close of the fiscal year December 31st, on account of production for the succeeding season's consumption and sale.............. 13,832,123.38		20,203,221.02
	$47,687,056.26	$53,399,926.84

SALES

The volume of total sales was larger than any former year in the history of the industry. The domestic trade increased 20 per cent and the foreign trade increased 13 per cent over last fiscal year. The higher ratio of gain in domestic sales is principally due to the fact that the Company's domestic trade suffered during the general business depression of 1908, which, however, caused no decline in the Company's foreign trade.

The sales of harvesting machinery, tillage implements, and twine increased approximately 10 per cent over 1908, and were slightly larger than 1907, which was the previous high mark. The sales of the new lines of wagons, manure spreaders, gasoline engines, cream separators, auto-buggies, and tractors aggregated 45 per cent higher than any previous year, and aided considerably in the improvement effected in the Company's earnings.

	Season 1907	Season 1908	Season 1909
Harvesting Machinery, Tillage Implements and Twine:			
United States	$35,417,092.88	$30,920,336.69	$34,616,558.74
Foreign Countries	21,582,557.01	21,419,866.16	22,894,797.55
	$56,999,649.89	$52,340,202.85	$57,511,356.29
Wagons, Manure Spreaders, Gasoline Engines, Cream Separators, Auto-Buggies, Tractors:			
United States	$10,985,492.17	$10,903,661.29	$15,480,606.95
Foreign Countries	2,895,987.16	3,384,927.22	5,239,578.11
	$13,881,479.33	$14,288,588.51	$20,720,185.06
Steel Products, Fiber Sales, etc	7,325,761.14	5,912,979.80	8,383,008.20
Total Sales	$78,206,890.36	$72,541,771.16	$86,614,549.55

WORKING CAPITAL

Following is the Working Capital condition compared with the previous fiscal year:

	December 31, 1908	December 31, 1909	Increase
Current Assets:			
Inventories.....................	$47,087,050.20	$ 53,399,920.84	$ 5,712,870.58
Receivables (Net)...............	36,311,230.01	46,212,035.80	9,900,805.79
Cash...........................	9,339,054.90	5,426,689.82	*3,912,365.08
	$93,337,341.17	$105,038,652.46	$11,701,311.29
Deduct:			
Current Liabilities:			
Purchase Money Obligations............		2,250,000.00	2,250,000.00
Bills and Accounts Payable.........	14,060,052.53	11,905,281.02	*2,100,771.51
Net Working Capital........	$79,271,288.64	$ 90,823,371.44	$11,552,082.80

*Decrease

The above increase of $11,552,000 in the net working and trading assets of the Company is derived entirely from the portion of 1909 earnings required to finance the expansion of the Company and therefore retained in the business.

The excess of $5,712,000 in inventories is attributable to the increased expenditures for material and labor after the close of 1909 season to provide machinery and implements in anticipation of the demand for 1910 harvest.

The excess of $9,900,000 in receivables is caused partly by the increased sales resulting in larger outstandings at the close of the year, partly by the extension of additional credit in Canada, Russia and Siberia to finance the heavy purchases of farm machinery required in the rapid development of farming operations in those countries, and partly by the amount of $3,000,000 due from employes on account of stock subscriptions, which amount is being repaid at the rate of approximately $750,000 per annum.

At the time of organization, October 1, 1902, the Working Capital of the Company was $75,805,000 compared to $90,823,000 at December 31, 1909, as shown above, an increase of $15,018,000 at the latter date. During the same period, the cash expended for permanent property, additional plant, buildings and equipment, aggregating $22,000,000 has been provided out of earnings.

As evidenced by the above figures, the Working Capital requirements of the Company are large; first, on account of the magnitude of the inventories, the output of harvesting machinery being in process of manufacture for many months ahead of the selling seasons, which are limited to the time immediately preceding the harvests and are necessarily short; second, because of the liberal credit extended to the farming community thus enabling them to buy machinery for prompt use which otherwise they might not be in position to purchase.

EMPLOYES PROFIT SHARING

There are two plans of profit sharing in operation with the employes: First: A percentage of the annual earnings of the Company, varying with the amount of profit earned, is distributed in cash among employes who have been found worthy of special recognition during the year. Each employe participating in this distribution is, in addition, afforded the privilege, if he so desires, of buying the Company's stock at less than the prevailing market prices. Second: Sale of the Company's stock to employes at a price below the prevailing market value, payments being made on an installment basis. In July, 1909, the Company offered to all employes its Preferred Stock at $115 per share and its Common Stock at $75 per share, each employe having the privilege of subscribing for an amount not exceeding his annual salary or wages, and of paying therefor in monthly installments not exceeding 25 per cent of each month's salary or wages. In addition to the regular dividends on the stock there is allowed an annual bonus of $4 on each share of Preferred Stock and $3 on each share of Common Stock each year for five years, the only condition being that an employe must be in good standing in the Company's service during each of these years and shall retain his stock during that period. 4,400 employes availed themselves of this offer subscribing for 17,684 shares of Preferred Stock and 16,410 of Common Stock. This plan offers employes a very satisfactory form of investment in the business in which they are employed, has tended to increase the spirit of co-operation and loyalty, and gives to the Company the great advantage of anchoring its organization to the business.

PENSION FUND

The Company now has fifty-five employes on the regular pension roll. These pensioners have averaged nearly thirty years of service; their average age is sixty-six years. Five pensioners died during last year. Pensions are paid solely out of funds donated by the Company, and a permanent pension fund is being established by appropriations from earnings until the accumulation of this fund is sufficient to provide revenue to discharge future pension payments. Following is a statement of the condition of the fund at December 31, 1909:

Pension Fund Appropriations:

From 1908 Earnings		$250,000.00
From 1909 Earnings		250,000 00
Total Appropriations to December 31, 1909		$500,000.00

Add:
Income from fund for year 1909	$12,284.00	

Less:
Pension payments during 1909	9,629.78	2,654.22
Balance at December 31, 1909		$502,654.22

EMPLOYES BENEFIT ASSOCIATION

OBJECT:

The object of the Benefit Association is to provide its members with a certain income when sick, or when disabled by accident, either on or off duty, and to pay to their families certain definite sums in case of death; to create and maintain a fund which shall belong to the employes, be used in payment of benefits to them and cost them the least money possible considering the benefits received.

MEMBERSHIP:

Membership in the Association is voluntary. The average membership during the first fiscal year (16 months) was 19,559. The growth of the Association has been very satisfactory to its Trustees as well as to the Officers of the International Harvester Company.

EMPLOYES' CONTRIBUTION:

Two per cent of wages received by the employe, except that no member shall be allowed to contribute or receive benefits on the basis of more than $2,000 annual compensation.

COMPANY'S CONTRIBUTION:

At the end of each year, if the average membership in the Benefit Association during that year has equaled fifty per cent of the average total number of employes in the manufacturing plants, the Company will contribute $25,000 to the fund, and if such average membership has equaled seventy-five per cent of such total number of employes, the Company will contribute $50,000 to the fund.

RESULTS OF FIRST FISCAL YEAR'S OPERATION:

The following statement shows the results of operation for the first fiscal year, covering the sixteen months from September 1, 1908 to December 31, 1909:

Operating Receipts......................................		$353,296 00
Operating Payments:		
Benefits Paid.........................	$232,232 60	
Expenses.............................	29,557.51	261,790.11
Cash on Hand, December 31, 1909		$ 91,505 89
Deduct:		
Liabilities for unsettled claims (partly estimated)		56,054.32
Estimated Surplus from Operations on December 31, 1909 ...		$ 35,451.57
Add:		
Contribution of International Harvester Company		50,000.00
Total Estimated Surplus..........		$ 85,451.57

WELFARE WORK

In June, 1909, the superintendents of the various plants and one other special representative, nineteen in number, were appointed an Advisory Board on Welfare. To be effective and satisfactory, both to employes and to the Company, Welfare Work must be conducted along practical lines, and it was therefore determined to place it in charge of a board of operating men. The results already obtained through the activity of this board are very gratifying.

Special efforts have been put forth during the past year to reduce the number of accidents at the plants. The protection and safeguarding of machinery and equipment has been an important part of the work of the Advisory Board. Its members interchange suggestions and ideas with a view of installing in every plant the most effective devices for protecting the employes. It is hoped that this concerted action will result in minimizing the danger of injury to the employes and in reducing the economic loss which this country at present suffers from industrial accidents.

Conditions affecting the health of the employes are also receiving very careful consideration. A high standard for sanitary equipment has been decided upon, and much has been done during the past year in installing new sanitary appliances and generally improving the sanitary conditions at the various works. Further improvements will be made during 1910.

The new Club House at the Deering Works is now completed and ready for use. It provides an Assembly Hall for entertainments, dances, meetings, etc., which is also equipped for a gymnasium. There are bowling alleys, billiard rooms, reading rooms and class rooms where instruction in technical subjects can be secured. The Club House fills a definite want at the Deering Works and it is hoped that the Hall will prove a popular place for neighborhood meetings.

During the year 1909, $110,047.04 was expended in the various branches of Welfare Work in addition to the Company's contribution to the Employes' Benefit Association and the Pension Fund.

EMPLOYES

The average number of employes of all companies during the past year was 28,493, and the total salaries and wages paid, together with the amounts expended or set aside for the benefit of employes, for Profit Sharing, Employes Benefit Association, and the Pension Fund, was $22,857,129.66.

During the year the Officers have been giving careful attention to the subject of Employers' Liability and compensation to employes for industrial accidents, with a view to adopting a plan which would be fair to both the Company and the employes. Substantial progress has been made along these lines and it is hoped that a comprehensive and satisfactory plan can soon be put in operation.

The sales of wagons, manure spreaders, gasoline engines, cream separators, auto-buggies, tractors and other new lines aggregated over $20,000,000 in the year 1909 and contributed largely to the increased earnings. These various lines have been developed at heavy expense and are becoming firmly established. The steadily increasing demand for the Company's products in foreign countries makes that trade a stable and permanent factor in the total earnings. Approximately 40 per cent of the 1909 sales of harvesting machinery, tillage implements and twine were in foreign countries, and the total foreign business has increased almost 100 per cent since the first year of the organization in 1902.

The new works at Croix, France, and Neuss, Germany, recently erected to supply the requirements of the French and German trade commenced partial operations in March, 1910.

The growth of the Russian trade in the past and the assurance of Russia's great future as an agricultural country has made it desirable to manufacture there at least a part of the requirements for the Russian harvest. A large plant comprising 40 acres has been purchased at Lubertzy, near Moscow. It is well built and is equipped with modern machinery for manufacturing gas engines. Plans are being made to add facilities for the manufacture of harvesting machines and tillage implements.

In July, 1909, the Company offered its preferred and common stock for sale to its employes on monthly installment payments. This plan was favorably received and 4,400 employes subscribed for 17,684 shares of Preferred Stock and 16,410 shares of Common Stock.

The bonus distribution to especially meritorious employes was again made in 1909 and 1,426 participated.

The Board takes pleasure in acknowledging that the increased success of the business is largely due to the loyal efforts of the organization.

By Order of the Board of Directors,

CYRUS H. McCORMICK,
President.

Chicago, April 9, 1910.

DECEMBER 31 1909

LIABILITIES

CAPITAL STOCK:

Preferred...	$60.000 000 00	
Common..	60,000,000 00	$120.000.000.00*

PURCHASE MONEY OBLIGATIONS .... | | 2.250.000.00

CURRENT LIABILITIES:

Bills Payable	$ 5.824.750 00		
Accounts Payable:			
Audited Vouchers, Accrued Interest and Taxes, etc...	$5.090.531.02		
Preferred Stock Dividend (payable March 1, 1910)	1,050,000.00	6.140.531.02	11,965,281.02

RESERVES:

Plant Depreciation and Extinguishment........	$ 6,510,674.76	
Special Maintenance....	1,038,741.06	
Collection Expenses on Receivables...	800,000.00	
Insurance Fund........	1,093,461.73	
Pension Fund............................	502,654.22	
Contingent	1,250,000.00	11,195,531.77

SURPLUS.. | 27,384,729.82*

$172,795,542.61

*NOTE.—In February, 1910, $20,000,000 of the Company's Surplus was transferred to the Common Stock of the Company, as explained on pages 4 and 8 of this report.

COMBINED BALANCE SHEET

ASSETS

PROPERTY ACCOUNT:

Real Estate and Plant Property, Ore Mines, Coal and Timber Lands at December 31, 1908..............	$62,941,304.49	
Net Capital Additions during 1909	2,716,584.31	
	$65,657,888 80	
Expenditures for Stripping and Development at Ore Mines	874,720 00	$66,532,608.86

DEFERRED CHARGES TO OPERATIONS:

Advanced Payments for Mine Royalties, etc	153,418.79

INSURANCE FUND ASSETS..................................... 1,070,862.50

CURRENT ASSETS:

Inventories:

Finished Products, Raw Materials, etc., at close of 1909 Season...............................	$33,130,705.82	
Subsequent Material Purchases and Manufacture for 1910 Season...............................	20,263,221.02	
	$53,399,926.84	

Receivables:

Farmers' and Agents' Notes.........	$29,752,945.15		
Accounts Receivable...............	19,103,716.45		
	$48,856,661.60		
Deduct:			
Accumulated Reserves for Contingent Losses.......................	2,644,625.80	46,212,035.80	
Cash...		5,426,689.82	105,038,652.46
			$172,795,542.61

COMBINED PROFIT AND LOSS ACCOUNT
FOR THE SEASON 1909

Sales of Harvesting Machinery, Tillage Implements, Engines, Cream Separators, Wagons, Manure Spreaders, Auto-Buggies, Twine, Steel Products, etc........	$86,614,549.55
Deduct:	
*Cost of Manufacturing and Distributing.............	67,669,233.94
	$18,945,315.61
Add:	
Miscellaneous Earnings and Charges (Net)	869,706.65
	$19,815,082.26
Deduct:	
Administrative and General Expenses................................	589,752.52
	$19,225,329.74
Deduct:	
Appropriation for Fire Insurance Fund...............................	$ 250,000.00
Appropriation for Renewals and Minor Improvements...................	567,151.85
Reserve for Pension Fund..	250,000.00
Reserves for Plant Depreciation and Ore Extinguishment..................	1,827,381.47
Reserves for Contingent Losses and Collection Expenses on Receivables	880,000.00
	$ 3,774,533.32
	$15,450,796.42
Deduct:	
Interest on Purchase Money Obligations and Current Loans...............	558,056.21
Net Profit.................................	$14,892,740.21

*NOTE:—The item of Cost of Manufacturing and Distributing includes the cost of manufacturing the products (exclusive of depreciation on plant property and ore extinguishment) the freight and duty charges paid, and all selling expenses incurred by the America Company in marketing the products.

HASKINS & SELLS

CERTIFIED PUBLIC ACCOUNTANTS
30 BROAD STREET
NEW YORK

LONDON, E. C.
30 COLEMAN STREET

CHICAGO	ST. LOUIS	CLEVELAND	PITTSBURGH
MARQUETTE BUILDING	THIRD NATIONAL BANK BUILDING	WILLIAMSON BUILDING	FARMERS BANK BUILDING

CABLE ADDRESS "HASKELLS"

New York, April 7, 1910.

The Board of Directors,

International Harvester Company,

Chicago, Illinois.

We have made an audit of the books, accounts and records of the International Harvester Company and of affiliated companies for the year ended December 31, 1909.

We have examined the charges to capital accounts, have verified the Cash and other Current Assets at December 31, 1909, including the inventories of Raw Materials and Supplies, Work in Progress, and Finished Product, and have verified the Income and Profit and Loss accounts.

We find that Raw Materials and Supplies in storerooms and in process of manufacture were priced at cost, which was lower than market values at December 31, 1909; that Finished Machines, Attachments, and Twine were inventoried at cost, and Repair Parts at proper percentages of list prices, with a reasonable allowance for depreciation of Finished Machines and Repair Parts on the territory.

The company has pursued a conservative policy in relation to charges to capital accounts. Adequate reserves have been provided for depreciation of fixed assets and for possible losses, and full provision has been made for all known liabilities.

WE HEREBY CERTIFY that, in our opinion, the Statement of Combined Assets and Liabilities submitted herewith reflects the true financial condition at December 31, 1909, and that the accompanying Statement of Profits is correct.

HASKINS & SELLS,
Certified Public Accountants.

23

1910

ANNUAL REPORT

OF

THE DIRECTORS

OF

AMERICAN TELEPHONE & TELEGRAPH COMPANY

TO THE STOCKHOLDERS

FOR THE

YEAR ENDING DECEMBER 31, 1910

NEW YORK, 1911.

American Telephone & Telegraph Company

OFFICERS

President
THEODORE N. VAIL

Vice Presidents
EDWARD J. HALL
U. N. BETHELL   WILLIAM R. DRIVER   N. C. KINGSBURY
B. E. SUNNY   H. B. THAYER   CHARLES P. WARE

Treasurer   *Secretary*
WILLIAM R. DRIVER   CHARLES EUSTIS HUBBARD

Comptroller   *General Counsel*
CHARLES G. DuBOIS   GEORGE V. LEVERETT

Chief Engineer
JOHN J. CARTY

DIRECTORS

CHARLES W. AMORY   CHARLES EUSTIS HUBBARD
THOMAS B. BAILEY   LEWIS CASS LEDYARD
GEORGE F. BAKER   JOHN J. MITCHELL
FRANCIS BLAKE   WILLIAM LOWELL PUTNAM
HARRY H. BRIGHAM   THOMAS SANDERS
ALEXANDER COCHRANE   SYLVANUS L. SCHOONMAKER
T. JEFFERSON COOLIDGE, JR. EUGENE V. R. THAYER
W. MURRAY CRANE   THEODORE N. VAIL
HENRY P. DAVISON   FRANK E. WARNER
RUDULPH ELLIS   JOHN I. WATERBURY
NORMAN W. HARRIS   MOSES WILLIAMS
HENRY L. HIGGINSON   ROBERT WINSOR
HENRY S. HOWE

REPORT OF THE DIRECTORS
OF
AMERICAN TELEPHONE AND TELEGRAPH COMPANY.

NEW YORK, March 13, 1911.

TO THE STOCKHOLDERS:

Herewith is respectfully submitted a general statement covering the business of the Bell system as a whole, followed by the report of the American Telephone and Telegraph Company, for the year 1910.

BELL TELEPHONE SYSTEM IN UNITED STATES.

SUBSCRIBER STATIONS.

At the end of the year the number of stations which constituted our system in the United States was 5,882,719, an increase of 740,027. 1,852,051 of these were operated by local, co-operative and rural independent companies or associations having sub-license or connection contracts, so-called connecting companies.

WIRE MILEAGE.

The total mileage of wire in use for exchange and toll service was 11,642,212 miles, of which 1,162,186 were added during the year. These figures do not include the mileage of wire operated by connecting companies.

4

TRAFFIC.

Including the traffic over the long-distance lines, but not including connecting companies, the daily average of toll connections was about 602,500, and of exchange connections about 21,681,500, as against corresponding figures in 1909 of 517,000 and 19,925,000; the total daily average for 1910 reaching 22,284,000, or at the rate of about 7,175,448,000 per year.

PLANT ADDITIONS.

82

The amount added to plant and real estate by all the companies, excluding connecting companies, constituting our system in the United States during the year 1910 was:—

Real Estate	$2,518,133
Equipment	19,628,357
Exchange Lines	13,409,546
Toll Lines	14,959,048
Construction Work in Process	3,067,734
	$53,582,818

PLANT ADDITIONS OF PREVIOUS YEARS.

The amount added in 1900 was $31,619,100; in 1901, $31,005,400; in 1902, $37,336,500; in 1903, $35,368,700; in 1904, $33,436,700; in 1905, $50,780,900; in 1906, $79,366,900; in 1907, $52,921,400; in 1908, $26,637,200; and in 1909, $28,700,100, making the total expenditure for additions to plant during the eleven years $460,755,700.

MAINTENANCE AND RECONSTRUCTION.

During the year $52,028,000 was applied out of revenue to maintenance and reconstruction purposes.

The total provision for maintenance and reconstruction charged against revenue for the last eight years was over $283,500,000.

CONSTRUCTION FOR THE CURRENT YEAR.

Estimates of all the associated operating companies and of the American Telephone and Telegraph Company for all new construction requirements in 1911 have been prepared. It is estimated that about $60,000,000 will be required for current additions to plant in 1911, of which amount some $30,000,000 will be provided by the existing and current resources of the companies. All who are responsible for these expenditures are working in complete understanding of these estimates and the limits set on their expenditures.

DEPRECIATION.   83

The question of depreciation has been considered very critically and analytically during the past year, by commissions and other bodies, in connection with studies on the rate question. While a depreciation reserve was generally favored, there seemed to be a disposition to apply experience and theories, gleaned from other lines of business, to the telephone business.

The telephone business is unique in that it supplies its own terminals, which are vast in number, are temporary in character, and call for large investment, unique in that a very considerable part of its plant is of a rapidly deteriorating character. Underground conduits and cables and aerial cables are fast changing this, but in the outlying rural and semi-urban districts and for long-distance lines construction will always have to be overhead on poles. There is nothing analogous to it in industrial or public utility service except the telegraph.

The entire disregard or underestimating of depreciation and future replacement, is the cause of nearly all the financial disasters that have occurred in the telephone business, and has been the common failing of newcomers in the telephone field from the beginning to the present time.

Current repairs on new plant, even of the old time temporary character, were small; no surplus or reserve was provided; profits were apparently large, as were dividends.

A false atmosphere of prosperity surrounded the business which was not dispelled until replacements of plant through decay or obsolescence became imperative; until the overhead gave way to the underground, until the individual board gave way to the multiple central office system, until central office energy supplanted the magneto system, until exacting construction requirements of long-distance speaking began, until expansion of business and extension into new fields, some unremunerative, were obligatory; until a condition existed where, to correct mistakes of the past, capital had to be expended without producing any corresponding increase in the revenue.

The inevitable was in some cases postponed by excessive charges to construction account, but came in time, as it is bound to come under such conditions. The apparent profits and dividends had been at the cost of the capital and, at the time of the greatest necessity, resources were at the lowest ebb.

Ignorantly or wilfully, every cause but the right cause was blamed, and although the management had been in the hands of the outside interests, the Bell parent company was given the responsibility, had to carry the burden, and assume the work of reconstruction and rehabilitation.

An illustration may make the necessity of depreciation reserve even clearer. If a carter or local expressman or hackman owning his own carriages, horses or motor cars, should consider as profit all revenue over and above his current expenses and costs of current repairs, and should spend it, saving nothing with which to replace his plant when worn out or damaged beyond repair, he would be called thriftless and improvident. He had enjoyed his capital, and had nothing upon which to raise more.

84

The present policy of the Bell System is to provide against every probable contingency and to base the amount and extent of such provision on past experience—not on future expectations. It is conjectured that the future will show a decrease in the depreciation or reconstruction due to decay, wear and tear, and obsolescence. Changes—improvements—are going on as rapidly as in the past, but the general character of plant and methods is assuming more permanency. The improvements are being evolved from, and are being grafted on to, the old system and methods. The disturbing and sometimes seemingly destructive conditions following the rapid development of high pressure power and transmission have been to a great measure overcome.

85

All this has been made possible through the unremitting study and research of the staff of the Engineering and Experimental Departments of the Company, who by close attention, observation and study, anticipate and provide for all such contingencies and conditions as can possibly be anticipated or provided for in advance.

Under these conditions there is small probability that any such causes as those which forced the wholesale reconstruction or rearrangement of plant in the past will again occur; it is, however, for the benefit of the public and of the corporation to have an ample reserve for any contingency which may happen.

Local telephone service up to the present requirements cannot be furnished by isolated or individual companies, and facilities for general service must be co-extensive with speaking limits, so that it is imperative for any system which pretends to be comprehensive to meet, and meet promptly, all demands for service. Its public usefulness as well as corporate existence and prosperity make it imperative to meet the continuing demand for extension which sometimes seems almost overwhelming in its magnitude.

Not only must this increase be met, but to be met economically or efficiently, it must be anticipated; subways cannot be built conduit by conduit, or filled wire by wire—cost would be prohibitive and service impossible. Central office buildings must be located and erected and connected by subway with the general system before switchboards or wires or equipment can be introduced. When built they must be built for the future. To build for present requirements only, and enlarge as demand comes, is impossible in much of this work; and, where possible, impracticable from service standpoint, or prohibitive from that of cost. Advance construction of this kind of the Bell Telephone System, including construction in process, December 31, 1910, was estimated at $180,000,000. Had no plant been built in advance of needs except that which was unavoidable the expenditure would have been reduced by $112,000,000, but the cost of the plant not built at first, if provided later and only as required, would have been $250,000,000 instead of $112,-000,000. In other words, not to provide for advance construction doubles the cost of the plant.

86

The capital for this advance construction must be provided by and at the cost of the present, as was the advance construction of the past provided by and at the cost of the past. To the extent that advance construction reduces the cost of necessary plant and anticipates reconstruction and replacement, to that extent the capital charge to be borne by present and future is reduced and to that extent it immediately puts the depreciation reserve to its intended use. The criticism that any excess of reserve is at the cost of the present for the benefit of the future is true, but only to the extent that it may be found eventually to be in excess of actual requirements. In any case it would be no more than might rightly be considered an insurance against obsolescence which cannot be foreseen.

FIGURES FOR THE YEAR.

The following tables show the business for the year of the Bell Telephone System including the American Telephone and Telegraph Company and its associated holding and operating companies in the United States, but not including connected independent or sub-licensee companies, nor the Western Electric Company and Western Union Telegraph Company except as investments in and dividends from those companies are included respectively in assets and revenue. All inter-company duplications are eliminated in making up these tables so that the figures represent the business of the system as a whole in its relations to the public.

87

The gross revenue collected from the public in 1910 for telephone service by the Bell System—not including the connected independent companies—was $165,-600,000; an increase of nearly $16,000,000 over last year. Of this, operation consumed $54,000,000; taxes, $8,000,000; current maintenance, $25,700,000; and provision for depreciation, $26,200,000.

The surplus available for charges, etc., was $51,000,-000, of which $11,550,000 was paid in interest and $25,-000,000 was paid in dividends to the public.

The total capitalization, including inter-company items and duplications, of the companies of the Bell System is $1,114,310,979. Of this $502,306,910 is owned and in the treasury of the companies of the Bell System. The capital stock, bonds and notes payable outstanding in the hands of the public at the close of the year were $612,000,000. If to this be added the current accounts payable $21,700,000, the total obligations of every kind were $633,700,000, as against which there were liquid assets, cash and current accounts receivable, of $53,600,000, leaving $580,100,000 as the net permanent capital obligations of the whole system outstanding in the hands of the public.

Against these obligations, the companies had property $696,700,000—an excess of $116,600,000, or 20 per cent.

There is a large additional surplus, which is legitimate and proper and which could be properly added to the book Surplus, representing as it does the value of intangible property, such as franchises, contracts, patents, rights of way, both public and private, which are not carried at any valuation in the book accounts.

In every case where the public authorities have appraised the plant of the companies, the valuation has been far in excess of the book valuation. It is within the bounds of conservatism to say that the obligations of all the companies outstanding in the hands of the public are represented by 150 per cent. of property at a fair replacement valuation of the plants and assets, not including public franchises.

88

In spite of these facts and figures shown from year to year in our annual reports; in spite of reports to the contrary of every public or semi-public body which has examined and reported on the value of the property of the Bell System; in total disregard of information at the disposition of every one, there are many who for some purpose or other—sometimes to induce credulous investors to take some worthless securities in hope of extraordinary and impossible returns; sometimes for political purposes; sometimes for sensation or notoriety—continue to spread the reports of fabulous over-capitalization of the Bell System as a whole and of its component parts, and gross and extortionate charges for service.

Particular attention, therefore, is invited to the tables following, and also to the one showing averages of operating units of associated companies, on page 13.

BELL TELEPHONE SYSTEM IN UNITED STATES.

COMPARISON OF EARNINGS AND EXPENSES, 1909 AND 1910.

(ALL DUPLICATIONS, INCLUDING INTEREST, DIVIDENDS AND
OTHER PAYMENTS TO AMERICAN TELEPHONE AND TELE-
GRAPH COMPANY BY ASSOCIATED HOLDING AND
OPERATING COMPANIES, EXCLUDED.)

	1909.	1910.	Increase.
Gross Earnings	$140,914,708	$165,612,881	$15,698,173
Expenses—Operation	$49,731,941	$54,235,449	$4,503,508
Current Maintenance	23,723,681	25,763,082	2,039,401
Depreciation	21,115,272	26,264,927	5,149,655
Taxes	6,976,306	8,355,015	1,378,709
Total Expenses	$101,547,200	$114,618,473	$13,071,273
Net Earnings	$48,367,508	$50,994,408	$2,626,900
Deduct Interest	10,221,383	11,556,864	1,335,481
Balance Net Profits	$38,146,125	$39,437,544	$1,291,419
Deduct Dividends Paid	23,910,603	25,160,786	1,250,183
Surplus Earnings	$14,235,522	$14,276,758	$41,236

COMBINED BALANCE SHEET, 1909 AND 1910.

(DUPLICATIONS EXCLUDED)

ASSETS:	Dec. 31, 1909.	Dec. 31, 1910.	Increase.
Contracts and Licenses	$7,212,781	$2,943,381	$4,269,400*
Telephone Plant	557,417,146	610,999,964	53,582,818
Supplies, Tools, etc	17,048,196	20,987,551	3,939,355
Receivables	49,744,919	26,077,802	23,667,117*
Cash	32,055,866	27,548,933	4,506,933*
Stocks and Bonds	38,166,284	64,766,089	26,599,805
Total	$701,645,192	$753,323,720	$51,678,528
LIABILITIES:			
Capital Stock	$352,904,063	$344,645,430	$8,258,633*
Funded Debts	187,685,339	224,791,696	37,106,357
Bills Payable	40,721,625	42,566,943	1,845,318
Accounts Payable	24,633,780	21,721,125	2,912,655*
Total Outstanding obligations	$605,944,807	$633,725,194	$27,780,387
Surplus and Reserves	95,700,385	119,598,526	23,898,141
Total	$701,645,192	$753,323,720	$51,678,528

*Decrease.

AVERAGE OPERATING UNITS OF ASSOCIATED

OPERATING COMPANIES.

(*See table on next page.*)

The table on the following page shows average operating revenue and expenses per station, operating ratios, unit plant costs, etc., of the associated operating companies (not including the American Telephone and Telegraph Company's long-distance lines), for the years 1895, 1900, 1905 and 1910.

It will be noted that there has been a steady decrease both in expenses and revenue per subscriber's station, so that now the average subscriber pays for a higher grade, more comprehensive service, less than half what he paid fifteen years ago for the much less useful service that was then possible.

This reduction in cost of service has made it possible for every one who needs a telephone to have one and to get the great advantage of being within reach of everybody by telephone.

The greatly decreased plant investment per station to which attention was called in the previous annual report has been still further reduced during the year to $142, notwithstanding the extensive additions to toll lines shown on page 4.

There is a steady increase in the proportion of wires underground, as shown on page 63, which indicates a greater permanence of plant and decreases the maintenance costs. This low cost of plant and this decreasing maintenance cost are only made possible by the central supervision of engineering and manufacturing of the Bell System and the advance construction referred to at length under the head of Depreciation.

The percentage of net profits to capital stock, although not so good as in the earlier years of the business, shows for 1910 an improvement over recent years.

Average Operating Units of Associated Operating Companies, 1895 to 1910.

(THIS TABLE COVERS THE COMPANIES OWNING ALL THE
EXCHANGES AND TOLL LINES OF THE BELL TELEPHONE
SYSTEM EXCEPT THE LONG-DISTANCE LINES OF
AMERICAN TELEPHONE & TELEGRAPH CO.)

Average per Exchange Station.

EARNINGS:	1895.	1900.	1905.	1910.
Exchange Service	$69.75	$44.68	$33.31	$31.28
Toll Service	11.35	12.60	9.95	9.47
Total	$81.10	$57.28	$43.26	$40.75
EXPENSES:				
Operation	$29.15	$21.63	$16.96	$15.14
Taxes	2.23	2.37	1.49	2.00
Total	$31.38	$24.00	$18.45	$17.14
Balance	$49.72	$33.28	$24.81	$23.61
Maintenance and Depreciation	26.20	17.68	13.91	13.46
Net Earnings	$23.52	$15.60	$10.90	$10.15
Per Cent. Operation Expense to Tel. Earnings	35.9	37.8	39.2	37.2
Per Cent. Telephone Expense to Tel. Earnings	71.0	72.8	74.8	75.1
Per Cent. Maintenance and Depreciation to Average Plant, Supplies, etc.	9.1	8.4	8.9	9.5
Per Cent. Increase Exchange Stations*	15.7	26.5	24.5	11.8
Per Cent. Increase Miles Exchange Wire*	15.9	33.2	27.2	12.0
Per cent. Increase Miles Toll Wire*.	21.3	25.2	12.4	11.5
Average Plant Cost per Exchange Station (including Exchange and Toll Construction)	$260	$199	$145	$142
Average Cost per Mile of Pole Line (Toll) (Including Wire)	$219	$348	$438	$688
Average Cost per Mile of Wire (Toll) (Including Poles)	$81	$71	$62	$66
Per Cent. Gross Telephone Earnings to Average Plant	33.4	31.7	31.7	29.3
Per Cent. Net Profits to Average Capital Stock	10.11	9.44	8.34	8.48
Per cent. Dividends to Average Capital Stock	5.07	6.19	5.75	6.31

*Increase during year shown, over previous year.

91

WESTERN ELECTRIC COMPANY.

The Western Electric Company occupies a unique position in the manufacturing business. It is in fact the manufacturing department of the Bell System.

To develop efficiency in service it was necessary to control the evolution of apparatus as well as of methods of operation. To control the quality and style of apparatus, to control the improvements which suggested themselves in the course of, and were the outcome of the experimental work and the development and improvement studies and experiments, it was necessary for the Bell System to control the manufacture of equipment and apparatus.

The present Western Electric Company was the outgrowth of this necessity.

This relation created the business of the Western Electric Company.

This relation of the Western Electric Company with the Bell System not only eliminated the expense which such companies must incur in the establishment of their business, but also largely reduced the operating or continuing expenses. Its business was either for the Bell Companies, or came to it because of its relation to the Bell Companies. Its manufactured products were made upon advance orders or to fill regular and definite continuing demands. A relatively small merchandise stock had to be carried.

There was no selling expense which, in the ordinary manufacturing business, absorbs such a large percentage of the manufacturing profits. There were no bad debts. The capital of the company was small and the floating debt large—at times much larger than the capital.

The growth had been so rapid that there had been no time to adjust the business to the changing conditions. It became apparent that some of these conditions must be changed for the permanent good of the company.

Before instituting any changes an offer was made to the outside shareholders of the Western Electric Company for an exchange or sale of their stock to the American Telephone and Telegraph Company. The offer was considered a liberal one and was accepted by a very large majority of the smaller holders and by a majority of the total shareholdings not held by the American Company.

A definite program of readjustment to new conditions was adopted and has been steadily pushed forward.

Outside lines of manufacture which were not only unprofitable but were absorbing a very large proportion of the capital of the company have been abandoned and the company's energy and efforts concentrated on the manufacture and sale of telephonic apparatus and auxiliary supplies.

The Hawthorne works have been enlarged and the Chicago City Clinton Street and Polk Street properties have been sold at a slight advance over their book values. The company's debt has been funded and it has ample working capital.

The prices charged to the Bell System are lower than the prices charged to other telephone customers. In the year 1910 the rate of gross profit on sales to the Bell System was 7.5% less than on sales to such other customers. This difference was offset by the lower expense in selling to the Bell Companies.

The relation between the Bell System and the Western Electric Company has the advantage of a ready made business, with none of the ordinary drawbacks and expenses and risks that other manufacturing companies have. Because of that relation, however, all investigations made as to the cost and expenses of the telephone business by public bodies include an investigation to ascertain whether or not the Bell System is getting, indirectly, abnormal profits through its manufacturing department by making excessive charges for apparatus and supplies. While all such investigations have, so far, ended satisfactorily, they bring into the discussion the profits of the company, its relations to public utilities, its profits, and the proportion of these profits which should be divided among the shareholders.

Everything indicates that the company can make satisfactory prices to the telephone companies for its products and maintain a 10 per cent. dividend. This rate has been started and it is not believed that existing conditions or a conservative policy would justify more.

REPORT OF THE AMERICAN
TELEPHONE AND TELEGRAPH COMPANY.

The improvement which has marked previous years still continues. The net revenue for the year was $31,-933,214.49, out of which were paid interest, $5,077,-321.33, and dividends, $20,776,822.12. The balance, $6,079,071.04, shows an increase, notwithstanding the large increase in dividends due to the exchange of convertible bonds for shares.

CONVERTIBLE BONDS.

At the close of business, December 31, 1910, $111,-059,000 of the $150,000,000 convertible bonds sold had been handed in for conversion, leaving outstanding at that date $38,941,000.

SHARE CAPITAL.

Due to the conversion of the bonds, there has been an increase of $6,860,300 in the outstanding share capital. This increase has been well distributed. The number of shareholders, 40,381, on December 31, 1910, shows an increase of 4,558 during the year. The distribution is general, there being 40,087 shareholders who hold less than 1,000 shares each, 266 who hold from 1,000 to 5,000 shares each and 28 who each hold 5,000 shares or more. The total holdings in blocks of 5,000 or more are less than 10 per cent. of the stock outstanding. A majority of the company's stockholders are women. Less than 8 per cent. of the stock was at December 31st in the names of brokers.

ISSUES OF CAPITAL STOCK AND BONDS.

There has been no issue of share capital during the year except in exchange for convertible bonds. The amount of these bonds still outstanding at the time of this report is about $30,000,000.

Some of the Collateral 4s have been issued in the course of the year in connection with the program for rearranging the territory, referred to last year, and other similar purposes.

It will be necessary, towards the close of the year, to do some financing, and should conditions remain much as they now are this will probably be done by an issue of share capital to the stockholders. The time and amount of the issue will be determined later in order that any change in conditions may be taken advantage of.

Last year we stated that the premiums received over the par value of capital issues were over $14,000,000. The conversion of bonds into stock during the year has increased this premium account to nearly $17,000,000.

96

GENERAL.

The business of the American Telephone and Telegraph Company is largely, but by no means entirely that of a holding company. It is an operating company in that it exercises centralized administrative functions over the associated companies and owns and directly operates the long-distance lines, binding this company into one system.

It is a developing and manufacturing company by reason of its control over the manufacturing of the Western Electric Company through the Experimental and Engineering Departments and its contract relations with and stock ownership in that company.

To get a proper comprehension of the business of the company as a whole, the combined balance sheet and earnings statement on page 11 must be considered rather than the balance sheet and earnings statement of the American Telephone and Telegraph Company alone.

The interest of the American Telephone and Telegraph Company in its associated operating companies is over 80 per cent., in addition to which it has its own earnings. The American Telephone and Telegraph Company's share of the surplus earnings of the Bell System is approximately 90 per cent., so that the showing of real interest to the security holders of American Telephone and Telegraph Company lies in the figures of the Bell System as a whole.

The combined statements of the Bell System show that during the year the property of the whole system increased $84,000,000. This includes plant, real estate, supplies, tools, stocks and bonds.

The cash and other liquid assets were reduced by $28,000,000. The intangible assets, such as contracts, patents, franchises, etc., were reduced by $4,270,000, leaving less than $3,000,000 on the books of all the companies against these items.

The net increase in assets, about $52,000,000, was provided by an increase in outstanding obligations of less than $28,000,000.

97

LEGAL.

The Legal Department reports that throughout the country the relations of this company and its associated companies with the Public Service Commissions of the several states have, on the whole, been of a very satisfactory character. The Commissions have recognized the fundamental correctness of our methods of operating, the soundness of our principles of accounting and the fairness of our dealings with the public.

There has, consequently, been but little difficulty in working harmoniously with these Commissions in solving the problems which, in a growing business, constantly demand attention.

In Oklahoma, where our associated company felt compelled to disagree with the State Commission, the Supreme Court of the State in the so-called Enid case has fully sustained our claims. That Court in its opinion has made a very valuable contribution to the law, recognizing, as it does, that in the telephone business large expenditures must be made in the establishment and development of an efficient telephone service which do not appear in the plant, but which contribute to the value of the business when established. This "going value" must always be added to the value of the physical plant in determining the investment upon which the telephone company is entitled to an income. The Court also recognized the necessity in the telephone business of making a liberal provision for depreciation, not only to provide for the decay and destruction of plant, but also to make the changes required to meet rapidly growing demands and to furnish the public with the improved facilities which the great development of the art has made necessary.

Our associated companies have been quick to respond to the public needs with these improved facilities and advanced methods of operating. In consequence they have had very little litigation with their subscribers and have been uniformly successful in such as has arisen.

In the Western Union case the United States Circuit Court has affirmed the report of the Master and the case will be appealed. Nothing has developed in this case which changes our view that the earlier decisions in this case were correct and that we have fully accounted for all that was due the plaintiffs under the contract of November 10, 1879.

98

PENSIONS AND SAVINGS.

During the year a great deal of attention has been given to some scheme for Pensions and Savings which would be of the greatest possible benefit and assistance to the employees, and if possible a substantial improvement on any scheme now in force.

The problem is an intricate and complicated one and the solution not easy.

At a conference of all the associated companies it was agreed that any plan adopted by the American Telephone and Telegraph Company would also be adopted by them, making it comprehensive and covering the Bell System as a whole, so that all changes of employees between companies would not affect their Pensions or Savings benefits.

In the meantime all cases which would come under Pensions or Savings plans will be acted upon individually by the company, so that in effect so far as the employees are concerned the delay does not postpone any benefit to them.

INDEPENDENT AND OPPOSITION COMPANIES.

Our policy in respect to the opposition and independent telephone systems has been consistently followed through the year. Wherever it could be legally done, and done with the acquiescence of the public, opposition companies have been acquired and merged into the Bell System.

Independent companies have been added to the System through sub-license or connecting contracts.

There is no question but that the public are tired of dual telephone exchange systems, and that so fast as confidence in protection against the real or imaginary evils of monopoly increases, opposition against mergers will decrease.

This condition can only be brought about by putting before the public the fullest and most detailed information as to the company, its policy and purposes.

PUBLIC RELATIONS.

In all times, in all lands, public opinion has had control at the last word—public opinion is but the concert of individual opinion, and is as much subject to change or to education.

It is based on information and belief. If it is wrong it is wrong because of wrong information, and consequent erroneous belief.

It is not only the right but the obligation of all individuals, or aggregations of individuals, who come before the public, to see that the public have full and correct information.

The Bell System gained 740,027 subscribers last year. Of the total number of subscribers over 1,000,000 were new during the year.

The American Telephone and Telegraph Company gained 4,558 shareholders last year. Of the total number of shareholders many more were new last year.

The excuse for setting forth at great length the policy, facts, beliefs and desires of the Bell System and those administering it, even to the extent of repeating much that has already been said and explaining some things familiar to many, is to inform the new public, the new subscribers, and the new shareholders.

Every fact that is stated is correct.

Every argument or reason is believed to be well founded and based on facts and is intended to be impartial.

The position of the Bell System is well known.

It is believed that the telephone system should be universal, interdependent and intercommunicating, affording opportunity for any subscriber of any ex-

change to communicate with any other subscriber
of any other exchange within the limits of speaking
distance, giving to every subscriber every possible
additional facility for *annihilating time or distance by
use of electrical transmission of intelligence or personal communication.* It is believed that some sort
of a connection with the telephone system should be
within reach of all. It is believed further, that this
idea of universality can be broadened and applied to
a *universal wire system* for the *electrical transmission of intelligence* (*written or personal communication*), from every one in every place to every one in
every other place, a system as universal and as extensive as the highway system of the country which
extends from every man's door to every other man's
door.

101

It is not believed that this can be accomplished
by separately controlled or distinct systems nor that
there can be competition in the accepted sense of competition.

It is believed that all this can be accomplished
to the reasonable satisfaction of the public with its
acquiescence, under such control and regulation as
will afford the public much better service at less cost
than any competition or government-owned monopoly
could permanently afford and at the same time be self-
sustaining.

The Bell System as at present constituted was
evolved first through the local exchange.

In the beginning of the business it was impossible
to get the necessary capital for development in any
large amount. In the place of large capital, small
capital and the optimism of individuals had to be
utilized. Small capital, large hopes and individual
effort brought about a development by limiting the
size of the exchange territory given to each individual
to his possibilities. In this way the country and
smaller cities were largely developed before much

was done in the larger cities. The capital to develop New York was estimated at less than $100,000, yet it was a long time before even that could be raised. Even if it had been possible to raise capital to exploit the whole country through one company, it would have been impossible to use it properly. The business was new. Those who constructed and operated it had to be educated. The policy of small units and individual effort, with concentration, application and resourcefulness brought a more rapid development and education than could have been had in any other way.

In this formative period, when the business was new, before distant speaking possibilities were shown, all communication was local. No two exchanges were either equipped or operated on the same lines or under the same methods, nor did they need to be; service, judged by present standards, was poor, but satisfied the local use; better service was not known. Later development of the toll line, of lines connecting exchanges, and of long-distance service made the deficiencies of the service glaring and the necessity of improvement imperative.

It will be remembered by many when the long-distance service was first introduced special connections had to be built for the users; now every telephone station or line can be equally well used for long-distance speaking.

With the extension of the speaking limits of the telephone over connecting lines came also the necessity for the extension of the territorial limits of the exchange systems, the necessity of standardization, uniformity of apparatus and operating methods, and an effective common control over all. The necessity for system was the beginning of the Bell System. The combination of the separate exchanges and lines into larger aggregations or organizations followed. It was necessary to have more effective organization with more effective administration and management, and with resources sufficient to make the changes which experiment and experience had found necessary.

It is impossible to define the territorial limitations of a telephone system because from every exchange center communication is wanted up to the talking limits in every direction.

This process of combination will continue until all telephone exchanges and lines will be merged either into one company owning and operating the whole system, or until a number of companies with territories determined by political, business or geographical conditions, each performing all functions pertaining to local management and operation, will be closely associated under the control of one central organization exercising all the functions of centralized general administration. But whatever may be the form of the operating organization, there is bound to be for legal purposes and the holding of franchises, some sort of subordinate state organization which will bring the business and property in each locality under the jurisdiction of the state in which it is situated and operated.

The American Telephone and Telegraph Company, which is the owner of all or part of each company forming the Bell System, is not simply a holding company. It is not a combination that has eliminated competition between the companies controlled by it. There can be no rivalry or competition between local exchanges in adjacent territory. Those desiring the service of exchanges in adjacent territory in addition to their own can get it much better and cheaper through their local exchange. To give direct individual wires from one exchange territory into another would be impractical from the multiplication of lines and prohibitive on account of cost. The American Telephone and Telegraph Company is a centralized general administration for all the

103

companies. It does the financing for the extension of the business. It furnishes the engineering, operating and other experts. It maintains a productive and protective organization so far as patents are concerned. It defends all the companies against all infringements. It undertakes to bring about improvements by working out the ideas and suggestions of others, both in and out of the business. Its agents keep each company fully informed of all that is going on in the field. It avoids all duplication of efforts, of experiments, of trial of new methods, apparatus, etc. It looks after the public relations of the companies. In other words, it performs all that service which is common to all, leaving to the local companies the local management. The organization is not unlike that of the United States, each local company occupying its own territory and performing all local functions, the American Telephone and Telegraph Company binding them all together with its long-distance lines and looking after all the relations between the local companies and between local companies and other companies. To have developed the telephone industry to its present state of efficiency would have been beyond the ability of any one of the local companies.

All independent systems which have been started have more or less followed the same lines, but within restricted areas, whether built by one company or interest, or by several. First, the local exchange, then the toll line to outlying points, and then the long-distance line connecting with other independent exchanges, tieing them together to form a system affording facilities for communication between the subscribers of one exchange and the subscribers of the other, but limited in scope, and without the community of interest necessary to a common system.

In other words we have the Bell System on the one side, developed on the lines of a universal, intercommunicating and interdependent service. We have the opposition on the other side, segregated exchanges or limited systems without universality, incomplete and inefficient, neither interdependent nor intercommunicating, except to a limited extent.

CORPORATE ORGANIZATION AND COMBINATION.

There is nothing of greater common interest, nothing which is exciting more comment and discussion at the present moment, than the questions of state control of corporate organizations and of combinations, especially of those controlling public utilities.

Corporate organization and combination are the necessary and logical solution of the problem of caring for the wonderful development which has been going on all over the world, and particularly in this country, in the recent past.

105

Combination only can cope with that industrial development of the present time which is far beyond the scope of individual effort or capital. In those good old times, one man, with his own capital, could carry on even the largest operations. The margin of profits due to low wages and large selling prices enabled the owners of such individual establishments to live and enjoy the best to be had in those times, and amass fortunes—fortunes relatively as large as any of the present—from an amount of gross business, the profits from which today would not be sufficient to pay the wages of a shop superintendent.

The development of the arts, the necessity of extensive laboratories and experimental departments, with technical staffs competent to keep abreast of modern progress and find out how to *utilize all of everything,* the large gross production at small margin of profit, the large capital requirements necessary to conduct business on these lines; all these place modern industrial enterprises either beyond the financial ability of any one individual, or far beyond the amount that any one individual wishes to have in any one venture.

Without attempting to discuss the history or evolution of "Company," "Corporation," or "Monopoly," and similar organizations or combinations of trade, it can be said that the first and oldest step towards corporate organization was partnership. Corporate combination is but a partnership wherein the partners are represented by shares held in various amounts by the various investors.

These corporate organizations and combinations have become a permanent part of our business machinery; the public would not, if it could, abolish them.

106

Who would ever consent, or would the requirements of business allow, that the railroads between the great sections of our country revert to the independent lines that once existed, with all the consequential delays, inconveniences and disadvantages to traffic and travel? Who would be content if the telegraph business should be carried on by the transfer of messages from one to another of the numerous companies, formerly independent, but now combined and giving direct transit over the whole country?

That there has been in large measure reason or cause for the existing unfavorable public opinion as to corporations, trusts and combinations, is beyond question, but it does not follow that there is reason or cause for the wholesale denunciation and condemnation of all corporations, trusts and combinations. Nor does it follow that all that is bad is centered in or confined to those prominent in the public eye.

Many of the practices most severely condemned are but the amplification or continuance of practices or customs common in the current affairs of business, practices or customs which were not wrong in themselves, but wrong in the abuse of them.

Public utility corporations and other combinations

have too frequently assumed that new laws and regulations were disastrous and ruinous without first giving them a fair trial, and legislators too often have displayed an ignorance or disregard of existing laws, spreading the idea that new legislation was a cure-all for any undesirable condition, while it was often only a political play, and the enforcement of the existing laws was utterly neglected. The results have been bad. While business will adjust itself to any condition if given time and opportunity, sudden change of conditions will result in disaster to some interest, but not as a rule to those at which the change was aimed.

107

There is too little consideration given to the fact, based on all experience, that no one interest can permanently prosper unless all other interests are in a prosperous condition, and to the fact that any sudden change in existing conditions will always be taken advantage of by some one interest to the detriment of other interests in general.

The proper use of corporate organization or combination under proper regulation or control cannot be objected to.

What is and should be condemned, prevented and punished, is the abuse made of corporate machinery to the detriment of public welfare and such abuse as has been and is being practised so extensively for purely speculative and oftentimes swindling enterprises.

It is largely this abuse by professional speculative promoters and swindling security vendors, mostly on a comparatively small scale, not in any way associated or connected with the general business organizations or systems, that has been the cause of most of the popular odium surrounding this necessary machinery of business. It does not seem possible that the only way of reaching such offenders is through penalties for "misuse of the mails," but however or by whomever the remedy is applied, he who does it should receive the heartiest thanks and appreciation of the community.

The large corporate combinations which often in popular opinion are supposed to be owned or wholly controlled by some one man or some few men, are, in fact, made up of thousands and tens of thousands of silent partners, the shareholders, who are the real owners. The existence of these real owners, these shareholders, is often obscured in the shadow of some one or more individuals who dominate these companies, not by large ownership, as popularly believed, but by administrative and operating aggressiveness and successful management. The shareholding owners are in the aggregate very numerous and, in any other country than America, would be frequently in evidence and heard from, would always take an active participation in all meetings, annual or special, and would in that way protect themselves and their holdings by associating the corporation or combination in the minds of the public with the particular and separate individual ownerships, or interests in them. In this way that same protection, recognition or consideration, to which all interests, whether individual or corporate, are alike entitled, would be assured.

PUBLIC UTILITIES.
THE "SERVED" AND THE "SERVERS."

Under the existing conditions the corporations or combinations represent the "servers." To the shareholders, dividends represent good management and desirable investment, but to many of the community, the community that is "served," profits which in individual enterprise would be considered reasonable are unreasonable and forced out of their pockets by unscrupulous management or illegal or dishonest practices.

The contest between the "served" and the

"servers," the "producer" and the "consumer," between "he-who-has" and "he-who-has-not," has been going on from the dawn of civilization, from the time when some one had more of some one thing than he wanted, while another had none, or less than he wanted.

From time immemorial efforts have been made in some way to control or restrict any accumulation, in the hands or in the uncontrolled possession of any individual or set of individuals, of those things which had become necessary to public wants, and to prevent necessities from in any way getting outside that control which natural competition, or the law of supply and demand under normal conditions exercises.

109

There has always been and will always be the laudable desire of the great public to be served rightly, and as cheaply as possible, which sometimes selfishly degenerates into a lack of consideration for the rights of those who are serving.

On the other hand there has always been the laudable desire of the "server," or the producer, to get a profit for his service or production, which sometimes degenerates into a selfish disregard or lack of consideration for those who are served.

This conflict, which originated with the first commercial transaction or exchange, has continued ever since and will continue to the end of time.

Until the state, or conditions under which society was organized, began to be complex there were very few things which were not and could not be regulated by the law of supply and demand, the law of substitution of one article for another in case of scarcity, or by the laws of competition. In the simple life, which was with the masses of the people until very recent years enforced, and is with all laudable, there were few articles which were in themselves necessities, and of these very few which did not have alternative articles of use, or substitutes, and, in fact, there was little that was not produced by the local

community or by the family. Those few things which,
in the growth of civilization, and particularly by the
increase of urban population, were of general use and
necessity for all, those few things in which the masses
of the public had an interest in receiving regularly
and reasonably, soon became the object of control or
regulation, and here was the beginning of and reason
for state control and regulation or state ownership.

Public Control.

Public control or regulation of Public Service Corporations by permanent commissions, has come and
come to stay. Control or regulation exercised through
such a body has many advantages over that exercised
through regular legislative bodies or committees. The
permanent commission will be a quasi-judicial body.
It should be made up of members whose duty it will be,
and who will have the desire, the time and the opportunity, to familiarize themselves with the questions
coming before them. It should act only after thorough
investigation and be governed by the equities of each
case. It would in time establish a course of practice
and precedent for the guidance of all concerned.

Experience also has demonstrated that this "supervision" should stop at "control" and "regulation"
and not "manage," "operate" nor dictate what the
management or operation should be beyond the requirements of the greatest efficiency and economy.

Management or operation requires intimate knowledge and experience which can only be gained by continuous, active and practical participation in actual
working, while control or regulation can be intelligently exercised, after judicial hearing, by those who
have not the knowledge or experience to operate.

State control or regulation should be of such character as to encourage the highest possible standard
in plant, the utmost extension of facilities, the highest

efficiency in service, rigid economy in operation, and
to that end should allow rates that will warrant the
highest wages for the best service, some reward for
high efficiency in administration, and such certainty
of return on investment as will induce investors not
only to retain their securities, but to supply at all
times all the capital needed to meet the demands of
the public.

Such "control" and "regulation" can and should
stop all abuses of capitalization, of extortion or of
overcharges, of unreasonable division of profits.

If there is to be state control and regulation, there
should also be state protection—protection to a corporation striving to serve the whole community (some
part of whose service must necessarily be unprofitable), from aggressive competition which covers only
that part which is profitable.

Governmental control should protect the investor as
well as the public. It should ensure to the public good
service and fair rates. It should also ensure fair
returns to the investor.

A public utility giving good service at fair rates
should not be subject to competition at unfair rates.

It is not that all competition should be suppressed,
but that all competition should be regulated and controlled. That competition should be suppressed
which arises out of the promotion of unnecessary duplication, which gives no additional facilities or service,
which is in no sense either extension or improvement,
which without initiative or enterprise tries to take advantage of the initiative and enterprise of others by
sharing the profitable without assuming any of the burden of the unprofitable parts or which has only the selfishly speculative object of forcing a consolidation or
purchase.

State control and regulation, to be effective at all,
should be of such a character, that the results from the
operation of any one enterprise would not warrant

111

the expenditure or investment necessary for mere duplication and straight competition. In other words, the profits should not be so large as to warrant duplication of capitalization in the competition for the same business.

When thoroughly understood it will be found that "control" will give more of the benefits and public advantages, which are expected to be obtained by state ownership, than could be obtained through such ownership, and will obtain them without the public burden of either the public office-holder or public debt or operating deficit. It is conceded that as a rule private management is better, more economical and more efficient than public management, and much more advanced and enterprising. The economical margin between public and private management has been shown by experience to be more than sufficient to secure the best private administration.

When through a wise and judicious state control and regulation all the advantages without any of the disadvantages of state ownership are secured, state ownership is doomed.

State control of public utilities should not prevent progress, should be sufficiently unrestricting to encourage the introduction and demonstration of the value of any new or novel enterprise, and should allow sufficient reward for the initiative, enterprise, risk and imagination of the adventurers behind such enterprises. It should discriminate between the useful adventurers or promoters, pioneers in fact, and those pirates or sharks who, on the strength of other successes, extravagantly capitalize undeveloped ideas, and exchange the worthless securities for the savings of deluded and credulous investors. Corporate control and restriction should always exist to a sufficient degree to prevent such speculative promoting, and such stock-jobbing schemes.

The regulation or control of any new or novel thing

which is a mere convenience and not a necessity can be left largely to the laws of trade; such a thing, if offered, must be offered at a price acceptable to the public, who are the customers, at a price which in the opinion of the purchaser leaves him a margin of profit either in convenience or enjoyment. Under such control private initiative can be depended upon for the introduction of everything believed to have possibilities.

The combination of the promoter, investor and capitalist, with their imagination, personality, optimism and desire, has been at the bottom of every development of every kind or nature which has benefitted the human race in the way of utilities, and still is the only way in which new utilities can be developed. Whenever any great works have been undertaken by governments they have been on lines of old development, based on experience of that which has been developed by the persistent genius and application of some individual or group of individuals.

State control or regulation, to be effective, should when exercised, be accepted and acquiesced in by the public. If all the decisions not in exact accord with the desire or contention of the public are condemned, if it is expected and required that all decisions be against the utilities controlled, if politics and political effect are to govern decisions, if decisions go for nothing with, and are not respected by the public, failure and disappointment are bound to follow, self-respecting men will refuse to act, the standard of appointments will fall and state control and regulation will become a disgrace, and the evils which it was intended to correct will multiply.

If any company gives good service, meets all the reasonable demands of the public, does not earn more than sufficient to provide for the maintenance of its plant up to the latest standard and for reconstruction of plant when worn out or obsolete, pays only fair dividends to its shareholders—if a company is only doing this its rates and charges to the public cannot be unreasonable.

COMPETITION VS. CONTROL OR REGULATION.

Effective, aggressive competition, and regulation and control are inconsistent with each other, and cannot be had at the same time.

Control or regulation, to be effective, means publicity; it means semi-public discuss on and consideration before action; it means deliberation, non-discrimination; it means everything which is the opposite of and inconsistent with effective competition.

Competition—aggressive, effective competition—means *strife*, industrial warfare; it means contention; it oftentimes means taking advantage of or resorting to any means that the conscience of the contestants or the degree of the enforcement of the laws will permit. To make competition effective great and uncontrolled latitude of action is necessary; action must be prompt and secret.

Aggressive competition means duplication of plant and investment. The ultimate object of such competition is the possession of the field wholly or partially; therefore it means either ultimate combination on such basis and with such prices as will cover past losses, or it means loss of return on investment, and eventual loss of capital. However it results, all costs of aggressive, uncontrolled competition are eventually borne, directly or indirectly, by the public.

Competition which is not aggressive, presupposes co-operative action, understandings, agreements. which result in general uniformity or harmony of action, which, in fact, is not competition but is combination, unstable but for the time effective.

Competing Exchanges.

Two local telephone exchanges in the same community are regarded as competing exchanges, and the public tolerates this dual service only in the fast disappearing idea that through competition in the telephone service some benefit may be obtained both as to rate and efficiency. Competition means that the same thing, or a satisfactory substitute, is offered. In this sense there can be no competing exchanges unless each exchange has substantially the same list of subscribers, which is in itself inconceivable.

It is not telephone service *per se* that an exchange affords; it is a particular, definite telephone connection between two people which can only be given between two parties connected with the same exchange or the same system. Each of the several independent exchanges in the same community offers you telephone service, but telephone service only with its particular list of subscribers.

Opposition exchanges compete in the same way as do two street railway lines, each starting in the center of the city, running a short distance through the same main street, and then branching off, each supplying an entirely different district of the city. Those traveling only from point to point on the main street can use either line, pay one fare; there is to this extent competition—there is a choice. Beyond that, to reach the other districts, there is no choice, there is no competition; one line or the other must be taken, depending on the particular district wished to be reached.

In the case of the street car service, payment is made only to the line used, when used.

To be in a position to obtain full telephone service where there are opposition exchanges, subscriptions to all are necessary.

In all other opposition utilities, to get the full service one or the other is paid—not both.

115

As before said, the purpose and object of an exchange is to afford a direct speaking circuit between parties at points distant from each other, to afford a highway for personal communication between any two. The exchange gives nothing but that connection, does nothing but provide that highway of communication, and place it at the service of the two parties desiring to communicate. The actual communicating is done by the parties themselves over this circuit placed at their exclusive service for the time being. To get this service, however, both parties must be connected with the same system; if not, the telephone circuit between the two parties cannot be made.

116
In two exchanges each having 2,000 subscribers, Messrs. A, B, C, D, E, F, G, H, I, J, K, L, M, N are connected with one, and Messrs. A, B, C, O, P, Q, R, S, T, U, V, X, Y, Z, connected with the other. Messrs. A, B, and C can use either exchange to connect with each other, but to connect with each other one exchange with one subscription and with but one payment would be sufficient. This is not competition; this is duplication.

Messrs. A, B, C can connect with all the others on both exchanges only by two subscriptions and two payments. There is no choice; there is no competition.

Any competition between opposition exchanges is confined to obtaining new subscribers—to increasing their subscription lists. Neither the same thing nor what could possibly be called a substitute is offered. Each exchange affords that connection between the subscribers on its particular list and that is all—between Messrs. A, B, C, D, E, F, G, H, etc., or between Messrs. A, B, C, O, P, Q, R, S, T, etc. A subscription to only one exchange is of no benefit when a connection with the other exchange is wanted, subscription to the other exchange is also necessary. This is not competition in any beneficial or any other sense.

When anyone decides to become a subscriber to an exchange he does not go to the one which offers any other inducement than the ability to connect with the people with whom it is the habit or necessity of the person subscribing to communicate. If it is his habit or necessity to communicate with some or all of those on both exchanges, subscriptions to both exchanges are necessary; in other words to get the advantage of complete local telephone service in a community, subscription to every local exchange in that community is necessary.

The fundamental idea of the Bell System is that the telephone service should be universal, intercommunicating and interdependent; that there are *certain people* with whom one *communicates frequently* and *regularly*; there are a *certain few* with whom one *communicates occasionally*, while there are *times* when it is *most necessary to get* communication with *some other one*, who, until the *particular necessity* arose, *might have been unknown and unthought of. It is this necessity, impossible to predetermine, which makes the universal service the only perfect service.*

On the assumption that a perfect telephone system must afford this direct highway of communication between any two desiring to converse, this system must reach everyone; must be universal, comprehensive. To the extent that any system does not reach everyone it is not perfect; to the extent that any system does not reach everyone, it is not in competition with the one that does; and to the extent that both systems reach everyone it is merely duplication; it is not competition.

Two exchanges may compete for subscribers, but not by offering the same list of subscribers; it would be impossible to keep the list of subscribers to any two opposition exchanges the same. One may offer a more desirable list of subscribers from your point of view than the other, therefore you will subscribe to that

117

one, but if both offer an equally desirable list of subscribers to you then you must choose between them, or you must subscribe to both exchanges.

One may call the carriage industry and the automobile industry competing. They are in a sense, or one is a substitute in a very general sense for the other. One might say the wholesale or retail flour merchant and the rice merchant are competing, as one is a substitute for the other, but two exchanges offering different lists of subscribers are not competing even in that sense, as neither is a substitute for the other, in that on one you may have communication with certain people, and on the other with certain other people; therefore they are not competing.

118

Two exchange systems in the same place offering identically the same list of subscribers, if such a thing can be imagined, are as useless as a duplicate system of highways or streets in a village not connecting with each other, but each reaching all the residents.

Physical Connections.

Physical connection. What is meant by it? And what object is it intended to accomplish?

Where there are two or more so-called competing local telephone exchanges in the same territory, each offers a particular service; each offers a connection with its particular list of subscribers.

Physical connection would connect these separate exchanges by trunk lines the same as exchanges belonging to one system are connected.

This in itself would be an easy matter in many cases, and would allow the subscriber to one local exchange speaking connection with the subscribers to the other local exchanges. A fairly satisfactory service could be given if all of the exchanges had the same general style of equipment, uniform operating methods, and if harmony and concert of action between the operators of entirely independent and rival exchanges could be assured.

But what has been accomplished? You have enabled any subscriber to any exchange to communicate with any subscriber to any other exchange. You have not avoided the objectionable duplication. You have not given service to all the exchanges for one subscription. This can only be done through merger or combination, not by physical connection. Physical connection implies separate and independent entities. For the privilege of this physical connection with the other exchanges the subscriber to any one of the exchanges must pay. This payment or toll must be more or less the equivalent of what the regular subscribers pay, otherwise there would be discrimination.

If the equipment and the operating methods of the opposition or independent exchanges physically connected are different, the service is bound to be unsatisfactory. No one of the exchanges can have any control over the operators of the other exchanges. There is bound to be strife and contention between the operators, resulting in delays and poor service. Each exchange must necessarily give preference and attention to its own service.

From the standpoint of local telephone exchange service, therefore, there can be nothing to gain from physical connection, either in economy or quality of service.

The most important matter to consider in connection with physical connection, the one that has the greatest bearing on the subject, is the character of such physical connection between telephone exchanges, and wherein it differs from regular exchange of service or physical connection between other public utility companies.

A telephone exchange does not furnish a commodity, does not transport goods, nor does it transmit messages.

What the telephone exchange does is to place at the disposition of any subscriber a telephone circuit, consisting of two wires, connecting such subscriber with another person at a distant point. This circuit enables them to carry on speaking communication with each other; it must be continuous and unbroken; it is for their exclusive use and while the circuit is at their service it cannot be used by any others desiring to communicate, or for any other telephone purpose. The employes of the exchange render no other service than selecting and connecting the wires together to form this circuit, and putting the parties in communication. To do this, and do it satisfactorily, the operators making up the circuit must have absolute control of the wires necessary for these circuits over the whole distance between the points of communication; that is, the operator at the starting point must have either control of or perfect working unity and harmony of action with all the operators of all the trunk lines and exchange lines necessary for this circuit.

120

These conditions can only exist where there is a strong, common interest or control.

Physical connection between independent or opposition exchanges means, therefore, the placing of the wires necessary to give it effect out of the control for the time being of the owning company and under the control of a competing, opposition company, to enable that competing, opposition company to give its subscribers the use of property, equipment, facilities, operating staff, other than its own, and for the time being depriving the owning company and its subscribers of the use of such facilities.

Physical connection demands the exclusive use of an integral part of the property and facilities and operating staff of one company for the customers of a competing company, no matter how urgent may be the owner's necessity for the immediate use of such property and facilities, nor how small the surplus facilities beyond the owner's requirements.

If the service consisted of carrying packages or transmitting messages along with other packages or other messages, or hauling cars to their destination, or accepting through tickets or transfers from connecting or cross lines of travel, it would be very different. In such cases the property, facilities and operation remain in the control of the owning company or its operating staff; no property intended for the benefit of the customers of one company is put to the exclusive use of another company; all that is done, is the same as is done with and for all comers. The package or passenger is carried, or the message transmitted, to its destination at the convenience of the company, along with other packages or messages.

So far we have considered only the local exchange. Physical connection between independent or opposition telephone systems or between an independent local exchange and a telephone system presents not only the same but many more complications, and is far more objectionable.

To better understand what is meant by physical connection and what it is meant to accomplish, a knowledge of the evolution and development and policy of the Bell System is necessary, and what that policy and belief is.

Repeating what has been said above, it believes that the telephone system should be universal, interdependent and intercommunicating, affording opportunity for any subscriber to any exchange to communicate with any other subscriber of any other exchange within the limits of speaking distance, giving to every subscriber every possible additional facility for *annihilating time or distance by use of electrical transmission of intelligence or personal communication.* It believes that some sort of a connection with the telephone system should be within reach of all.

This is what the Bell System aims to be—one **system with common policy, common purpose and**

121

common action; comprehensive, universal, interdependent, intercommunicating; like the highway system of the country, extending from every door to every other door; affording *electrical communication of every kind,* from every one at every place to every one at every other place.

To create this system has been the policy of the Bell interests from the beginning. It is the only way by which a satisfactory telephone service—satisfactory to the public or profitable to its owners—can be maintained.

The Bell System as established is as advanced and extended as the country as a whole will warrant. Its policy of extension carries it a little in advance of the public demands. In any effort to cover the whole country many unremunerative exchanges and toll lines have to be constructed and operated. Some of these will in time become remunerative; some never will, and those, for the benefit of the whole system, will have to be carried at the cost of the whole system.

Most of the opposition exchanges have been built up in a selected territory with capital obtained by the promise of, or in anticipation of large profits; as a rule capitalized far in excess of the plant value or construction cost. Subscribers have been obtained by promises of improved service at low rates. Many of such exchanges owe what success they have, where there is any success, to personal local influence or interest. Many, if not all, have been a disappointment. The day of local telephone exchanges or limited telephone systems has gone. This is recognized and fully appreciated by those who have exploited or are operating them.

The idea of physical connection is born of a desire to get for these local and isolated competing or opposition exchanges or these comparatively limited exchange systems, the advantage of the more extensive, comprehensive Bell System. To get for the subscrib-

122

ers of these so-called competing, opposition exchanges the connections which their own systems do not give them, to get for their subscribers all the advantages enjoyed by subscribers of the Bell exchanges by giving them the use of a part of the Bell System.

Physical connection would force the Bell System to place at the disposal of and under the control of any opposition company, Philadelphia for instance, for the time being, one of its circuits from Chicago to Philadelphia, to connect that Bell circuit with the circuits and system of the opposition company and disconnect it, for the time being, from the circuits of the Bell System.

This is not carrying packages or transmitting messages for the subscribers of the opposition Philadelphia exchange; it is turning over to that exchange for the use of its subscribers the property of the Bell System.

The fact that the opposition exchange could get such facilities would enhance its importance at the expense of the Bell System.

Physical connection would force the comprehensive Bell System, which has been built up with foresight and enterprise and is being maintained in its completeness at the cost of maintaining unremunerative exchanges and unremunerative lines, to turn over to, and put under control of, any opposition system for its use and benefit, for the time being, a physical part of the property of the Bell System and at the same time deprive the subscribers to the Bell System of the use of such property. Physical connection would oblige any system to construct and maintain surplus facilities and employ a surplus staff of operators for the benefit of any so-called competing or opposition—but less enterprising—company.

No possible compensation would be adequate for such service or such deprivation.

One of the arguments for physical connection is that

123

it will stop duplication. How? All agreements as to territory, rates or character of opposition; all arrangements which would come under the head of combination or pooling; all understandings or anything that would be equivalent to consolidation or combination, must be eliminated; this is not what is meant by and is not a part of, physical connection. Leaving all understandings out of consideration what effect would physical connection have on the local opposition exchanges? Neither exchange could stop competing for subscribers. The exchange that did would soon dwindle to a point of absolute undesirability; in other words, to a point where the subscription list would offer no inducements to others to join. Consequently activity must be maintained, each exchange making every effort not only to retain all on its list of subscribers but to add more. The same territory must be covered, the consequent duplication of conduits, pole lines, central and branch offices must continue; in fact the strife or competition would have to be more severe.

It is claimed that physical connection would bring about one system, where any one telephone subscriber could obtain connection with any other telephone subscriber within the limits of possible communication. With physical connection that would be the case, after a fashion, but what kind of a system would it be? It would be imperfect in that it would still be a dual system, with dual charges, made up of heterogeneous units of exchanges and lines, operated under independent managements with different operating methods and interests, with no common control over operators, without which service can not be satisfactory; in fact with all those imperfections that it has taken the Bell interests years to correct—imperfections which can be removed only by combination, agreement, understanding, which would be in effect consolidation.

Such demand as there may be for physical connection from opposition exchanges is a recognition of superior facilities and comes from a desire to get the benefits of those superior facilities.

So far as it comes from the public it is an expression of weariness with dual service or so-called competition.

Is there anything in practice, law or precedent that can compel one system, built upon a comprehensive basis, and trying to meet all the requirements of the public, to turn over its physical property for the use of so-called competitors—opposition exchanges built in selected territory with selfish views or motives? Is there anything to compel one to share the prosperity of a business created by enterprise and advanced policy with those who wish to appropriate the benefits of such work? Can any public utility company be compelled to divest itself of the operating control of its own property which was created for and may be needed at any time in the conduct of its own business? This is not the kind of interchange of business contemplated by the rules governing common carriers. It is not co-operation. It is pure and simple confiscation.

125

126

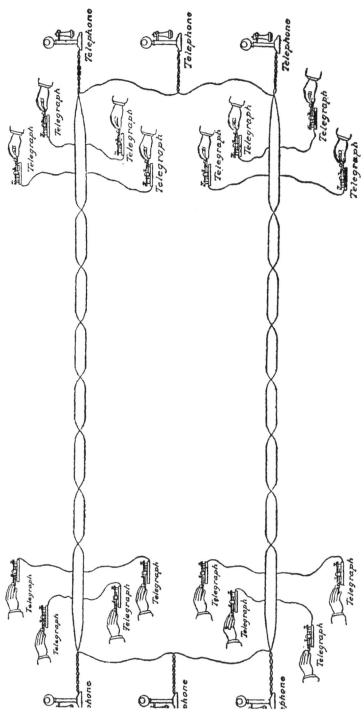

TWO TELEPHONE CIRCUITS IN DAILY USE BETWEEN NEW YORK AND CHICAGO CARRYING THREE TELEPHONE CONVERSATIONS AND EIGHT TELEGRAPH MESSAGES SIMULTANEOUSLY WITHOUT INTERFERENCE WITH EACH OTHER.

TELEPHONE AND TELEGRAPH.

The relations between the telephone system and the telegraph system are complementary.

Telephone service is furnishing for the personal use of the public an electrical circuit for personal communication between distant points. Nothing is carried by the telephone company, no commodity furnished, nothing transmitted by its staff, and nothing done except to make up a direct circuit between, and place it at the disposal of, the parties.

It annihilates distance in that it brings parties at distant points into speaking distance with each other.

Telegraph service is the electrical transmission, by the operating staff of the telegraph company, of written communications for others.

It annihilates time in that it instantaneously transmits written messages between different points.

The telephone provides something to be used by the public themselves.

The telegraph performs a distinct service for the public.

A telephone "circuit" consists of two copper wires of superior construction, arranged in a particular relation to each other, forming a metallic circuit equipped with auxiliary apparatus, loading coils, etc., connected with a switchboard—all very complicated and elaborate.

A telegraph "circuit" consists of one wire at most— a grounded circuit. This wire can be divided into several distinct "circuits."

A telephone "circuit" cannot be used for telephone purposes by any but the two parties in communication, during the time of such communication, but the same telephone "circuit" can, at the same time it is being

127

used for telephone service, be divided into two, four or
even eight telegraph "circuits," each of which can be
used for the transmission of telegraph messages.

While the existing telephone toll and long-distance
lines can be used for telegraph purposes, the existing
telegraph lines cannot be used for telephone toll and
long-distance purposes until reconstructed and arranged as described above.

There are two factors which determine the cost of
both services—Plant Cost and Operating Cost.
The total of these costs must be distributed over
the actual service performed, and the cost of each
item of service, whether telephonic communication or
telegraph message, varies directly with the total
amount of that service. The more the capacity of the
plant in service is utilized the less the cost of each particular item of service.

The plant cost is the fixed charge on capital invested
in plant, the cost of its maintenance and the depreciation reserve.

The operating cost is more or less a constant initial
charge on each item of service, i. e., telephone connection or telegraph message. In the telephone service
it is the cost of the time of the operators in putting up
the circuit or connection for the use of the parties, and
getting them into communication with each other. It
is relatively small in that one set of operators can care
for a number of circuits. In the telegraph service
there is a large constant initial cost, for each message,
made up of the cost of the skilled and expert operators
on each circuit, offices with clerical and messenger staff
for the collection and delivery, receiving, recording and
preparing messages for transmission, insurance against
mistakes in transmission or delay in delivery, etc.*

128

---

* NOTE. It seems unreasonable that a telegraph company should have
a possible liability of many thousands of dollars for a single message at
ordinary rates. There is no other business where there is not some
additional charge for insurance beyond a minimum.

The possible use—the number of hours during which a telephone circuit can be used as well as the number of items of service, i. e., communications or connections, which can be given within those hours—is limited by the necessity of the *personal presence* on the circuit of the parties communicating; by the time necessary to get both parties on the circuit; by the time taken by the communication; and by the intervals lost while waiting for parties.

This limited capacity, together with the costly character of the telephone circuit, makes the plant cost of each connection or communication very large. The operating cost is relatively very small in that one set of operators can take care of the connections of a number of circuits.

The relatively small operating cost and large plant cost make *distance* the important controlling element in the cost of telephone toll line or long-distance service.

In the telegraph service the messages are transmitted by the operating staff, one after another, with the speed of writing. There are no lost intervals during the busy hours. The plant cost of each item of service, i. e., the telegraph message, is relatively very small, while the operating cost, for reasons given above, is relatively very large for each message.

The relatively large operating cost and small plant cost per telegraph message make distance a subordinate factor in the cost of telegraph service.

The ratio of the possible number of telegraph messages over the same wires compared to the possible number of telephone communications is very large.

It is possible to "telephone" messages, but while the operating cost would be somewhat larger than in the case of "telegraphing," the plant cost would make telephoning messages prohibitive over long distance under ordinary conditions. The use of the telephone for that purpose is therefore limited economically to short distances, or some situation where the plant cost would be almost or entirely negligible.

The small operating but very large plant cost of the telephone communication and the large operating but relatively small plant cost of the telegraph message limit the possibility of either being used indiscriminately or interchangeably to *very short distances, or to other particular situations.*

Under existing conditions or the present state of the art, the "telephonic" transmission of written messages cannot take the place of "telegraphic" transmission in the regular conduct of the business.

130

In a large way the complementary character exists in the joint occupancy and joint use for both purposes of the trunk line plant of both companies. For the general service of each the operating staffs of the telephone and of the telegraph are in every respect distinct and different, and not in the slightest degree interchangeable. Each function requires an independent operating organization, made up largely of experts in each particular business, complete in every respect. Any attempt on the part of a telephone company to do a regular "telegraph business" would necessitate a "telegraph" operating organization in addition to its "telephone" operating organization.

Before a telegraph company could do a "telephone business" it would be necessary to reconstruct and rearrange its entire wire plant; to construct and equip central offices, distributing subways and lines, subscribers' connections and stations, at a cost of several times its existing telegraph wire plant, and also to create a distinct "telephone" operating organization.

While the large economies are in the joint occupancy and the joint use of the trunk "wire plant," there are great advantages and large economies in the utilization for both purposes of other plant and operating facilities which must be maintained for a single purpose in any case, and which could bear the additional burden of the service of the other without an additional cost. There are in the distributing and branch lines of both services large plant and operating facilities which are only being utilized to a small part of their capacities; where the business of either company is not sufficient to maintain either office or operating staff; where to maintain any office there must be utilized the office and employees of some business which has first claim on the service and attention of such employees. Under these conditions satisfactory service is impossible, and to a great degree affects the reputation of the whole service, particularly that of the telegraph. This large economic waste incident to separate service could be almost entirely eliminated by joint use or occupancy, and by bringing the business entirely under one common control or influence the efficiency and the reputation of the service could be greatly improved.

The utilization of plant and operating staff not fully employed makes it possible to collect and deliver messages by telephone and to connect exchanges and subscribers' stations by telephone toll lines with the night telegraph offices at other points.

To the extent that these waste facilities are utilized for public benefit and private profits, just to that extent regular standard service could be cheapened or *new service* and *additional facilities* given to the public.

The idea of universality has been referred to in connection with the telephone system. This idea can be broadened and applied to a wire system. We believe that the future development of the wire system in the United States will afford facilities for the annihilation of both *time and distance* by the general use of *electrical transmission* for *written or personal communication,* and will afford electrical communication of every kind of intelligence from everyone at every place to everyone at every other place. It will be comprehensive, universal.

131

To do this efficiently and economically means the combination of every kind of electrical transmission of intelligence into one system in order that new and additional uses may be developed and that the wire plant and other facilities may be utilized to their fullest extent.

Cheap service comes from full loads. In the wire service this can only be had by employing the plant to its full capacity, *all the time*. The charts on pages 56 and 57 will show to what a limited extent this is now being done.

In some lines of business like the transportation of passengers, where the unit of service is the car mile, and the overload capacity of the car is large, the average load can be greatly increased by making use of the "overload" during the few hours of maximum business. In no other way could the prevailing cheap fares be afforded for such long hauls.

In the electrical transmission of intelligence each item of service, the "message" or "telephonic connection" occupies the wires and the time to the exclusion of all else, and the law of increasing returns therefore works within the narrow limits of the capacity of the line. There can be no overload. *Cheaper service can only be given by the development of new or additional uses which can be distributed over the time now unused.* In the telephone business what can be done in this direction is restricted by the necessity of the personal presence of the parties using the telephone, which limits the use of circuits for telephone purposes to certain hours of the day. In the telegraph and cable business, under present conditions, it is different. There is a large capacity unused waiting to be utilized.

132

Expedited service means a large surplus plant to meet maximum demands, unutilized at all other times. The cost of the unutilized facilities must be borne by the expedited service. The result is high charges, due to small average load with consequent large plant cost,

Up to the present time the telegraph and cable business has been developed wholly on lines of *expedition* and the business that has been developed is such as will stand the extra cost of expedition. Theoretically at least, there should be no possibility of any further expedition, of any rush or special service, beyond what should be, if it is not now being given.

To do anything which would retard the expedition of the business as now developed would be detrimental to the social and business organization of the world; as in expedition lies the prime value of the present service.

Under a universal wire system operated on the lines and in the manner indicated above, the additional services will be given to the public at rates commensurate with the value of such services, and in the great possibilities of electrical transmission of intelligence some uses will be found or developed to absorb and utilize this enormous waste, and also relieve any congestion now suffered by the more important business by furnishing a service which would be satisfactory to such of the existing business as has heretofore had no alternative, but would prefer the new service.

The Night Letter—the first attempt—met with popular reception and is filling a definite place in the business and social world. The Day Letter, so recently introduced that its possibilities cannot yet be determined, will doubtless find its place. Depending upon the reception of these, other services will be introduced.

It is also intended to extend some of these new classes of service to the transatlantic cables as soon as

133

W. U. Telegraph Chart

SHOWING

RANGE OF SENT AND RECEIVED BUSINESS

AT

NEW YORK.

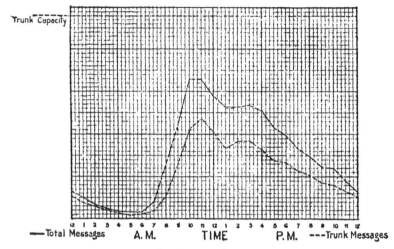

Trunk Capacity

——Total Messages   A. M.   TIME   P. M.   ---Trunk Messages

Cable Chart

OF

Transatlantic Business

SHOWING THE

CAPACITY OF OPERATING FORCE

AND THE

RANGE OF BUSINESS DONE.

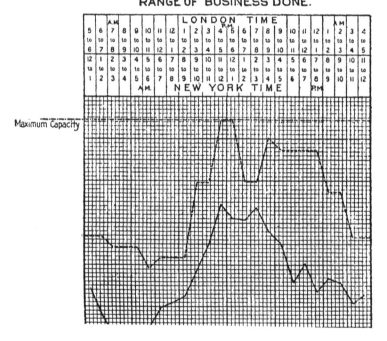

Maximum Capacity

TELEPHONE CHART
TYPICAL LONG DISTANCE TRAFFIC RECORD

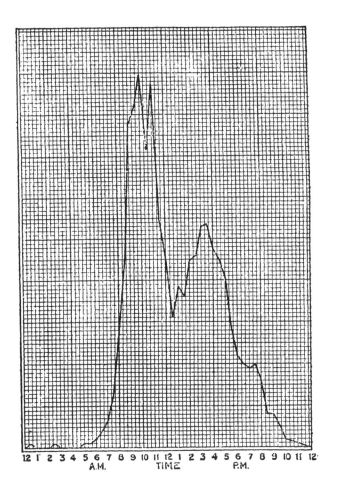

it is made possible by the completion of negotiations and arrangements now pending.

Until the economies, which may result from the joint occupancy or joint use and the consequent utilization of these now unutilized facilities, are determined, there will be no changes made in the present conduct of expedited or regular service. Whether all or only part of the economic waste will be absorbed in the other classes of service is a question yet to be answered; until answered anything that might result adversely either to the quality of the service, the extension and introduction of new service, or to the reasonable profits to which the companies are entitled, would be foolish and uncalled for.

136

RESUME AND CONCLUSION.

The following condensed summary of some of the principal things shown in this and previous reports is made with the purpose of taking away any excuse for further repetition or publication of those misstatements, distorted facts and erroneous conclusions which, for various reasons, are circulated from time to time.

It is shown that the total outstanding obligations of the Bell System in the United States, not including the manufacturing company, amount to $580,000,000. All the capital of the various companies composing the System not included in this consists of inter-company items and duplications.

It is shown that the book value of the property representing these outstanding obligations is $696,700,000, $116,000,000 in excess of the outstanding obligations. It is shown that in all cases of official appraisement the actual value of this plant has been found to be above the book value.

It is shown that there is no water in the capital of the American Telephone and Telegraph Company; that each $100 of outstanding obligations is represented by more than $100 cash paid into the treasury; that the excess of cash paid into the treasury over the outstanding obligations at the close of the year amounted to nearly $17,000,000.

It is shown that the construction costs of the Bell System are small. The cost per exchange station is but $117.12. The cost per exchange station, including the extensive system of toll lines, is but $142.13. This valuation includes the first class exchanges and exchange construction. All or substantially all of the cheaper class of construction, the rural co-operative and association lines, is embraced in the sub-licensee or connected companies, constructed on the basis of giving a low-cost local service.

It is shown that the cost of construction per exchange station has steadily decreased from $199.00 in 1900 to $142.00 in 1910, notwithstanding the great increase in the investment in real estate, underground construction, toll line construction and copper wire.

It is shown that instead of increasing and oppressive rates there has been a continual decrease of the average annual charge for exchange service from an average of $44.68 in 1900 to $31.28 in 1910.

It is shown that the taxes paid in the year 1910 by the Bell System amount to over 5 per cent. of its gross earnings, 16.4 per cent. of its net earnings, and 1.4 per cent. of the value of its telephone plant.

It is shown that the control of the company is not vested in any one interest nor has it been used for the

137

benefit of any individual or group of individuals; that the shareholders, recognizing an uninterrupted administration of their affairs in their interest have continued the Directorate on the same lines or the lines of natural succession from the beginning.

It is shown that the American Telephone and Telegraph Company is not in the accepted sense a trust nor has it been built up by absorbing competing companies or in restraint of business. That while the Bell System is made up of separate corporations, these corporations are not, never have been, and never could be in competition, and also that under any system of organization or under one ownership, separate companies are necessary for purposes of State jurisdiction.

That a universal and comprehensive telephone system cannot have any operating limits, but must give unbroken, continuous, connecting circuits under one control, from every subscriber's station in every direction to the limits of telephone speaking possibility.

It is shown that bona fide competition between local exchanges cannot exist, owing to the peculiarities of the service rendered by these exchanges.

It is shown that physical connection does not and cannot bring about any economical or beneficial result and increases instead of decreases the evil of dual construction and subscription.

That physical connection would give to subscribers of an opposition exchange the service and use of property provided for the use of others, and for which others pay.

We are charged with maintaining a large experimental and patent organization largely for the purpose of suppressing new inventions and improved methods. The Bell System does maintain a large experimental and engineering department, but for the purpose of developing the value and efficiency of anything that is new; what it really does is demonstrated by the fact that the construction, equipment and operating methods of the Bell System are the standard the world over. That the equioment of the exchanges of the whole world is either the same as, or is modeled upon that of the Bell System. And that no construction, equipment or operating methods rejected or "suppressed" by the engineering experts of the Bell System have ever yet come into permanent use.

We are charged with making abnormal profits on the equipment, supplies, etc., furnished the operating companies by the Western Electric Company, and in this way increasing the cost of service to the public. It is shown that the profits on Western Electric sales to the operating companies of the Bell System are less than on sales to the independent companies, to the extent at least of the saving in the cost of selling to the operating companies.

It is also shown that the telephone service and the telegraph service are complementary, not competitive; that each has its own proper place; that joint use and joint occupancy of wires will reduce operating cost, maintenance charges and construction investment. That utilizing the unutilized facilities of both will make possible large economies and improvement in the wire service as well as new, additional and useful services of both telephone and telegraph, for the benefit of both the corporations and the public.

For the Directors,

THEODORE N. VAIL,
President.

BELL TELEPHONE SYSTEM IN THE UNITED STATES.

	Dec. 31, 1895.	Dec. 31, 1900.	Dec. 31, 1905.	Dec. 31, 1909.	Dec. 31, 1910.	Increase, 1910.
Miles of Exchange Pole Lines	25,330	30,451	67,698	113,893	120,175	6,282
Miles of Toll Pole Lines	52,873	101,087	145,535	164,111	167,827	3,716
Total Miles of Pole Lines	78,203	131,538	213,233	278,004	288,002	9,998
Miles of Underground Wire	184,515	705,269	2,345,742	5,337,436	5,992,303	654,867
Miles of Submarine Wire	2,028	4,203	9,373	22,698	24,636	1,938
Miles of Aerial Wire	488,872	1,252,329	3,424,803	5,119,892	5,625,273	505,381
Total Miles of Wire	675,415	1,961,801	5,779,918	10,480,026	11,642,212	1,162,186
Comprising Toll Wire	215,687	607,599	1,265,236	1,804,552	1,963,994	159,442
Comprising Exchange Wire	459,728	1,354,202	4,514,682	8,675,474	9,678,218	1,002,744
Total	675,415	1,961,801	5,779,918	10,480,026	11,642,212	1,162,186
Total Exchange Circuits	237,837	508,262	1,135,449	1,829,942	2,082,960	253,018
Number of Central Offices	1,613	2,775	4,532	4,968	4,933	35†
Number of Bell Stations	281,695	800,880	2,241,367	3,588,247	4,030,668	442,421
Number of Bell Connected Stations	27,807	55,031	287,348	1,554,445	1,852,051	297,606
Total Stations	309,502	855,911	2,528,715	5,142,692	5,882,719	740,027
Number of Employees	14,517	37,067	89,661	104,956	120,311	15,355
Number of Connecting Companies				10,354	12,300	1,946
Exchange Connections Daily	2,351,420	5,668,986	13,543,468	19,925,194	21,681,471	1,756,277
Toll Connections Daily	51,123	148,528	368,083	517,341	602,539	85,198

* Includes Private Line Stations.　　† Decrease.

141

BELL TELEPHONE SYSTEM IN THE UNITED STATES.

ALL DUPLICATIONS BETWEEN COMPANIES EXCLUDED.

COMBINED BALANCE SHEETS AT FIVE YEAR INTERVALS, 1885-1910.

	Dec. 31, 1885.	Dec. 31, 1890.	Dec. 31, 1895.	Dec. 31, 1900.	Dec. 31, 1905.	Dec. 31, 1910.
ASSETS:						
Contracts and Licenses	$16,732,100	$18,925,700	$20,005,300	$14,794,300	$13,313,400	$2,943,381
Telephone Plant	38,618,600	58,512,400	87,858,500	180,699,800	368,065,300	610,999,964
Supplies, Tools, etc.	348,500	1,021,800	1,810,000	6,464,400	11,069,500	20,987,551
Receivables	1,450,900	1,761,600	3,746,600	13,644,000	26,220,800	26,077,802
Cash	1,792,600	1,183,300	2,484,100	3,223,000	11,005,900	27,548,933
Stocks and Bonds	1,138,800	2,697,400	4,480,500	11,400,400	23,041,200	64,766,089
Total	$60,081,500	$84,102,200	$120,385,000	$230,225,900	$452,716,100	$753,323,720
LIABILITIES:						
Capital Stock	$38,229,200	$43,792,800	$57,462,700	$130,006,900	$238,531,100	$344,645,430
Funded Debts	367,400	6,473,100	10,074,100	44,137,900	93,079,500	224,791,696
Bills Payable	2,618,900	1,323,000	2,000,000	7,000,000	35,000,000	42,566,943
Accounts Payable		3,301,100	6,138,000	13,583,300	22,407,500	21,721,125
Total Outstanding Obligations	$41,215,500	$54,890,000	$75,674,800	$194,728,100	$389,018,100	$633,725,194
Surplus and Reserves	18,866,000	29,212,200	44,710,200	35,497,800	63,698,000	119,598,526
Total	$60,081,500	$84,102,200	$120,385,000	$230,225,900	$452,716,100	$753,323,720

BELL TELEPHONE SYSTEM IN THE UNITED STATES.

ALL DUPLICATIONS BETWEEN COMPANIES EXCLUDED.

COMPARATIVE EARNINGS AT FIVE YEAR INTERVALS, 1885-1910.

	Year 1885.	Year 1890.	Year 1895.	Year 1900.	Year 1905.	Year 1910.
EARNINGS:						
Gross Earnings	$10,033,600	$16,212,100	$24,197,200	$46,385,600	$97,500,100	$165,612,881
Expenses	5,124,300	9,067,600	15,488,400	30,632,400	66,189,400	114,618,473
Net Earnings	$4,909,300	$7,144,500	$8,708,800	$15,753,200	$31,310,700	$50,994,408
Interest	27,700	278,700	655,500	2,389,600	5,836,300	11,556,864
Balance	$4,881,600	$6,865,800	$8,053,300	$13,363,600	$25,474,400	$39,437,544
Dividends	3,107,200	4,101,300	5,066,900	7,893,500	15,817,500	25,160,786
Surplus Earnings	$1,774,400	$2,764,500	$2,986,400	$5,470,100	$9,656,900	$14,276,758

American Telephone and Telegraph Company.
Balance Sheet, December 31, 1910.

ASSETS.

Stocks of Associated Companies	$356,662,338.33	
Bonds of Associated Companies	2,885,000.00	
Capital Advances to Associated Companies	34,165,499.20	$393,712,837.53
Telephones	$11,568,966.04	
Real Estate	2,184,730.44	
Long Distance Telephone Plant	45,948,391.62	59,702,088.10
Cash and Deposits	$13,109,340.32	
Short Term Notes	627,466.52	13,736,806.84
Special Demand Notes		16,970,229.34
Current Accounts Receivable		6,093,415.42
Treasury Bonds		17,300,000.00
		$507,515,377.23

LIABILITIES.

Capital Stock		$263,335,600.00
Four Per Cent. Collateral Trust Bonds, 1929	$78,000,000.00	
Four Per Cent. Convertible Bonds, 1936	38,941,000.00	
Five Per Cent. Coupon Notes, 1907	5,000.00	
Five Per Cent. Coupon Notes, 1910	22,000.00	
Other Notes Payable	13,150,000.00	
Indebtedness to Western Union Telegraph Co. for New York Telephone Co. Stock payable 1912 to 1915	16,500,000.00	146,618,000.00
Dividend Payable January 15	$5,266,712.00	
Interest and Taxes Accrued, but not due	2,163,658.83	
Current Accounts Payable	593,895.44	
Reserve for Unearned Revenue	2,758.99	8,027,025.26
Depreciation Reserve	$37,425,080.08	
Surplus	52,109,671.89	89,534,751.97
		$507,515,377.23

CHARLES G. DuBOIS, *Comptroller.*

American Telephone and Telegraph Company.
Comparative Statement of Earnings and Expenses
For the years 1909 and 1910.

	1909.	1910.
EARNINGS:		
Dividends..........................	$15,949,213.73	$19,205,494.35
Interest and other revenue from Associated Companies..............	10,661,431.03	10,838,442.84
Telephone Traffic (net)............	4,360,104.94	4,893,513.39
Real Estate	95,723.97	95,119.69
Other Sources	1,694,867.76	325,758.44
Total.	$32,761,341.43	$35,358,328.71
EXPENSES..........................	2,570,575.57	3,425,114.22
NET EARNINGS......................	$30,190,765.86	$31,933,214.49
Deduct Interest	7,095,377.34	5,077,321.33
Balance...................	$23,095,388.52	$26,855,893.16
Dividends Paid	17,036,275.64	20,776,822.12
Balance...................	$6,059,112.88	$6,079,071.04
Carried to Reserves................	$3,000,000.00	$3,000,000.00
Carried to Surplus	3,059,112.88	3,079,071.04
	$6,059,112.88	$6,079,071.04

CHARLES G. DuBOIS, *Comptroller.*

145

American Telephone and Telegraph Company.
Annual Earnings and Dividends.

Year.	Net Revenue.	Dividends Paid.	Added to Reserves.	Added to Surplus.
1900	$5,486,058	$4,078,601	$937,258	$470,198
1901	7,398,286	5,050,024	1,377,651	970,611
1902	7,835,272	6,584,404	522,247	728,622
1903	10,564,665	8,619,151	728,140	1,217,374
1904	11,275,702	9,799,117	586,149	890,435
1905	13,034,038	9,866,355	1,743,295	1,424,388
1906	12,970,937	10,195,233	1,773,737	1,001,967
1907	16,269,388	10,943,644	3,500,000	1,825,744
1908	18,121,707	12,459,156	3,000,000	2,662,551
1909	23,095,389	17,036,276	3,000,000	3,059,113
1910	26,855,893	20,776,822	3,000,000	3,079,071

CHARLES G. DuBOIS, *Comptroller.*

WESTINGHOUSE ELECTRIC & MANUFACTURING COMPANY

ANNUAL REPORT

MARCH 31, 1911

MEETING, JULY 26, 1911

OFFICERS AND DEPARTMENTS

OFFICERS

Robert Mather, Chairman of Board, New York.
Edwin F. Atkins, President, New York.
E. M. Herr, First Vice-President, Pittsburg.
L. A. Osborne, Second Vice-President, Pittsburg.
Charles A. Terry, Third Vice-President, New York.
G. W. Hebard, Acting Vice-President, New York.
H. D. Shute. Acting Vice-President, Pittsburg.
James C. Bennett, Comptroller and Secretary, New York.
Warren H. Jones, Assistant Secretary, New York.
T. W. Siemon, Treasurer and Assistant Secretary, Pittsburg.
H. F. Baetz, Assistant Treasurer, Pittsburg.
S. H. Anderson, Acting Assistant Treasurer, Pittsburg.   149
F. E. Craig, Auditor, Pittsburg.
W. B. Covil, Jr., Assistant Auditor, Pittsburg.

MANUFACTURING DEPARTMENT

Tracy Lyon, Assistant to First Vice-President.
Alexander Taylor, Manager of Works.
C. B. Auel, Assistant Manager of Works.
J. McA. Duncan, Assistant Manager of Works.
C. W. Johnson, Assistant Manager of Works.
E. R. Norris, Assistant Manager of Works.
E. F. Harder, Superintendent of Newark Works.

ERECTING DEPARTMENT

W. K. Dunlap, Assistant to First Vice-President.
G. W. Canney, Superintendent of Erecting.

ENGINEERING DEPARTMENT

H. P. Davis, Ass't to First Vice-President and Manager of Engineering.
B. G. Lamme, Chief Engineer.
Chas. F. Scott, Consulting Engineer.

SALES DEPARTMENT

S. L. Nicholson, Sales Manager.
C. S. Cook, Manager, Railway and Lighting Department.
Charles Robbins, Manager, Industrial and Power Department.
G. Brewer Griffin, Manager, Detail and Supply Department.
Maurice Coster, Manager, Export Department.

WESTINGHOUSE ELECTRIC & MANUFACTURING COMPANY

Operating Plants at

EAST PITTSBURG, PA.
NEWARK, N. J.
PITTSBURG, PA.
CLEVELAND, OHIO

MAIN OFFICES, East Pittsburg, Pa.
NEW YORK OFFICES, 165 Broadway.

SUBSIDIARY MANUFACTURING COMPANIES

WESTINGHOUSE LAMP COMPANY
WALTER CARY, General Manager

Operating Plants at

BLOOMFIELD, N. J.
NEW YORK CITY

MAIN OFFICES, Bloomfield, N. J.

THE BRYANT ELECTRIC COMPANY
THE PERKINS ELECTRIC SWITCH MANUFACTURING COMPANY
W. C. BRYANT, President, Treasurer and General Manager

Operating Plants at

BRIDGEPORT, CONN.

MAIN OFFICES, Bridgeport, Conn.

R. D. NUTTALL COMPANY
F. A. ESTEP, President and Treasurer

Operating Plant at

PITTSBURG, PA.

MAIN OFFICES, Pittsburg, Pa.

To the Stockholders of the

WESTINGHOUSE ELECTRIC & MANUFACTURING COMPANY:

The Directors respectfully present herewith their report of the operations of your Company and of its subsidiary Companies for the fiscal year ended March 31, 1911. The Income Account for the year, which includes the operations of all the subsidiary Companies—sales between Companies, however, being eliminated—is as follows:

GROSS EARNINGS:

Shipments Billed		$38,119,312.01

COST OF SHIPMENTS:

Factory Costs, including all Expenditures for Patterns, Dies, New Small Tools and Other Betterments and Extensions; also Inventory Adjustments and all Selling, Administration, General and Development Expenses		32,510,546.87

NET MANUFACTURING PROFITS ... $ 5,608,765.14

OTHER INCOME:

Interest and Discount	$ 272,055.28	
Dividends and Interest on Sundry Stocks and Bonds Owned	615,299.40	
Miscellaneous—Royalties Etc.	628,177.13	1,515,531.81

TOTAL INCOME ... $ 7,124,296.95

DEDUCTIONS FROM INCOME:

Interest on Bonds and Debentures	$1,076,553.71	
Interest on Collateral Notes	416,000.00	
Miscellaneous Interest	92,933.04	
Property and Plant Depreciations Charged against Income	371,668.19	
Proportion of Expenses Incidental to Bond and Note Issues	76,666.66	
Miscellaneous	209,369.37	2,243,190.97

NET INCOME—SURPLUS FOR THE YEAR ... $ 4,881,105.98

151

The year's business, both in gross earnings and net income, was the largest in the history of the Company. The gross earnings exceeded those of the preceding fiscal year by $8,870,630 and were greater by $5,093,072 than the earnings of the best previous year in the Company's existence. A condensed comparative statement of gross earnings and net profits for the past six years, adjusted to the basis of the foregoing statement of income, follows:

	YEAR ENDED MARCH 31,					
	1906	1907	1908	1909	1910	1911
Gross Earnings—Shipments Billed	$24,081,601	$33,026,240	$32,844,829	$20,606,592	$29,248,682	$38,119,312
Cost of Shipments—Includes all Selling, Administration and General Expenses	21,390,059	28,846,665	$30,301,147	19,955,808	25,695,704	32,510,547
Net Manufacturing Profits	$ 2,691,542	$ 4,179,575	2,543,682	$ 650,784	$ 3,552,978	$ 5,608,765
Other Income	959,786	1,256,335	1,555,697	986,293	1,616,561	1,515,531
Total Income	$ 3,651,328	$ 5,435,910	$ 4,099,379	$ 1,637,077	$ 5,169,539	$ 7,124,296
Less—Inventory Adjustments, Inactive Apparatus and Material Scrapped, Bad Accounts and Extraordinary Items of Expense charged to Income	493,081	1,070,383	1,087,453	841,321	419,692	657,704
Net Income Applicable to Interest and other charges	$ 3,158,247	$ 4,365,527	$ 3,011,926	$ 795,756	$ 4,749,847	$ 6,466,592
Interest Charges	$ 1,137,592	$ 1,592,353	$ 2,061,091	$ 2,200,771	$ 1,689,183	$ 1,585,487
Net Income—Surplus for the Year	$ 2,020,655	$ 2,773,174	$ 950,835	$ 1,405,015 (Deficit)	$ 3,060,664	$ 4,881,105

Your Directors feel that the satisfactory results of the past year, reached as they were during a period of somewhat less than normal activity in other lines of industry, afford sound basis for continued hope in the future of the electrical manufacturing industry and in the maintenance by your Company of its position in that field. It is, on the other hand, a fact that the volume of business now offering is on a diminishing scale, and the results of the last year, therefore, are no certain indication of a continuance for the future of gross earnings and net profits such as the past twelve months have produced. The business taken by the Company during February and March, 1911— the last two months of the fiscal year covered by this report—was somewhat less than that taken during the same months of 1910, and the value of the orders booked since the close of the fiscal year does not compare favorably with that of the corresponding period a year ago.

The value of unfilled orders as of March 31, 1910, was $11,256,196, as of March 31, 1911, this value stood at $7,616,058.

Certain other conditions affect the estimate for the immediate future of the earning power of your Company. On March 31, 1896, your Company entered into an agreement with the General Electric Company whereby for a period of fifteen years thereafter each Company licensed the other under the patents controlled by it during the term of the agreement, with provision for the payment of royalties by each on the basis of its use of the patents of the other. For the past few years under the operation of this agreement your Company has received substantial sums by way of royalties. This agreement expired by limitation of time on April 30, 1911. No renewal of it is contemplated. This source of revenue, therefore, cannot now be counted upon.

Other patent license agreements with manufacturers of mining locomotives, small motors, fuses, switches and sockets, under which your Company has been working for some years, have recently been cancelled on the suggestion that they might be questioned as being in violation of the Federal anti-trust laws, notwithstanding they were originally made and have been maintained under advice of counsel that assured your Company of their validity.

Your Directors have had steadily in mind the purpose of strengthening your Company's position in every possible direction. To that end they have authorized considerable increase in the expenditures of the selling organization, for increasing the number of salesmen in the field, for remuneration to its representatives adequate to secure the best effort on their part, for the extension of advertising, and to provide for proper warehouse facilities for carrying stocks at distributing points. This has added considerably to the aggregate selling expense, but the results we believe, have been justified in the increased volume of business obtained. It is a matter of simple computation, on the basis of the operations of the past two years, to ascertain the point at which the volume of gross business fails to provide a surplus over operating expenses and fixed charges. It is vital that your business should not drop to that point.

6

With the same purpose in view fairly large expenditures have been authorized for the work of new development and for improvement in current types of apparatus. This work has been particularly marked with respect to the redesigning of direct current motors, alternating current and direct current mill and crane motors, small power motors, high speed turbo-generators, circuit breakers, railway equipment and heating and cooking apparatus. Your Directors feel that this is an item of expenditure which, owing to the position of your Company, it would be unwise at any time to curtail. It must be borne in mind that your Company must keep pace in technical skill and inventive ingenuity with its competitors even though their combined capital and manufacturing facilities are greatly in excess of yours. The cost of all new development and redesigning is charged monthly as a part of the current costs.

During the past year additional real estate adjoining the Newark plant has been acquired, so that your Company now owns substantially all of the city square on which the factory is located. Upon part of this additional real estate an extension to the plant is in course of construction upon a plan which contemplates ultimately occupying all the newly acquired area with an harmonious structure. The extension now being built will increase the manufacturing floor space of this plant about 30 per cent.

The New York City plant is now in full operation by the Westinghouse Lamp Company in the production of Tungsten lamps, the equipment of the building for that purpose, referred to in the last report, having been fully completed.

The additions to the Bridgeport, Conn., plant under way at the end of the previous fiscal year have also been carried to completion.

During the year the R. D. Nuttall Company, which has heretofore occupied rented premises in Pittsburg, completed negotiations for the purchase of an existing manufacturing plant on Fifty-Fourth Street, in Pittsburg, Pa., comprising approximately five acres. This plant, with some additions to its equipment now in progress, will furnish the Nuttall Company with ample facilities for many years to care for its growing business This transaction will be taken on the books of the Company during April 1911.

Your Company operates an iron foundry at Pittsburg, Pa., on leased premises. In anticipation of the termination of its lease, and because the plant is poorly adapted to the Company's needs, plans have been completed during the year for the erection of a new foundry at Trafford City, about six miles east of the main factory of your Company at East Pittsburg. Approximately sixty-three acres of land have been acquired for this and other possible purposes, at a total cost of $184,500. Your Company has further acquired, for the purpose of insuring communication between the proposed new foundry and its plant at East Pittsburg, sixty per cent of the capital stock of the Interworks Railway Company, owning and operating a line of railway between East Pittsburg and Trafford City. Plans have been prepared for the erection of foundry and pattern buildings at Trafford City, at an aggregate cost of approximately $1,250,000.

Your Company was made party defendant, together with the General Electric Company, the National Lamp Company and a number of other lamp manufacturers, to

153

a bill in equity recently filed by the United States under the provisions of the Sherman anti-trust law. This bill proceeds on the theory that certain agreements and acts of the lamp manufacturers, defendants in the suit, constitute a combination in restraint of trade. While it would not be proper to discuss in this report the matters involved in this proceeding, your Directors feel justified in saying that your Company's operations have been such that the outcome of the suit is not likely to seriously affect the conduct of its lamp business.

The surplus as of March 31, 1910, was $5,668,948.23. This has been increased during the year by various items of profit detailed in the statement of Profit and Loss, to $6,349,255.92. Adding the net income for the year, $4,881,105.98 there resulted a surplus with which your Directors had to deal as of the end of the fiscal year, of $11,230,361.90.

154

Against this surplus have been charged dividends on the Preferred Stock, for the year at the rate of 7 per cent per annum and a balance of 8¾ per cent accumulated but unpaid in previous years, together aggregating $629,795.25. In the adjustment of the account Property and Plant (hereinafter referred to) and in establishing a direct liability for bonds of the Walker Company guaranteed by your Company (hereinafter explained), there resulted charges against Surplus aggregating $1,193,297.79, the items comprising which are shown separately in the statement of Profit and Loss. Charges against Surplus in connection with reserves for notes and accounts receivable were made during the year aggregating $589,774.05. Miscellaneous charges against Profit and Loss amounted to $355.00. The total of the charges enumerated is $2,413,222.09. There were also written off as depreciations of investments, the following:

STOCKS:
    Westinghouse Electric Company, Ltd., London . . . . $ 500,000.00
    Societe Anonyme Westinghouse (French Company) 218,974.00
    The Westinghouse Machine Company 93,538.60

BONDS:
    Lackawanna & Wyoming Valley Rapid Transit Co. 2,000,000.00

MISCELLANEOUS STOCKS AND BONDS 40,402.31

                TOTAL $2,852,914.91

As a result of these depreciations the Surplus as of March 31, 1911, shown in the Balance Sheet, is $5,964,224.90.

The Consolidated Balance Sheet as of March 31, 1911, follows:

ASSETS		LIABILITIES		
PROPERTY AND PLANT:		**CAPITAL STOCK:**		
Factory Plants, including Real Estate, Machinery, Equipment Etc..	$17,692,145 61	Preferred		$ 3,996,700.00
		Assenting—In Hands of Public.... $35,187,587 50		
		In Treasury . 1,507,000 00	36,694,587 50	
SINKING FUND:		TOTAL CAPITAL STOCK.		$40,693,287 50
With Trustee for Redemption of Convertible Sinking Fund, 5%, Gold Bonds......	445 48	**FUNDED DEBT.**		
		Convertible Sinking Fund, 5%, Gold Bonds, due January 1 1931		
INVESTMENTS:		In Hands of Public.. $19,691,000.00		
Stocks, Bonds, Debentures, Collateral Trust Notes etc., including those of Affiliated European and Canadian Westinghouse Companies	24,034,035.99	In Treasury .. 266,000 00	$19,957,000.00	
		Debenture Certificates, 5%, due July 1, 1913....	1,800,000 00	
		Bonds—Walker Company, due January 1, 1916, Guaranteed by W. E. & M. Co...	850,000 00	
CURRENT ASSETS:		TOTAL FUNDED DEBT....		22,607,000 00
Cash.. . $6,634,677.07		**COLLATERAL NOTES:**		
Cash on Deposit to Pay Interest Coupons.... 27,340.00		Six Per Cent Collateral Notes, due August 1, 1913 . $ 4,000,000.00		
Cash on Deposit to Pay Dividends on Preferred Stock 940 82		Five Per Cent Collateral Notes, due October 1, 1917 2,720,000 00		
Notes Receivable... 2,946,531 46		TOTAL COLLATERAL NOTES .		6,720,000 00
Accounts Receivable. 9,694,731 06		**LONG TERM NOTES:**		
Due from Subscribers to Capital Stock 53,924 77		Four Year 5% Notes due January 1, 1913 . . $ 429,900.00		
TOTAL CURRENT ASSETS .	19,158,168 98	Five Year 5% Notes due January 1, 1914 429,500.00		
		Six Year 5% Notes due January 1, 1915. 425,500.00		
		Fifteen Year 5% Notes due January 1, 1924 98,750.00		
WORKING AND TRADING ASSETS:		TOTAL LONG TERM NOTES.		1,383,650.00
Raw Materials and Supplies, Finished Parts and Machines, Work in Progress, Goods on Consignment and Apparatus with Customers....	14,321,474 01	**REAL ESTATE MORTGAGES ASSUMED IN PURCHASE OF PROPERTY.**		228,200 00
		CURRENT LIABILITIES:		
		Accounts Payable . $ 2,454,674 83		
OTHER ASSETS:		Interest Taxes, Wages, Rebates etc., Accrued, Not Due 572,803 75		
Patents, Charters and Franchises $6,074,985 17		Dividends on Preferred Stock, Payable April 15, 1911 139,954 50		
Insurance, Taxes etc., Paid in Advance... 120,321 78		Unpaid Dividends on Preferred Stock 940 62		
Deferred Charge—Expenses Incidental to Issue of Bonds and Notes . 993,333.34		TOTAL CURRENT LIABILITIES .		3,168,373 70
TOTAL OTHER ASSETS	7,188,640 29	**RESERVE**		
		For Adjustment of Inventories, Notes and Accounts Receivable Etc		1,630,774 26
TOTAL ASSETS . . .	$82,395,510 36	**PROFIT AND LOSS.**		
		Surplus . .		5,964,224.90
		TOTAL LIABILITIES		$82,395,510 36

Note—There is a Contingent Liability for Notes Receivable discounted by Subsidiary Companies amounting to $16,703 87.

Your Directors present the following explanation of important items in the Balance Sheet, with the view of informing the Stockholders as fully as possible, without entering into unnecessary details, as to the character and value of the Company's assets and the extent and nature of its liabilities. This information is given both in recognition of the duty of corporate directors to give their stockholders the fullest practicable publicity as to the corporation's affairs and for the purpose of enabling the stockholders to form for themselves an intelligent judgment as to the advisability of distributing the Company's current earnings by way of dividends on the assenting stock.

ASSETS

I—Property and Plant—$17,692,145.61

This item represents the present value of the real estate, buildings, machinery and equipment comprising your manufacturing plants at East Pittsburg, Pa., Newark, N. J., Pittsburg, Pa., Cleveland, Ohio, Bloomfield, N. J.. New York, N. Y. and Bridgeport, Conn.; also storage and warehouse properties at distributing points throughout the country.

During the past year your Directors caused to be made by the American Appraisal Company of Milwaukee. Wisconsin, a complete inventory and appraisal of the buildings, machinery and equipment of all your plants. A like appraisal of the real estate was made through local agencies. The appraisal of the buildings, machinery and equipment was made to ascertain, first, the cost as of the date of appraisal of reproducing the buildings, machinery and equipment, new; and second, the present **sound values,** after charging against the reproductive cost all depreciations in buildings, machinery and equipment as determined by the judgment and estimate of the Appraisal Company. These **sound values** thus ascertained by the Appraisal Company, are the figures appearing in the Balance Sheet.

The aggregate of the item Property and Plant in the Balance Sheet as of March 31, 1910, was $14,974,629.20. There is an increase in this item of $2,717,516.41. This increase is chiefly due to the following: Your plants at Newark, New York City and Cleveland have heretofore appeared in the Balance Sheet, not under "Property and Plant", but under "Investments", for the reason that your Company's control of these properties was represented by the ownership of securities of other corporations that held title to them. Title to the Newark plant was held by The United States Electric Lighting Company, all of whose stock is now owned by your Company, to the New York plant by The Consolidated Electric Light Company, substantially all of whose stock is likewise owned, and to the Cleveland plant by the Walker Foundry Company, all of whose stock your Company also owns. The Cleveland plant is subject to the lien of a mortgage securing $850,000 of bonds of the Walker Company, a former owner of the plant. These bonds, though guaranteed as to principal and interest by the Westinghouse Electric & Manufacturing Company, have never appeared as a direct obligation of your Company, though reference has been made in former reports to this guaranty as a contingent liability. During the past year title has been taken by the Westinghouse Electric & Manufacturing Company to the Cleveland plant, subject to the $850,000 bonds. Steps are in progress to convey to the Westinghouse Electric & Manufacturing Company the Newark plant and it is intended that similar action shall be taken with reference to the New York City plant. In view of this situation it was determined to write into the account "Property and Plant", the appraised value of the buildings, machinery and equipment comprising each of these plants, eliminating from investments the items heretofore representing your stock control of these properties, and taking upon the books of the Westinghouse Electric & Manufacturing Company as its direct obligation, its guaranty of the Walker Company bonds. This difference between former book values and present appraised values, aggregating $1,193,297.79, has been charged against Surplus, partly as depreciation of Investments, and partly as an adjustment due to establishing on the books as a direct liability the guaranty of the bonds of the Walker Company.

Your Directors have determined that for the current fiscal year depreciation charges to provide for obsolescence of buildings shall be made monthly at the annual rate of two per cent of the reproductive cost thereof, providing for all other depreciations of Property and Plant by charging monthly to operating expenses the cost of all renewals, replacements and maintenance of both buildings and machinery and equipment. As to the former, this is a new policy. As to the latter, this determination is but a continuance of past practices, as a result of the application of which to the operations of the past year, $2,271,471.41 were charged out of earnings, as part of current operating expenses, on account of depreciation of buildings, machinery and equipment.

II—Sinking Fund—$445.48

This item represents the balance uninvested of sinking fund payments made to the Trustee, in accordance with the requirements of the indenture controlling the Company's issue of Convertible Sinking Fund Five Per Cent Gold Bonds.

III—Investments—$24,034,635.99

A—Securities of Westinghouse Electric & Manufacturing Co.

There are included in this account securities of Westinghouse Electric & Manufacturing Company carried at their face values as follows:

Capital stock—assenting	$1,507,048.00
Convertible sinking fund bonds	266,000.00
Bond scrip	1,150.50
Total	**$1,774,198.50**

The assenting capital stock was acquired partly by the several subsidiary Companies in settlement of accounts due them by the Westinghouse Electric & Manufacturing Company at the time of the receivership, and partly in settlement of disputed relations existing at and after the receivership between the Westinghouse Electric & Manufacturing Company and Security Investment Company. The stock is carried as an investment with the intent that at a favorable time it shall be resold.

The convertible sinking fund bonds have been acquired and are held in anticipation of sinking fund requirements. The bond scrip represents scrip purchased to be exchanged for bonds, also to be held for sinking fund purposes.

B—Securities of Subsidiary Companies

The following are known as the "Subsidiary Companies" of Westinghouse Electric & Manufacturing Company:

Westinghouse Lamp Company;

The Bryant Electric Company (The Perkins Electric Switch Manufacturing Co.);

R. D. Nuttall Company;

Westinghouse Electric & Manufacturing Company of Texas.

None of these Companies has any funded debt. All the shares of stock of each of them is owned by Westinghouse Electric & Manufacturing Company, but none of these stocks appear as investments in the consolidated balance sheet herewith presented. Instead, the assets and liabilities of each of the subsidiary companies are included under their several appropriate headings in the consolidated balance sheet.

The ownership by The Bryant Electric Company of all the capital stock ($125,000) of The Perkins Electric Switch Manufacturing Company, is carried on the books of The Bryant Electric Company at $2,000,000. This item is included in "Investments" in the consolidated balance sheet, after deducting the par amount of the outstanding capital stock, at..**$1,875,000.00**
This item can be considered as having value only as goodwill.

C—Foreign Companies

Since 1889 your Company has from time to time invested large amounts of its capital in establishing and maintaining companies for the manufacture and sale of Westinghouse electrical apparatus in foreign countries. Since no detailed report of these efforts and of their results has heretofore been made to the stockholders, your Directors deem this an opportune time to inform the stockholders concerning them, and also as to the values at which the resulting investments now stand upon the books.

The first foreign Company, organized July 11, 1889, was

Westinghouse Electric Company, Limited
(a corporation of Great Britain)

Its issued capital consists of:

Preference shares................	£189,550 ($ 919,317.50)
Ordinary shares................	£275,000 ($1,333,750.00)

The entire issued capital of this company was eventually acquired by Westinghouse Electric & Manufacturing Company, and as of March 31, 1909, was carried as an investment on your books at an aggregate book value of **$1,773,084.05**. This book value represented expenses incurred from 1889 to 1906 in the efforts to establish the manufacture and sale of your Company's apparatus in foreign countries. This expense included the cost of taking out and maintaining patents in foreign countries on the inventions and improvements of the home company. From time to time the patents issued by the various foreign countries in which manufacturing companies were organized, as hereinafter described, were transferred to such companies. As of March 31, 1910, the assets of Westinghouse Electric Company, Ltd., consisted (aside from some small holdings of shares in other companies, of little or no value) of the patents owned by it in Germany, Austria, Hungary, Norway, Sweden and Denmark, and in certain licenses granted by it under some of these patents. The income of the company is and has long been insufficient to pay the expenses of its operations and the upkeep of its patents. During the fiscal year ended March 31, 1910, your Directors deemed it wise to write off from the book value of this item $773,084.05 and during the fiscal year just ended there has been written off an additional $500,000.00 making a total depreciation of this item of $1,273,084.05, leaving the book value of this investment as of March 31, 1911..**$500,000.00**
Further depreciation of this item must be contemplated.

The next foreign company, organized July 10, 1899, was

The British Westinghouse Electric & Manufacturing Co., Ltd.
(a corporation of Great Britain)

This company by 1903 had completed the construction and equipment of immense works for the manufacture of electrical apparatus, steam turbines and gas engines. The buildings comprise machine shops, an iron foundry, a steel foundry and forge, a brass foundry, a malleable iron foundry and office buildings, at Trafford Park, near Manchester, England. The company's buildings occupy a total floor area of 27 acres. Its real estate holdings comprise 133 acres which it holds under an annual rent charge of £7,740 ($37,539) to be increased on January 1, 1915, in perpetuity, to £8,845 ($42,-898.25). The company's original capital, issued from time to time from 1900 to 1906, consisted of

Ordinary shares	£ 750,000	($ 3,637,500)
Preference shares	£2,500,000	($12,125,000)
4% Mortgage debenture stock	£1,241,353	($ 6,020,562)
Total	£4,491,353	($21,783,062)

The ordinary shares were issued in payment for patents, manufacturing information and territorial rights. The preference shares and the mortgage debenture stock were sold for cash at substantially par, and the aggregate of their face value, £3,741,353 ($18,145,-562), represents approximately the amount of money spent in producing the facilities of the British Company and in paying the losses incurred in its operations prior to 1907. In January 1907, because of losses thus far incurred, the capital of the company was reduced by £1,375,000 ($6,668,750). In 1908 there was a further authorized issue of £300,000 ($1,455,000) of 6% prior lien debentures, of which £250,000 ($1,212,500) were issued. Of this issue £16,400 ($79,540) have been retired under sinking fund provisions leaving outstanding £233,600 ($1,132,960) as of December 31, 1910.

The present capitalization is:

Preference shares	£1,500,000	($ 7,275,000)
Ordinary shares	£ 375,000	($ 1,818,750)
4% Mortgage debenture stock	£1,241,353	($ 6,020,562)
6% Prior lien debentures	£ 233,600	($ 1,132,960)
Total	£3,349,953	($16,247,272)

The operations of the British Company have been quite uniformly unprofitable, as is shown by the table of gross earnings and net income, which follows:

	YEAR ENDED DECEMBER 31						
	1904	1905	1906	1907	1908	1909	1910
Gross Earnings—Shipments Billed	£1,464,695	£1,334,815	£1,054,199	£1,121,432	£1,068,539	£ 984,709	£1,206,366
Net Profit from Operations	4,289	126,784 (loss)	310,524 (loss)	17,536 (loss)	12,626	51,623	62,372
Other Income	2,813	3,228	1,231	1,668	2,760	17,435	19,891
TOTAL INCOME	7,102	123,556 (loss)	309,293 (loss)	16,168 (loss)	15,386	69,058	82,263
Interest Charges	37,298	43,476	56,764	64,033	62,607	64,556	64,184
Net Surplus for the Year	£ 30,196 (loss) ($146,450)	£ 167,032 (loss) ($810,105)	£ 366,057 (loss) ($1,775,376)	£ 80,201 (loss) ($388,974)	£ 47,221 (loss) ($229,021)	£ 4,502 ($21,834)	£ 18,079 ($87,683)

A further reduction of the British Company's capital seems to be forecasted by the necessity for providing for payment of an award against it aggregating with costs substantially more than £100,000 ($485,000), in an arbitration proceeding, recently decided, between the British Company and the London Underground Railway.

The Income Account for the year ended December 31, 1910, follows:

	£	s.	d.		£	s.	d.
To Interest on 6 per cent. Prior Lien Bonds to 31st December, 1910	14,358	0	0	By Profit for year, including estimated profit accrued to date on contracts in progress, interest received etc., after providing for the expenses of management, directors' fees, for bad and doubtful debts, maintenance of buildings, machinery etc., and all other working charges	110,133	17	8
To Proportion of Issue expenses of 6 per cent. Prior Lien Debentures written off	660	0	0				
To Interest on 4 per cent. Mortgage Debenture Stock	49,654	2	4				
To Expenses on surplus land and buildings	5,364	13	5				
To Amount written off works, machinery, plant etc. £ 9,423 11 6				By interest on deposits and loans	2,370	7	3
To Additional sum reserved for general depreciation 15,000 0 0	24,423	11	6	By transfer fees	34	15	0
To profit for year including Prior Lien Redemption account	18,078	12	8				
	£112,538	19	11		£112,538	19	11

160   The improved situation and prospects of the British Company reflected by the results of its operations for the past year, seem to assure the ability of the company to meet its fixed charges represented by the interest on its two classes of debentures, but do not give promise of an early return on either its preference or ordinary shares. The balance sheet of the company as of December 31, last, follows:

ASSETS

PROPERTY AND PLANT:

Buildings, fixtures and land	£	935,182
Machinery, plant and furniture, tools and dies, patterns, drawings etc., Trafford Park		752,258
Office furniture and equipment—London and branch offices		4,199
TOTAL	£1,691,639	

INVESTMENTS:

Clyde Valley Electrical Power Company, Ltd.—Shares	£	200,790
Traction & Power Securities Company, Ltd.—Shares		56,950
Miscellaneous shares and debentures		28,674
TOTAL	£	286,414

CURRENT ASSETS:

Cash at bankers and on loan	£	92,792
Cash with cashiers, agents and others		21,744
Notes receivable		6,753
Accounts receivable		559,628
TOTAL	£	680,917

WORKING AND TRADING ASSETS:

Materials and supplies, finished product, work in progress etc.	£	516,100

OTHER ASSETS:

Patents and good-will	£	375,000
Insurance, taxes and royalties paid in advance		14,039
Suspense account—prior lien debenture issue expenses		12,977
Development of Rateau turbines		6,894
TOTAL	£	408,910
TOTAL ASSETS	£3,583,980	

LIABILITIES

CAPITAL:

Share capital:

Preference shares		£1,500,000
Ordinary shares		375,000
TOTAL	£1,875,000	

Debentures:

6% Prior lien	£	233,600
4% Mortgage stock		1,241,353
TOTAL	£1,474,953	

CURRENT LIABILITIES:

Current accounts	£	130,615
Taxes and rents, royalties etc.		17,585
Advances received on contracts in progress		2,009
Interest accrued		28,331
TOTAL	£	178,540

RESERVE ACCOUNTS AND SURPLUS	£	55,487
TOTAL LIABILITIES	£3,583,980	

Of the outstanding capital of the British Company the Westinghouse Electric & Manufacturing Company owns the following:

Preference shares	£536,112 ($2,600,143)
Ordinary shares	£190,230 ($ 922,615)
4% Mortgage debenture stock	£675,000 ($3,273,750)

Of these, the ordinary shares do not appear on your books as an investment of any value. The preference shares, having a par value (after the reduction of capital in 1907) of $2,600,143 were carried on your books as an investment until 1910 at a book value, representing the original cost of acquisition, of $4,458,083. As of March 31, 1910, your Directors wrote off for depreciation of this item the sum of $3,564,563. Its book value as of March 31, 1911, is..**$893,520.00** The shares have a present market value on the London Stock Exchange of 21 shillings per share of the par value of £3 each, which makes the present aggregate market value of this item approximately the book value.

The 4% Debenture stock, having a par value of $3,273,750 is carried on the books as an investment at the cost of acquisition.......................**$3,137,104.84** It yields a return of 4% on par. Recent sales on the London Stock Exchange have been at the price of 62% of par.

On November 28, 1901, there was organized under French law

Societe Anonyme Westinghouse, of Paris

(French Company)

Its outstanding capital is

Preference shares............Frs. 10,000,000 ($1,930,000)
Ordinary shares.............Frs. 10,000,000 ($1,930,000)
5% Debentures..............Frs. 7,500,000 ($1,447,500)

161

The French Company operates a factory at Havre, France, where it manufactures a general line of electrical apparatus and certain condensing apparatus for steam engines and turbines. It also has a factory at Freinville, near Paris, where it manufactures Westinghouse air brakes. Its territory includes France, Belgium, Holland, Switzerland, Spain and Portugal. The operations of the company have been steadily unprofitable; and, while it earns and pays the interest on its debentures, only once, for the year 1908, has it paid a dividend on its preference shares. It underwent one reduction of capital in 1907, whereby its ordinary shares were reduced from Frs. 20,000,000 ($3,860,000) to Frs. 10,000,000, ($1,930,000). In 1909 it increased its issue of preference shares by Frs. 5,000,0000, ($965,000). Since January 1, 1911, it has increased its 5% debenture issue from Frs. 7,500,000 ($1,447,500) to Frs. 10,000,000 ($1,930,000). It proposes at its annual general meeting in June 1911, again to reduce its capital by a reduction of the ordinary shares from Frs. 10,000,000 ($1,930,000) to Frs. 4,000,000 ($772,000). Statement of its gross and net earnings for the years 1906 to 1910 inclusive, follows:

	YEAR ENDED DECEMBER 31				
	1906	1907	1908	1909	1910
	Francs	Francs	Francs	Francs	Francs
Gross Earnings—Shipments Billed....	9,864,092	10,350,733	15,184,819	13,207,311	14,031,636
Net Profit from Operations.............................	730,021	1,183,941	670,785	288,125 (loss)	23,243 (loss)
Other Income...	83,581	183,163	211,629	726,120	412,205
TOTAL INCOME...............................	646,440 (loss)	1,000,778 (loss)	882,414	437,995	388,962
Interest Charges..........................	29,825	351,644	604,881	513,327	397,359
Net Surplus for the Year................................	676,265 (loss) ($130,519)	1,352,422 (loss) ($261,017)	277,533 ($53,563)	75,332 (loss) ($14,539)	8,397* (loss) ($1,620)

*Preliminary—final reports not yet received.

A condensed preliminary balance sheet of the French Company as of December 31, 1910, which does not take into account the increase in its debenture issue, or the proposed reduction of share capital, follows:

ASSETS	FRANCS	LIABILITIES	FRANCS
PROPERTY AND PLANT:		**CAPITAL STOCK:**	
Real Estate and buildings..	3,621,769	Ordinary shares	10,000,000
Machinery, tools, patterns, fixtures and office furniture...	4,537,979	Preference shares	10,000,000
Patents	3,985,000	5% Debentures	7,500,000
TOTAL	12,144,748		
		TOTAL CAPITAL AND FUNDED DEBT	27,500,000
INVESTMENTS:			
Italian Company	*2,969,694		
Miscellaneous	748,949		
TOTAL	3,718,643		
CURRENT ASSETS:		**CURRENT LIABILITIES:**	
Cash with bankers	157,258	Notes payable	473,091
Cash with cashier, agents et al	84,559	Accounts payable	3,207,077
Cash guarantees and advances	224,287	Advances on account of apparatus to be delivered	1,090,559
Notes receivable	36,250	Interest etc.	193,062
Accounts receivable	8,466,677		
TOTAL	8,969,031	TOTAL	4,964,389
WORKING AND TRADING ASSETS:			
Raw materials and supplies, finished product, work in progress etc.	7,342,535	RESERVES, PROFIT AND LOSS ETC.	389,069
DEFERRED CHARGES	178,501		
TOTAL ASSETS	32,853,458	TOTAL LIABILITIES	32,853,458

*1000 Shares (par value Lire 250,000) deposited with Bankers as security for guarantees on contracts undertaken.

NOTE:—As of December 31, 1910, the French Company had a contingent liability for guarantees and endorsements made for account of the Italian Company to the amount of Frs. 1,570,014.

Of the outstanding capital of the French Company, the Westinghouse Electric & Manufacturing Company owns:

        Preference shares.............Frs. 4,628,750 ($ 893,348)
        Ordinary shares...............Frs. 2,883,750 ($ 556,563)
        5% Debentures................Frs. 7,500,000 ($1,447,500)

With the exception of Frs. 3,478,750 ($671,398) of preference shares, these were all acquired prior to 1907. During the Receivership of your Company (1907-1908) the Court authorized the Receivers to advance $1,300,000 to the French Company. These advances were not actually made during the Receivership, but in 1909 your Company took at par Frs. 3,478,750 ($671,398) of the preference shares issued that year.

The debentures are carried on your books as an investment at cost.... **$1,430,730.37**

The preference shares are likewise carried among investments at cost.. **$896,536.51**

Prior to March 31, 1910, the ordinary shares were carried as an investment at cost $494,032.21. During the year ended March 31, 1910, there was written off as depreciation of this item $275,057.21. During the last fiscal year there was written off a further sum of $218,974.00, leaving the book value of the ordinary shares as of March 31, 1911.. **$1.00**

Your Directors hope that with careful management the debentures and the preference shares of the French Company may be made worth their face values. There is no market quotation for any of these securities.

On March 11, 1907, there was organized under Italian law, as a subsidiary of the French Company,

Societa Italiana Westinghouse
(Italian Company)

The outstanding capital of this company consists of
        Ordinary shares.............Lire 4,000,000 ($772,000).
Of these the French company owns approximately Lire 3,000,000 ($579,000).

16

162

For the purpose of capitalizing certain advances recently made to it by the French Company and the Westinghouse Electric & Manufacturing Company, the Italian Company is about to create an issue of Lire 4,000,000 ($772,000) of 5% debentures. Of this issue approximately Lire 1,500,000 ($289,500) will be received by the French Company and Lire 2,500,000 ($482,500) by the Westinghouse Electric & Manufacturing Company. These debentures will in next year's balance sheet of your Company appear among Investments; meanwhile the amounts advanced as of March 31, 1911 appear in the balance sheet under the items Notes and Accounts Receivable at $289,746.12.

The Italian Company in 1907-8 constructed a factory at Vado, Ligure, Italy, for the primary purpose of executing important contracts for the electrification of certain of the Italian State Railways. Delays by the Italian Government in carrying out its program for the improvement of its railway lines has temporarily disappointed the expectations with which this company was organized and its plant created, so that it is now looking to the general market for orders for electrical apparatus to keep its works in operation.

Statement of its earnings and profits and its balance sheet as of December 31, 1910, follows:

	YEAR ENDED DECEMBER 31		
	1908 Lire 2,325,678	1909 Lire 2,899,713	1910 Lire 3,688,241
Gross Earnings—Shipments Billed			
Net Profit from Operations	104,611	318,786	121,590 (loss)
Other Income	141,210	173,653	469,033
TOTAL INCOME	245,821	492,439	347,443
Deductions from Income—Interest and Other Charges	75,077	255,225	518,121
Net Surplus for the Year	170,744 ($ 32,953)	237,214 ($ 45,782)	(loss) 170,678 ($ 32,940)

ASSETS		LIABILITIES	
PROPERTY AND PLANT:	LIRE	**CAPITAL STOCK:**	LIRE
Real estate and buildings	1,329,626	Ordinary Shares	4,000,000
Other real estate	665,148		
Machinery, tools, patterns, fixtures and furniture	2,466,522		
Patents	1,049,917	**CURRENT LIABILITIES:**	
Total	5,511,213	Notes payable	
		Issued for cash	3,091,014 (1)
CURRENT AND WORKING ASSETS:		Miscellaneous	361,579
Cash with cashier and banks	22,174	Accounts payable	2,563,643 (2)
Cash with agents etc.	110,319	Bank overdraft	93,191
Cash guarantees etc.	367,831	Miscellaneous—including interest	50,155
Accounts and notes receivable	2,995,850		
Inventories	1,146,004	Total	6,159,582
Total	4,642,178		
DEFERRED CHARGES	61,765	LEGAL RESERVE AND PROFIT AND LOSS	55,574
Total Assets	10,215,156	Total Liabilities	10,215,156

(1) Includes notes for L. 1,500,000 held by American Co. for cash advanced. The balance is held almost exclusively by Italian banks and in part is secured by guarantee of the French Co.
(2) Includes account due the French Co. amounting to approximately L. 1,250,000.

In July 1906 there was organized under the laws of France
Societe Electrique Westinghouse de Russie
(Russian Company)
The outstanding capital of this Company is

Cash shares..................Frs. 7,000,000 ($1,351,000)
Apport shares..............Frs. 13,000,000 ($2,509,000)
5% Debentures.............Frs. 14,000,000 ($2,702,000)

17

This company was organized primarily to execute a contract amounting to over Rs. 10,000,000 ($5,150,000) for the electrification of the St. Petersburg tramways. For the purpose of this work the Russian Company acquired the electric manufacturing plant in Moscow of the Compagnie Centrale d'Electricite of Paris. Part of the purchase price was deferred and secured by a mortgage on the plant of which there is still due approximately Frs. 750,000 ($144,750) maturing in three nearly equal instalments on July 25, 1911, January 25, 1912, and July 25, 1912. Upon the organization of the Russian Company the Westinghouse Electric & Manufacturing Company advanced to it sums aggregating $895,888.12, of which there remains due to this Company $290,000.00. The Westinghouse Electric & Manufacturing Company purchased from the Russian Company its issue of Frs. 14,000,000 ($2,702,000) of 5% debentures at 83% of par, the cost aggregatinlg $2,243,243.24. It also subscribed for Frs. 3,600,000 ($694,800) cash shares of the Russian Company at par, the payment for this subscription aggregating $696,322.35. The apport shares of which your company owns Frs. 1,240,000 ($239,320) par value, cost $198,962.05. The Russian Company owes the Westinghouse Electric & Manufacturing Company on open account for materials $32,355.81. There remains unpaid also the interest on the debentures from October 1, 1908 to April 1, 1911, aggregating $324,324.30. The total investment in and accounts due by the Russian Company at the close of the last fiscal year therefore aggregate $3,785,207.75. Of this, prior to March 31, 1910, there were carried on your books as Investments

Cash shares at cost......................	$ 696,322.35
Apport shares...........................	198,962.05
5% Debentures at cost...................	2,243,243.24

As of March 31, 1910, the investment in the cash and apport shares was written off to $1.00 for each class of shares, leaving as of March 31, 1911, the book value of this investment **$2,243,245.24**
Further depreciation of this investment may be required.

Other items are carried against the Russian Company in other accounts as follows:

Accounts Receivable.......................$	32,355.81
Notes Receivable...........................	290,000.00

The unpaid interest on the debentures has not been entered on the books of your Company.

The execution of the St. Petersburg contract resulted in a loss of approximately Rs. 2,000,000 ($1,030,000). In its other operations the losses of the Russian Company have aggregated Rs. 1,584,425 ($815,978). The aggregate losses in the operations of the Russian Company to date therefore are in excess of $1,800,000. There are other losses not yet definitely ascertained, due to the difference between the actual value of the Moscow plant and the price paid for it, and to depreciations occurring since the property was acquired not yet entered on the books.

The City of St. Petersburg is withholding from the amount due by it to the Russian Company an aggregate of over Rs. 700,000 ($360,500) by way of fines imposed for alleged delays in the performance of the contract and the company is urging a large claim for extras. There is reason to hope that the fines may be substantially remitted. Until these disputes are adjusted and payment made, it is obviously impossible to predict how much of our investment in the Russian Company can be realized. The maintenance of the company as a going concern is necessary pending the negotiations with the Municipality of St. Petersburg, and for this purpose your Directors have found it necessary to provide it with funds. These advances, approximating $110,322 to March 31, 1911, are secured by mortgage. During the past year, improvement in the operations and increase of the business of the Moscow plant encourage the hope that it may at least earn its operating expenses.

On September 6, 1906 there was organized under Austrian laws

Westinghouse Metallfaden-Gluhlampen-Fabrik Gesellschaft, m.b.H.
(Austrian Company)

The outstanding capital stock of this company is Kronen 1,600,000 ($324,800). Of this Kronen 1,230,000 ($249,690) are owned by the Westinghouse Electric & Manufacturing Company and Westinghouse Lamp Company and are carried among investments at the cost of acquisition aggregating...**$250,626.75**
The Austrian Company operates a factory for the manufacture of tungsten lamps at Atzgersdorf near Vienna. Its operations have so far been measureably profitable, and the shares owned by your Company may safely be considered worth their book value.

The balance sheet of the Austrian Company as of February 28, 1911, follows:

ASSETS		LIABILITIES	
PROPERTY AND PLANT:	Kronen	**CAPITAL:**	Kronen
Real estate and buildings............................	503,137	Capital stock..............	1,600,000
Machinery, tools, patterns, fixtures and furniture.........	827,634		
Patents...	1	**CURRENT LIABILITIES:**	
Total.....	1,330,772	Accounts payable...................................	836,836
CURRENT AND WORKING ASSETS:		Loan—Union Bank..................................	30,000
Cash with bankers................................	3,343	Dividend...	240,000
Cash with cashiers etc...............................	35,414		
Accounts receivable................................	850,107	Total......................................	1,106,836
Inventories.......................................	1,011,264		
Insurance, taxes etc., paid in advance.................	11,000		
Total Current and Working Assets..........	1,911,128	RESERVE ACCOUNTS, PROFIT AND LOSS ETC..........	535,064
Total Assets..............................	3,241,900	Total Liabilities...........................	3,241,900

At the time of the organization of the Austrian Lamp Company, there was organized

The Westinghouse Metal Filament Lamp Company, Ltd.
(London Lamp Company)

with a capitalization of £ 10,000 ($48,500) of which 80% is owned by the Westinghouse Lamp Company, one of your subsidiary companies, and is carried on the books of that company at cost..**$38,800.00**

The London Lamp Company was organized to control the patents covering the tungsten lamp manufacturing processes for the territory outside of that of the Austrian Lamp Company. It is believed that the book value of this investment will be realized.

At various times from 1903 to 1908 the Westinghouse Electric & Manufacturing Company acquired shares in

Canadian Westinghouse Company, Limited
(organized under the laws of Canada)

Capital—Authorized.............$5,000,000.00
      —Issued................. 4,376,600.00

Of the latter the Westinghouse Electric & Manufacturing Company owns $1,710,000, of which $500,000 was acquired in consideration of the transfer of patent rights and manufacturing information for Canada. The balance, $1,210,000, has been acquired from time to time at par for cash. The shares are carried on your books as an investment at par..**$1,710,000.00**

166 Canadian Westinghouse Company, Ltd., operates a manufacturing plant at Hamilton, Ontario, Canada. It manufactures a general line of electrical apparatus and in addition the Westinghouse air brake. It has been uniformly and increasingly successful and has paid dividends regularly since 1903 at the rate of 6% per annum, with an extra 1% paid for 1910. The shares may safely be considered worth in excess of their book value. The general balance sheet and statement of profit and loss both as of December 31, 1910, follow:

GENERAL BALANCE SHEET

ASSETS		LIABILITIES	
Cash...	$ 376,565.29	Capital stock..............	$4,376,600.00
Accounts and bills receivable	1,276,527.14	Accounts payable............	501,846.51
PROPERTY AND PLANT:		Reserve for depreciation of property and plant......	400,000 00
(Includes Air Brake and Electric Properties, Real Estate, General Office Building, Equipment, Sundries and Patents, Rights and Licenses)..	2,764,403 05	Reserve for inventory adjustment...........	50,000.00
		Profit and loss account...	726,613.22
Inventory of materials and products on hand, December 31st, 1910..... ...	1,626,384.31		
Insurance unexpired and taxes paid in advance	10,679.94		
TOTAL ASSETS....	$6,055,059 73	TOTAL LIABILITIES.....	$6,055,059.73

PROFIT AND LOSS ACCOUNT

Balance Brought Forward January 1st, 1910.			$ 536,103.87
Net Earnings, Fiscal Year Ended December 31st, 1910.		$697,393.56	
Less—			
Dividends 1910.............	$306,362.00		
Reserve for General Depreciation of Property and Plant.......	100,000.00		
Reserve for Inventory Adjustment.......	30,000 00		
Written off Property and Plant....	70,522.21	506,884.21	190,509.35
Balance Carried Forward January 1st, 1911....			$ 726,613.22

D—OTHER MANUFACTURING COMPANIES
The Westinghouse Machine Company

On February 28, 1910 the Westinghouse Electric & Manufacturing Company acquired $250,000 par value, of the capital stock of The Westinghouse Machine Company, as part consideration of the adjustment of relations heretofore referred to between your Company and the Security Investment Company. These shares were taken on the books at the time of acquisition at a value of $218,538.60. As of March 31, 1911 your Directors wrote off for depreciation of this item $93,538.60, leaving the book value of these shares in investments at..**$125,000.00**

20

Nernst Lamp Company

On October 28, 1909 the Westinghouse Electric & Manufacturing Company acquired $500,000 of Nernst Lamp Company 5% first mortgage bonds at par. These were taken in pursuance of the terms of an adjustment by the Nernst Lamp Company with all of its creditors, by virtue of which it was discharged from the hands of receivers. The claim thus adjusted represented in part moneys advanced and materials furnished to the Nernst Lamp Company, and in part an unpaid balance on the sale in 1907 by the Westinghouse Electric & Manufacturing Company to the Nernst Lamp Company of the property known as the Garrison Alley factory in Pittsburg, Pa. These bonds are carried on your books at par.......................................**$500,000.00**

The Nernst Lamp Company is a subsidiary of The Westinghouse Machine Company, which owns all of its capital stock.

E—THE TRACTION & POWER SECURITIES COMPANY, LTD.

The Receivers of the Westinghouse Electric & Manufacturing Company on December 31, 1907, acquired at par £169,150 ($820,377), of the capital stock of The Traction & Power Securities Company, Ltd., from The British Westinghouse Electric & Manufacturing Company, Ltd., in payment of certain notes, open account and interest.

The Traction & Power Securities Company. Ltd., was organized in 1901 under the laws of Great Britain as a securities holding company. Its issued and outstanding capital is

Ordinary shares...................£854,100 ($4,142,385)

The assets of The Traction & Power Securities Company, Ltd., consist almost wholly of:

(a) £620,000 ($3,007,000) face value 4% prior lien debentures of the Mersey Railway, an electrically operated railway extending through the tunnel under the Mersey River, from Liverpool to Birkenhead. The Mersey Railway earns a small surplus over and above the interest on these debentures. Market sales of the debentures have recently been made in small lots at about 81.

(b) £344,470 ($1,670,679) par value, ordinary shares of The Clyde Valley Electrical Power company. The latter company owns and operates two power plants, one at Motherwell and the other at Yoker, on the Clyde River near Glasgow, Scotland. For additions to its plant the Clyde Valley Company has recently incurred indebtedness, secured by mortgage to The Traction & Power Securities Company, of over £140,000 ($679,000) which will probably be increased before the work is completed, to £200,000 ($970,000). Some adjustment of its capital to provide for the funding of this temporary loan will be necessary before the Clyde Valley Company can pay dividends, although it is now earning substantial profits above its operating expenses and fixed charges. There is no present market for the shares and no exact basis on which to estimate their value.

It is obvious that the value of The Traction & Power Securities Company's shares owned by your Company depends upon the future of the Mersey Railway and The Clyde Valley Electrical Power Company. Until there can be established a market value for the debentures of the former and the shares of the latter, the value of The Traction & Power Securities Company shares is undeterminable. It is believed, that eventually they may be made worth substantially par, but there is at present no market for them. These shares are carried on the books of your Company as of March 31, 1911 at **$820,135.00**

Niagara, Lockport & Ontario Power Company

Your Company owns $912,000, par value, of the First Mortgage 5% bonds, and $1,000,000, par value, of the five year 5% coupon notes of Niagara, Lockport & Ontario Power Company, and owns or controls substantially 55% of the outstanding capital stock of that company. These securities are carried on your books as investments, the

bonds at **$912,000.00**

the notes at **907,219.64**

and the stock at **2.00**

These bonds, notes, and stock were acquired, chiefly in exchange for collateral notes of the Iroquois Construction Co. bought by your Company in October, 1907, and partly in payment of advances made prior to and during the receivership of your Company to finance the construction of the transmission line of the Niagara, Lockport & Ontario Power Company, extending from Niagara Falls to Syracuse and intermediate points. This company is engaged in the transmission and sale of electric power generated at Niagara Falls by the Ontario Power Company, in which your company has no interest. The Niagara, Lockport & Ontario Power Company is earning and paying the interest on both its notes and bonds and its business shows a continuous growth. It would seem that the book values of these investments should eventually be realized. Following is a comparative statement of the operations and earnings of the company during the three and one-half years ended December 31, 1910.

	Total Receipts	Gross Income	Net Income
Six months ended December 31, 1907	$ 196,226.63	$ 7,876.63*	$ 67,811.51*
Year ended December 31, 1908	592,103.10	216,525.87	42,876.39
Year ended December 31, 1909	863,773.80	448,513.31	251,956.47
Year ended December 31, 1910	1,051,521.50	555,634.12	351,521.10

*Deficit

Atlanta Water & Electric Power Company

On October 1, 1907, the Westinghouse Electric & Manufacturing Company acquired at par $400,000 of the capital stock of the Atlanta Water & Electric Power Company, being part of an issue of $1,500,000 outstanding. These shares are carried on your books at cost..**$400,000.00** This book value should eventually be approximately realized but there is no present market for the shares.

This company operates an hydraulic electric power plant near Atlanta, Ga. Its power is sold on long term contracts to the company operating the local traction lines and the light and power company in Atlanta. It earns regularly a surplus over and above the 4% dividend paid on its stock. A statement of its earnings for six years ended December 31, 1910, follows:

	YEAR ENDED DECEMBER 31					
	1905	1906	1907	1908	1909	1910
Gross earnings	$134,609.28	$177,994.89	$170,265.03	$176,908.02	$183,981.03	$181,783.58
Operating expense and taxes	28,024.94	35,900.37	30,756.99	34,633.91	39,423.52	33,917.06
Net earnings	$106,584.34	$142,094.52	$139,508.04	$142,274.11	$144,557.51	$147,866.52
Other income		1,339.97	2,388.04	2,832.12	2,569.02	6,578.07
TOTAL INCOME	$106,584.34	$143,434.49	$141,896.08	$145,106.23	$147,126.53	$154,444.59
Interest (5% on $1,350,000 bonds)	$67,500.00	$67,500.00	$67,500.00	$67,500.00	$67,500.00	$67,500.00
Reserve for depreciation			25,000.00	25,000.00	15,000.00	15,000.00
Other income charges	1,500.00	625.00	176.00	72.07	748.20	79.87
TOTAL INCOME CHARGES	$69,000.00	$68,125.00	$92,676.00	$92,572.07	$83,248.20	$82,579.87
Surplus for the year	$37,584.34	$75,309.49	$49,220.08	$52,534.16	$63,878.33	$71,864.72

Your Company owns and carries as investments the following securities of other power companies:

		PAR VALUE	BOOK VALUE
Catskill Illuminating & Power Co. stock	$	25,350.00	$ 25,223.24
Sierra Power Co............... "		9,000.00	8,100.00
Telluride Power Co............ "		5,000.00	1,250.00
Cascade (1906) Power Co....... "		45,607.44	2,000.00
Idaho-Oregon Light & Power Co. bonds		30,000.00	21,000.00
" " " " " " stock		2,500.00	500.00
Central Georgia Power Co...... bonds		180,500.00	153,424.00
" " " " stock		90,250.00	1.00
Total book value............			**$211,498.24**

These bonds and stocks were practically all acquired in payment for apparatus sold. It is expected that the book values will be realized in time.

The ownership of the securities of power companies above described constitutes the sole foundation in fact for the statements from time to time appearing in current periodicals and Government reports of the connection of your Company with a so-called "water power trust."

G—TRACTION COMPANIES
Lackawanna & Wyoming Valley Rapid Transit Company

On various dates in 1904 and 1908 the Westinghouse Electric & Manufacturing Company acquired at par 5% bonds of the Lackawanna & Wyoming Valley Rapid Transit Company to an aggregate face value of $6,174,000.00. Until March 31, 1911, these bonds were carried in Investments at cost, $6,147,042.07, but on that date your Directors authorized that there be written off this item for depreciation the sum of $2,000,000.00 making the book value in the present balance sheet........**$4,147,042.07**
At this value it is hoped that this investment may eventually be liquidated.

Your Company also owns $4,885,600 (out of a total issue of $6,000,000) of the capital stock of the Lackawanna & Wyoming Valley Rapid Transit Co., carried on the books at **$1.00**

The Lackawanna & Wyoming Valley Rapid Transit Company owns all the securities of five subsidiary companies, which in turn own a line of double track, electrically operated railway extending from Wilkes-Barre to Scranton, Pa., a total distance of operated double track of 22.63 miles. The cost of constructing and equipping this property was $7,097,091. There are two issues of 5% bonds outstanding against the property. Of the first issue, secured by a prior lien upon most of the property, there are $888,000 outstanding, of which $100,000 are included in the $6,174,000 stated above as owned by your Company, and the others are owned by outside interests. The company's net earnings have never been sufficient to pay the entire interest on its outstanding bonds. A consolidated statement of the operations of its subsidiary companies follows:

	YEAR ENDED JANUARY 31				
	1907	1908	1909	1910	1911
Gross earnings..................	$457,174.16	$511,491.31	$545,122.58	$561,990.38	$590,959.46
Operating expense and taxes....................	253,416.87	270,443.73	333,006.47	344,108.44	350,278.85
Net earnings.................................	$203,757.29	$241,047.58	$212,116.11	$217,881.94	$240,680.61

Your Company owns also the following securities of other traction and miscellaneous companies, the final realization of which it is believed will approximate the book values:

NAME	DATE ACQUIRED	BOOK VALUE AT DATE ACQUIRED	BOOK VALUE MARCH 31, 1911
Grand Rapids, Grand Haven & Muskegon Railway Co. (Bonds, par value $500,000.)	Oct. 1, 1907	$500,000.00	$500,000.00
Indianapolis & Cincinnati Traction Co. (Bonds, par value $164,000)	Jan. 23, 1911	139,400.00	139,400.00
Pittsburg & Westmoreland St. Rwy. Co. (Stock, par value $100)	May 25, 1910	100.00	100.00
Rock Island Southern Railway Company (Bonds, par value $57,000.)	Mar. 31, 1911	52,100.00	52,100.00
Richmond Light & Railroad Co. (Bonds, par value $3,000)	Sept. 23, 1902	2,490.00	2,490.00
Spokane & Inland Empire Railway Co. (Stock, par value $150,000)	1906 & 1907	100,000.00	85,000.00

MISCELLANEOUS COMPANIES

NAME	DATE ACQUIRED	BOOK VALUE AT DATE ACQUIRED	BOOK VALUE MARCH 31, 1911
Consumers Electric Company (Bonds, par value $7,000)	Mar. 23, 1908	3,990.00	3,990.00
Cutter Electrical & Manufacturing Co. (Stock, par value $57,800)	Oct. 29, 1909	59,865.00	59,865.00
H-O Company, The (Bonds, par value $24,700) (Stock, par value 3,458)	Dec. 1, 1909	24,700.00	24,700.00
Laurentide Mica Co., Ltd., The (Stock, par value $25,000)	Dec. 31, 1904	25,000.00	25,000.00
Lehigh Valley Transit Co. (Stock, par value $1,224.00)	Oct. 17, 1906	1,224.09	300.00
Montgomery County Rapid Transit Co. (Bonds, par value $13,600)	May 9, 1910	100.00	100.00
Portales Irrigation Co. (Bonds, par value $160,600)	Feb. 16, 1911	126,167.50	126,167.50
Prescott Company, The (Stock, par value $190)	Jan. 20, 1910	190.00	100.00
Sing Sing Electric Lighting Co. (Bonds, par value $25,000)	Oct. 22, 1895	25,000.00	25,000.00
Southern Iron & Steel Co. (Bonds, par value $ 870.56) (Stock, par value 1,305.85)	Dec. 2, 1909	1,740.13	871.56
Titan Steel Casting Co. (Stock, par value $202,200)	June 14, 1910	41,801.00	41,801.00
Toledo & Indiana Railway Co. (Bonds, par value $2,500)	Feb. 24, 1910	1,722.49	1,722.49
United Water, Gas & Electric Co. (Stock, par value $135.87)	Jan. 17, 1910	135.87	25.00
Walker Electric Co. (Stock, par value $28,700)	Oct. 29, 1909	28,665.00	28,665.00
Whitewater Electric Light Co. (Stock, par value $4,000)	June 30, 1901	4,000.00	1,600.00
Miscellaneous Companies—Bonds and Stocks at $1.00 each, total			14.00

MISCELLANEOUS INVESTMENTS

East Pittsburg Club and Casino properties, East Pittsburg, Pa.................... 32,726.34
Interworks Railway Company... 105,810.94
    (This investment has already been referred to under Property and Plant)
Vacant real estate at Bloomfield, N. J..................................... 4,426.00

    TOTAL BOOK VALUE OF ALL INVESTMENTS............................ $24,034,635.99

IV—CURRENT ASSETS—$19,158,168.98

Little comment seems required upon this item of the balance sheet. It is the established practice of your Company to create monthly on a fixed basis a reserve for notes and accounts receivable. During the year the amount credited to this reserve in excess of bad debts charged off was $89,774.05. As of March 31, 1911, your Directors created an additional reserve for notes and accounts receivable of $500,000 making the aggregate of this reserve at the end of the fiscal year $589,774.05. It is believed that this adequately provides for all probable shrinkage in the book value of notes and accounts receivable, except, possibly, in respect of a note of Security Investment Company carried at a book value approximating $600,000, which may call for further consideration when the affairs of that company become more definitely adjusted.

V—WORKING AND TRADING ASSETS—$14,321,474.01

These figures represent actual present values at cost or less, based on an actual inventory carefully taken as of December 31, 1910.

VI—OTHER ASSETS—$7,188,640.29

Of this total $6,074,985.17 is the cost of patents, charters and franchises. Considering the important relation which the Company's patents in the aggregate bear to its business, your Directors are not now disposed to recommend a reduction of their book value.

The deferred charges, representing discount and other expenses incidental to the issuance of your convertible bonds and collateral notes, are being written off in stated monthly amounts adequate to amortize the account during the life time of the respective issues.

LIABILITIES

The only item on the liabilities side of the balance sheet that calls for any comment is that of Collateral Notes. The $6,000,000 six per cent notes outstanding a year ago were reduced to $4,000,000 by the payment of $2,000,000 on August 1, 1910.

The collateral securing the six per cent notes maturing August 1, 1913, is as follows:

$6,000,000 face value 5% first lien and consolidated mortgage gold bonds of the Lackawanna & Wyoming Valley Rapid Transit Company.

$950,000 par value assenting capital stock of the Westinghouse Electric & Manufacturing Company.

£675,000 face value 4% mortgage debenture stock of The British Westinghouse Electric & Manufacturing Company, Ltd.

£236,100 par value preference shares of The British Westinghouse Electric & Manufacturing Company, Ltd.

$500,000 face value 5% first mortgage bonds of the Grand Rapids, Grand Haven & Muskegon Railway.

$160,000 par value capital stock of the Canadian Westinghouse Company, Ltd.

The collateral securing the $2,720,000 five per cent notes maturing October 1, 1917, is as follows:

Frs. 10,500,000 face value 5% debentures Societe Electrique Westinghouse de Russie (Russian Company).

Frs. 7,395,000 face value 5% debentures Societe Anonyme Westinghouse, of Paris (French Company).

25

$322,000 par value capital stock of the Canadian Westinghouse Company, Ltd.

$21,000 face value 5% convertible bonds of the Westinghouse Electric & Manufacturing Company.

$699.45 cash.

The Long Term Notes aggregating $1,383,650 are unsecured.

By reference to the foregoing description of the securities comprising the collateral for the six per cent and five per cent collateral notes it will be seen that, with the possible exception of the shares of assenting capital stock of the Westinghouse Electric & Manufacturing Company, the collateral securing these notes is not readily saleable. Your Company must therefore contemplate the necessity, as these notes mature, either of extending them with the same collateral, or of providing other means of meeting them than through the sale of the collateral. There can, in the nature of things, be but two such other sources: **first,** through the issuance of additional capital securities either by way of bonds, securities or stock; or, **second,** through the use of the Company's earnings.

This is a question seriously to be considered before the earnings of your Company, gratifying as they have been for the last year and satisfactory as they were for the preceding year, are applied to the payment of dividends on the assenting stock.

After a careful consideration of all of the circumstances, having due regard for the true condition of your balance sheet, hereinbefore minutely described to you, the elements of uncertainty as to the immediate future of your Company's business, the need for cash for new foundry facilities, for extension of the Newark plant and other factory improvements, and the necessity of making wise provision for shortly maturing obligations, your Directors have felt that it is not wise at the present time to weaken your Company's position by diverting its surplus earnings, even in part, to the payment of dividends on the assenting stock. Whenever a change in conditions shall lead your Directors to feel that a different attitude can safely be assumed, the question will be reconsidered and determined in the light of such change; meanwhile your Directors trust that, with the aid of the very intimate information which this report gives as to the situation and affairs of their Company, the stockholders in general will be led to the same conclusion.

The books and accounts of the Company and of its subsidiary companies have been audited by Messrs. Haskins & Sells, Certified Public Accountants, and their certificate is made a part of this report.

The thanks of the Board are extended to officers and employes for the loyal and enthusiastic service that has made the results of the year possible.

By order of the Board of Directors.

ROBERT MATHER,
Chairman.

172

HASKINS & SELLS

CERTIFIED PUBLIC ACCOUNTANTS

30 BROAD STREET

NEW YORK

LONDON, E. C.
30 COLEMAN STREET

CHICAGO   ST. LOUIS   CLEVELAND   PITTSBURGH   BALTIMORE
HARRIS TRUST BUILDING   THIRD NATIONAL BANK BUILDING   WILLIAMSON BUILDING   FARMERS BANK BUILDING   EQUITABLE BUILDING

CABLE ADDRESS "HASKSELLS"

NEW YORK, May 22, 1911.

To the Board of Directors,

Westinghouse Electric & Manufacturing Co.,

New York.

We have made an audit, for the year ended March 31, 1911, of the books and accounts of the Westinghouse Electric & Manufacturing Company and the following subsidiary companies, viz.: Westinghouse Lamp Company, The Bryant Electric Company, The Perkins Electric Switch Manufacturing Company, the R. D. Nuttall Company and the Westinghouse Electric & Manufacturing Company of Texas.

We have verified the Cash, the Notes Receivable and the Stocks and Bonds owned, by count or by proper certificates from the depositaries. We have also verified, from the companies' records, the Accounts Receivable.

The investments are stated at the book value, which is considerably less than their aggregate cost.

The inventories of Raw Materials and Supplies, Finished Parts and Completed Apparatus, and Work in Progress were accurately and properly taken at cost, and

We Hereby Certify that, on the basis stated, the accompanying Consolidated General Balance Sheet of March 31, 1911, of the Westinghouse Electric & Manufacturing Company and subsidiary companies named above, properly represents the financial condition on that date, that the accompanying statement of Income and Profit and Loss for the year ended March 31, 1911, correctly states the result of operations for that period, and that the books of the companies are in agreement with these statements.

(Signed)   Haskins & Sells,

Certified Public Accountants.

173

Consolidated General Balance Sheet, March 31, 1911

ASSETS		LIABILITIES		
PROPERTY AND PLANT:		**CAPITAL STOCK:**		
Factory Plants, including Real Estate, Machinery,		Preferred	$ 3,998,700 00	
Equipment Etc.....	$17,692,145 61	Amounting—In Hands of Public . . $35,187,587 50		
		In Treasury 1,507,000 00	36,694,587 50	
SINKING FUND:		TOTAL CAPITAL STOCK...........		$40,693,287 50
With Trustee for Redemption of Convertible Sinking		**FUNDED DEBT:**		
Fund, 5%, Gold Bonds.....	445 45	Convertible Sinking Fund, 5%, Gold Bonds, due		
		January 1, 1931-		
		In Hands of Public $19,691,000 00		
INVESTMENTS:		In Treasury................ 266,000 00	$19,957,000 00	
Stocks, Bonds, Debentures, Collateral Trust Notes etc.,		Debenture Certificates, 5%, due July 1, 1913....	1,800,000 00	
including those of Affiliated European and Canadian		Bonds—Walker Company, due January 1, 1916		
Westinghouse Companies	24,034,635 99	Guaranteed by W. E. & M. Co..	850,000 00	
		TOTAL FUNDED DEBT....		22,607,000 00
CURRENT ASSETS.		**COLLATERAL NOTES**		
Cash	$6,634,577 07	Six Per Cent Collateral Notes, due August 1, 1913.	$ 4,000,000 00	
Cash on Deposit to Pay Interest Coupons...	27,340 00	Five Per Cent Collateral Notes, due October 1, 1917	2,720,000 00	
Cash on Deposit to Pay Dividends on Preferred Stock	940 62	TOTAL COLLATERAL NOTES		6,720,000 00
Notes Receivable	2,946,551 46	**LONG TERM NOTES:**		
Accounts Receivable.	9,494,731 06	Four Year 5% Notes due January 1, 1913.	$ 429,900 00	
Due from Subscribers to Capital Stock	53,928 77	Five Year 5% Notes due January 1, 1914	429,500 00	
TOTAL CURRENT ASSETS	19,158,168 98	Six Year 5% Notes due January 1, 1915	425,500 00	
		Fifteen Year 5% Notes due January 1, 1924	98,750 00	
WORKING AND TRADING ASSETS:		TOTAL LONG TERM NOTES....	1,383,650 00	
Raw Materials and Supplies, Finished Parts and		**REAL ESTATE MORTGAGES ASSUMED IN PURCHASE**		
Machines, Work in Progress, Goods on Consignment		**OF PROPERTY**		225,200 00
and Apparatus with Customers	14,321,474 01	**CURRENT LIABILITIES:**		
		Accounts Payable	$ 2,454,674 83	
OTHER ASSETS:		Interest, Taxes, Wages, Rebates etc., Accrued, Not		
Patents, Charters and Franchises	$6,074,985 17	Due	572,803 75	
Insurance, Taxes etc., Paid in Advance......	130,321 78	Dividends on Preferred Stock, Payable April 15, 1911	139,954 50	
Deferred Charge—Expenses Incidental to Issue of		Unpaid Dividends on Preferred Stock	940 62	
Bonds and Notes	993,333 34	TOTAL CURRENT LIABILITIES	3,168,373 70	
TOTAL OTHER ASSETS	7,198,640 29	**RESERVE:**		
TOTAL ASSETS	$82,395,510 36	For Adjustments of Inventories, Notes and Accounts		
		Receivable Etc		1,630,774 96
		PROFIT AND LOSS:		
		Surplus............		5,964,224 90
		TOTAL LIABILITIES		$82,395,510 36

NOTE—There is a Contingent Liability for Notes Receivable
discounted by Subsidiary Companies amounting to $16,703 87.

174

WESTINGHOUSE ELECTRIC & MANUFACTURING COMPANY AND SUBSIDIARY COMPANIES IN THE UNITED STATES

Consolidated Statement of Income and Profit and Loss for the Year Ended March 31, 1911

GROSS EARNINGS:

Shipments Billed..		$38,119,312.01

COST OF SHIPMENTS:

Factory Costs, including all Expenditures for Patterns, Dies, New Small Tools and Other Betterments and Extensions; also Inventory Adjustments and all Selling, Administration, General and Development Expenses.. 32,510,546.87

NET MANUFACTURING PROFITS... $ 5,608,765.14

OTHER INCOME:

Interest and Discount..	$ 272,055.28	
Dividends and Interest on Sundry Stocks and Bonds Owned...........................	615,299.40	
Miscellaneous—Royalties Etc..................................	628,177.13	1,515,531.81

TOTAL INCOME.............. $ 7,124,296.95

DEDUCTIONS FROM INCOME:

Interest on Bonds and Debentures............	$1,076,553.71	
Interest on Collateral Notes...................	416,000.00	
Miscellaneous Interest.............................	92,933.04	
Property and Plant Depreciations Charged against Income...........	371,668.19	
Proportion of Expenses Incidental to Bond and Note Issues..............	76,666.66	
Miscellaneous.......................................	209,369.37	2,243,190.97

NET INCOME—SURPLUS FOR THE YEAR.. $ 4,881,105.98

PROFIT AND LOSS CREDITS:

Profit and Loss—Surplus, March 31, 1910...........	$5,668,948.23	
Profit on Bonds and Debenture Certificates Purchased...........	5,200.43	
Adjustment of Property and Plant Accounts to Appraised Values............	459,399.10	
Collection of Accounts Receivable previously written off.......	172,335.75	
Miscellaneous......................................	43,372.41	6,349,255.92

GROSS SURPLUS... $11,230,361.90

PROFIT AND LOSS CHARGES:

Dividends on Preferred Capital Stock:			
For the Current Year......		$ 279,909.00	
Accumulated prior to the Current Year.........		349,886.25	
Depreciation of Securities:			
The United States Electric Lighting Company—Stock......	$431,091.61		
The Consolidated Electric Light Company—Stock and Bonds..........	307,121.27	738,212.88	
Difference between direct liability established for Walker Company Bonds and appraised, sound value of property mortgaged........		455,084.91	
Depreciation of Securities Owned.......		2,852,914.91	
Reserved for Notes and Accounts Receivable...........		589,774.05	
Miscellaneous.............		355.00	5,266,137.00

SURPLUS, MARCH 31, 1911, per Balance Sheet......................... $ 5,964,224.90

Financial Statement Analysis

The Reports of American Corporations.

Hereafter THE JOURNAL OF ACCOUNTANCY will contain a department devoted to a critical review of the reports of American Corporations whose stocks and bonds are of such character as cause them to be regularly dealt in on the Investment Market. Approaching a subject so delicate, the point of view of the editors will be: " What is the investor entitled to know?" The investor is the proprietor of the corporation, or of the assets in which the corporation holds equities.

The purpose of reports is to furnish accurate and authoritative information necessary to the exercise of intelligent investment control. Under the provisions of the Company's Acts of Great Britain the accuracy of such information is guaranteed by requiring that the stockholders at the regular meeting shall elect an independent auditor, who is held criminally and civilly responsible for statements made. Under the British system the auditor reports to the stockholders—this is the answer given by Parliament to the demand for publicity, and as a result it may be said that for the last half century Britain has been more free from corporate scandal than any of the strong commercial nations.

Following *laissez faire* doctrine, the United States has recognized no duty of corporate proprietorship and has provided no method for giving to investors adequate information in order that their judgments with respect to trusted agents may be an intelligent one. The officers having been placed in charge of the corporate estate and management have been permitted to render such an account and report of their stewardship as they may deem fit. Demands for publicity have not proceeded from investors, nor has it looked toward intelligent judgment of efficiency and economy of management. It has proceeded from a public conscience which is shocked by corporate immorality. Publicity is asked for in order that the State may exercise the proper police control. Our sense of business immorality and justice would be protected. If, however, we are to have corporate control which looks toward efficiency and economy the intelligence necessary to such control must come to the administration through the accounts, and must be regularly produced to the investor in the form of authoritative reports. While critical in our analysis, the aim and purpose of the department will be educational, looking toward a constructive result.

179

Reviews of Corporation Reports.

Corporate control is of three kinds, viz.: (1) the control exercised by the stockholder, (2) the control exercised by the board, (3) the control exercised by the officer. The purpose of accounts and reports is to make control intelligent. Do the reports rendered to stockholders contain such information as will enable them to exercise intelligent judgment with respect to the fidelity, efficiency and economy of corporate trustees and agents? This is the viewpoint of criticism and analysis appearing in this department of THE JOURNAL.

The Chicago and Northwestern Report.

180

A. is a stockholder of the Chicago and Northwestern Railway Company. Being desirous of voting intelligently at the annual election of the Board of Directors, he picks up a copy of the company's annual report for the fiscal year ending June 30, 1906, and seeks information which will throw light on the character and efficiency of the management during the past year. Will he find in this report all the information which is necessary for this purpose?

The printed report consists of two parts, one a descriptive report signed by the president of the company, the other a section of "Accounts and Statistics" containing the balance sheet, income account, physical statistics and various comparative statements compiled by or from the accounting department. The latter section should contain in statistical form all the information that is necessary for the stockholders to have to form an intelligent judgment as to the character and efficiency of the management, and the financial results; the section devoted to the president's report should merely present this information in more popular form. An examination of the report, however, reveals not only the fact that much of the statistical matter that ought to be presented in the statistical section is presented in the president's report instead, but that the matter which is contained in both sections is not presented in the form most conducive to bringing out the information desired.

For instance, the statistics of train movements, passengers and freight carried, average train-load, charges, quantity of ties and rails replaced, bridges rebuilt, and track reballasted are found only in the president's report. There are no statistics of engine-, passenger car- and freight car-mileage, nor, with the exception of the last item, can they be ascertained by computation; yet this information is necessary for a judgment as to the efficiency of train management.

Neither the president's report nor the statistical section is addressed to anyone in particular, nor is the latter signed. The last is especially important. If the balance sheet, income account, and statistical tables were compiled by an independent accountant after a careful audit, they might be very valuable to the stockholder or director who is seeking information in them, which would enable him to vote or act intelligently. But if they were compiled by the accounting department of the company itself their value would be much lessened for various reasons; the source is not disinterested, the information may be incomplete or presented in a form calculated to conceal the desirable information and to mislead. This criticism may be aimed at the reports of many other railway companies also. The importance of an independent audit of railway accounts cannot be over-emphasized. The stockholders will receive information which is information only when they insist on having the accounts of their companies audited and certified by reputable and independent accounting firms, who shall make their reports to the stockholders themselves and not to the officials of the company. The statistical section of the Northwestern's report probably has been compiled by the company's accounting department.

181

Assuming that these statistics are correct, what information can be obtained from them? Holding stock as an investment, A. is interested in the Northwestern's earning capacity and turns to the Income Account. This is what he finds: (See Table 1.)

This statement shows neither the net earnings for the year. nor the net income after payment of fixed charges applicable to the payment of dividends, these being merged with a stated profit and loss surplus, under the name of " Balance of Income Account," brought forward from previous years, an item which may represent a real surplus or nothing. These items could be

Table I.

INCOME ACCOUNT, JUNE 30, 1906.
(7,428.77 Miles.)

Debit			Credit		
June 30, 1906: To Operating Expenses.....		$39,789,099.17	June 30, 1905: By balance of income acc't June 30, 1905,		$11,640,181.01
To Taxes.........		2,427,176.68	June 30, 1906: By Gross Earnings, viz.: Passenger Earnings........	$14,441,415 07	
To Interest on bonds and interest	$7,845,329.34		Freight Earnings	45,802,852.58	
Less Dividends rec'd on C., St. P. M. & O. Stock	1,029,000.000	6,816,329.34	Express, Mail and Mdse......... ..	3,237,310.33	63,451,577.98
To Sinking Fund Accts. (itemized)		225,500.00	By Other Income		577,080.09
To Dividends on Stock (itemized)		6,483,913.50			
To Amt. of Expenditures for Construction, etc, deducted from Surplus net income by authority of Board of Directors		6,000,000			
To Balance of Income Account....		13,956,820.30	By Bal. to Credit of Income Acc't		$75,698,838.99
		$75,698,838 99			$13,956 820.30

182

made to stand out clearly as in the following rearranged account:

INCOME ACCOUNT, JUNE 30, 1906.

Debit			Credit		
To Operating Expenses		$39,789,099.17	By Gross Earnings, viz.: Passenger Earnings	$14,441,415.07	
To Balance, Net Earnings for year per contra......		23,692,478.81	Freight Earnings.	45,802,852.08	
		$63,481,577.81	Express, Mail & Miscellaneous..	3,237,310 33	$63,481,577 98
To Fixed Charges, Taxes...........		$2,427,176.68			$63,481,577.98
Interest on Bonds	7,845,329.34		By Balance, per contra		$23,692,478.81
Less Dividends on C., St. P., M & O. Stock..., ...	1,029,000.00		Other Income......		577,080.00
	$7,816,329 34				
To Sinking Funds..	225,500.00				
		$9,469,006.02			
To Balance, net income, per contra.		14,800,552.79			$24,269,555.81
		$24,269,558.81			
Dividends (itemized)		$6,483,913.50	By Balance, Net Income Available for Dividends, per contra		$14,800,552.79
Expenditures for Construction, Improvements, etc., deducted from Surplus Income by authority of the Board or Directors		6,000,000.40			$14,800,552.79
Balance, Surplus, net Income for year..............		2,316,639.29	By Balance, etc....		$2,310,639.29
		$14,800,552.79	By Surplus Income, June 30, 1905..:		11,640,181.01

From this statement it appears that the net earnings from operation for the year were $23,692,478.81, which together with other income and after the deduction of fixed charges left $14,-800,552.79 available for distribution in dividends. The 8 per cent. dividends on preferred and 7 per cent. on common stock used up less than 44 per cent. of this, leaving $8,316,639.29, which might have been carried to the surplus account. Six millions of this was written off, however, to cover the cost of new construction and improvement.

On its face this is a very good showing and justifies the high market price of Northwestern stock. A. seeks to verify this result by seeing whether sufficient allowances have been made for maintenance of way and equipment. As items in a subsequent table he finds:

Renewals of rails	$ 398,565.52
Renewals of ties	858,528.22
Repairs of roadway and track	3,703,983.66
Total maintenance of way	6,864,897.78
Repairs of locomotives	3,140,532.15
Repairs of passenger cars	564,559.63
Repairs of freight cars	4,592,976.80
Total maintenance of equipment	9,032,135.43

The cost of "maintenance of way" was nearly $6,900,000, and of "maintenance of equipment" over $9,000,000. Were these adequate? Were they insufficient, meaning ultimate impairment of the earning capacity of the property? Were they excessive, leading to a concealed surplus, which, because it is secret, leaves the market price of Northwestern stock lower than it otherwise would be, thus allowing "insiders" an opportunity to profit at the expense of the stockholder by speculating on the future advances of the stock?

The following statements may assist in answering these questions:

Aver. (estimated) number of locomotives in use during year	1,325
Aver. (estimated) number of passenger cars in use during year	1,165
Aver. (estimated) number of freight cars in use during year	54,074
Average number of miles of track operated	7,428.27
Tons of freight carried one mile	5,156,074,115
Aver. number tons of revenue freight per loaded car per mile	14.46
Total mileage of freight trains	19,634,933
Total mileage of passenger trains	15,797,903
New steel rails laid in renewals, in tons	22,889
Usable steel rails laid in renewals, in tons	6,294
Cost of new steel rails	$641,475.34
Cost of usable steel rails	$130,386.25

Value of old rails and other items	$463,296.07
Miles of track relaid with rails	256.96
No. of ties laid in renewals	1,964,045
Miles of track ballasted with crushed stone.................	9.00
Miles " " " " gravel	505,23
Miles " " " " cinders and slag	80.63
No. of steel bridges replacing wooden structures...........	63
Length of steel bridges, in feet...........................	2,947
Tons of bridge metal contained in steel bridges..............	2,618
Length of wooden structures filled in, in feet..............	9,296

Only the data as to equipment are obtainable from the " Accounts and Statistics " section; much of the remainder must be dug from the context of the president's report. Now to make use of these data.

Comparing the item, tons of freight carried one mile, with the item, average number of tons of revenue freight per loaded car per mile, it is seen that the total loaded car mileage for the year was 356,574,974 miles, which, for the average of 57,074 cars in service, amounts to 18.07 miles per day per loaded car. There is no means of ascertaining the empty car mileage; the Northwestern's report is deficient in this respect. But if a sufficient empty car mileage be assumed to bring the average run per car per day up to 30 miles, which is only average speed, this would bring the total car mileage for the year up to 592,037,503 miles. Probably this is far in excess of the actual mileage, but if not, the stated cost of repairs to freight cars, $4,592,976.80, represents a cost of about 7.7 mills per car mile; Woodlock allows 5 to 6 mills as sufficient for keeping freight equipment intact and in good condition. This sum also amounts to about $85 per year per car, as compared with $40 allowed as probably sufficient by the late Thomas L. Greene. It would seem that the freight cars which the Northwestern has bought to replace the cars sent to the bone-yard have been larger and more costly cars.

The report is again deficient. Although the passenger train mileage is stated, there are no data to enable one to ascertain the passenger car mileage and thus estimate the cost in repairs and renewals per passenger car mile. Nor is the helping and switching engine mileage stated, so that the inquiring stockholder understands the cost per engine mile of repairs and replacements of locomotives. By comparing the total cost of repairs to locomotives, $3,140,532.15, with the average number of locomotives. 1,325, he observes that the average cost per locomotive for the

year was $2,370.21 ; in the present age of heavy and costly loco-
motives, this probably is not very excessive. In a similar manner the repairs to passenger cars cost $493 per car, which is
about the average. The equipment has been more than maintained in condition and capacity.

Turning attention to maintenance of way statistics, the new
steel rails, at the stated total value, cost about $28 per ton, Steel
Trust values; the " usable " steel rails cost nearly $21 per ton,
which seems high. The total of 29,183 tons of rails relaid in
256.96 miles of track shows an average weight of the rails of
only 64½ lbs. per yard, which seems light in comparison with
the 90 and 120 lb. rails being laid in the main track of other
railroads; probably the new steel rails laid in the main line were
about 70 lbs. per yard, the average being brought down by the
much lighter " usable " rails which were laid in the tracks of
branch lines. The report should explicitly state the weight of
rails used in the main and branch lines.

The 256.96 miles of track relaid with rails constitute only
about one twenty-ninth of the total average mileage in operation. In this age of the rapid replacement of medium by heavy
rails, the proportion should be at least double this. The 1,964,-
045 ties laid in renewals average 264 ties per mile of road
operated. Allowing 2800 ties per mile of road, and seven years
as the average length of life of a tie, the number relaid each
year should be about 400. Probably ties last much longer in
the arid regions in which a part of the Northwestern's lines lie,
but the number 264 seems small. At a total cost of $858,528,
these ties averaged 43.7 cents each, which is probably not excessive.

The total cost for maintenance of way and structures, $6,-
864,898, allows only an average of $925 per mile, which is cer-
tainly not more than is necessary to keep the property in good
physical condition. On many roads this allowance exceeds
$2,000 per mile.

From the available physical statistics the inquiring stockholder judges that the fixed property has just about been maintained, while the rolling stock has been somewhat improved, the
cost being charged to operating expenses. Revising his judgment by taking into account the $6,000,000 expended in " con-
struction, improvements, and new permanent structures " and

185

charged against "Surplus Income," he decides that, if this item represents anything tangible, the property has been more than adequately maintained. This will be taken up later in connection with the Balance Sheet and " Construction Account."

Stockholder A. notes that the equipment has been increased during the year by the purchase of 35 new locomotives, 50 passenger cars and 3,586 freight and work cars. He desires to investigate the efficiency of train and car management and to see whether this additional equipment was really needed. For this purpose he brings together the following statistics, part of which has been stated or computed above:

186

Aver. number of tons of revenue freight per train per mile...	262.60
Aver. number of revenue freight per loaded car per mile.....	14.46
Aver. rate per ton per mile, in cents......................	0.89
Aver. earnings per freight train mile......................	$2.34
Passenger train mileage	15,797,903
Passengers carried one mile	703,176,138
Aver. number of passengers per train per mile...........	44.51
Aver. rate per passenger per mile, in cents..............	2.05
Aver. earnings per passenger train mile...................	$1.10
Aver. number of miles traveled by each loaded car per day...	18.07

Cost of motive power per train mile:

Repairs to engines	$0.059	
Fuel	0.151	
Engineers and firemen	0.101	
Oil and waste	0.005	$0.316

Increase in tons of freight carried, per cent..............	14.97
Increase in tons of freight carried one mile, per cent.........	20.12

The last four items, which are computed, should be shown for the engine mile; but in the absence of statistics of helping and switching engine mileage it is impossible to do this. The average train load of 263 tons is light for the territory through which the Northwestern runs; it should be considerably over 300 tons. The two items of $2.34 earnings per freight train-mile and $1.10 per passenger train-mile are about the average, as also are the rates of 8.9 mills per ton-mile and 2.05 cents per passenger-mile. The average carload for both loaded and empty car mileage should be about 15 tons; the stated figure of 14.46 tons per loaded car mile seems small; it may indicate that the freight equipment consists mostly of cars of comparatively small capacity. The average capacity per car, and the number of cars of each capacity should be stated in the equipment statistics.

The average number of passengers per passenger train-mile is obtained by comparing "Passengers carried one mile" by "Passenger train mileage"; the result, 44.51, is the average for that section of the country. Since the passenger car mileage and therefore the average number of cars per train are not known, there is no way of judging the need of the 50 new passenger and baggage cars purchased except by noting the growth of the passenger traffic. Passenger train mileage increased 5.77 per cent., passenger mileage 6.33 per cent. and the number of passengers 6.79 per cent. The passenger equipment was increased less than 5 per cent. Both the average freight car load and the average freight train load increased 9 and 10 per cent. in spite of the increase of nearly 7 per cent. in the number of freight cars; the tons of freight carried having increased nearly 15 per cent., and ton-mileage over 20 per cent.

On the whole, probably the new equipment was needed, although this could be judged better if data were at hand to show the average number of passengers per car mile. the average capacity of the freight equipment, and the average number of miles per day traveled by freight cars, loaded and empty. The last item is needed to show the efficiency of car management, whether they are loaded and emptied rapidly and kept moving, or let stand on private spurs and sidings. Neither the efficiency of freight, nor of passenger car management can be ascertained.

Turning to the balance sheet the stockholder finds a statement which tells him very little. It is a combination of the balance sheets of all the companies in the Northwestern system, whose lines are owned by the Chicago & Northwestern Railway Company, either directly or indirectly through ownership of the stock of proprietary companies. Neither the balance sheets nor the income accounts of these proprietary companies individually are shown, although the stockholder would be interested in the right management and successful operation of each. The main headings of this condensed balance sheet are shown in Table 3, next page.

As a technical matter the accountant might criticise the practice of exhibiting a sinking fund or an equipment renewal fund as a liability. It is seen that the "Operating Assets" exceed the "Current Liabilities" and the "Income Balances" combined, which is as it should be.

187

Table 3.

CONDENSED GENERAL BALANCE SHEETS, JUNE 30, 1906.

Dr.

Cost of Property

Balance June 30, 1905 ....$224,443,271.76		
Construction and equipment expenditures for year 3,311,024.67		
	$227,754,296.43	
Trustees of sinking funds	8,980,839.54	
General Assets (Itemizing Securities of C. & N. W. Ry. Co., subsidiary and other companies owned	37,393,831.77	
Operating Assets (Materials, Bills Receivable, Cash, etc.)	23,801,326.15	
	$297,990,293.89	

188

CONDENSED GENERAL BALANCE SHEETS, JUNE 30, 1906.

Cr.

Capital Stock

Common stock $97,577,862.92		
Preferred stock 2,337,837.61		
	$99,915,700.53	
Funded debt	164,214,000.00	
Sinking funds paid	8,980,839.54	
Equipment renewal fund	1,148,681.39	
Current liabilities	9,531,401.24	
Income balances		
Railroad income acc't............... $13,956,820.30		
Land income acc't 242,850.89	14,199,671.19	
	$297,990,293.89	

Other than this, this balance sheet yields practically no information. It would not have been difficult to print a comparative balance sheet, showing the amounts of the various items for two and possibly a longer period of years. Such a balance sheet would have been valuable to the stockholder by enabling him to trace the changes in these items from one year to another. By comparing the balance sheet for 1906 with that of 1905, and tabulating the changes, the following schedules are obtained:

PURPOSES FOR WHICH EXPENDITURES WERE MADE.

Increase in certain assets:

Cost of property	$3,311,024.67
Trustees of sinking funds	449,897.50

General Assets:

C. & N. W. bonds on hand	4,880,000.00
Sundry bonds fundable for C. & N. W. B'ds............	131,000.00
Cost of securities and advances on acc't of sundry proprietary companies	5,774,545.12
41,000 shares Union Pacific preferred stock	3,840,000.00

Operating Assets:
Due from agents and conductors 29,603.16
Due from U. S. Gov't 28,146.28
Due from various persons 15,916.94
Cash on hand 10,233,895.42
Decrease in Certain Liabilities:
Common stock in hands of company 4,535.00
Sundry bonds held in sinking funds................. 149,000.00
Bonds outstanding 3,862,000.00
Current Liabilities
Supply bills 1,350,182.12
Due other companies 110,979.50
Unpresented coupons and old dividends 9,064:00
Accrued interest 56,637.51
Land Income Account 2,972,721.82

$37,209,149.04

SOURCES OF FUNDS FOR EXPENDITURES.

Decrease in Certain Assets:
General—Common stock scrip in treasurer's hands..... $4,535.00
Operating Assets:
Materials, rails, ties, fuel, etc........................ 87,544.62
Bills receivable 80,048.66
Increase in Certain Liabilities:
Common stock outstanding 26,846,805.00
Bonds owned by company 4,880,000.00
Bonds owned by company fundable into C. & N. W. B'ds 131,000.00
Sinking funds paid 449,897.50
Equipment renewal fund 1,138,681.39
Current Liabilities:
Payrolls 217,453.44
Dividends declared 937,681.50
Drafts drawn by agents, outstanding 118,862.64
Railroad Surplus Income Acc't 2,316,639.29

$37,209,149.04

189

The significant change in the second schedule is the increase in the capital stock. A comparison of the two schedules and the elimination of the common items show that this increase in the liabilities is represented by the increase in the "Cost of Property," "Cost of Securities and Advances to Proprietary Companies," Union Pacific stock and cash, and a decrease in "Bonds Outstanding." The first item is adequately accounted for in a "Construction Account," which also accounts for the $6,000,000 expended on extensions and improvements and charged against "Surplus Income" in the Income Account. This "Construction Account" is found only in the president's report, however. The large increase of $5,774,545.12, in "Cost of Securities and Advances to Proprietary Companies" requires explanation. What companies are these, for what purposes were these advances, et cetera, made, and are they justified from the standpoint of the Northwestern's stockholders? The president's report creates the inference that they were made for the purpose of construction and improvement of lines, but no further information is anywhere vouchsafed.

An item which comes into prominence in these schedules and almost escapes attention in the balance sheet as published is that of "Land Income Account," which shows a decrease in one year's time of nearly $3,000,000, leaving a total of less than a quarter of a million in the 1906 Balance Sheet. What caused this large decrease? How does this account arise? Do the stockholders get the benefit of this income? It is not included in the general Income Account of the system. There is nothing in the report to throw light on this subject. There is a report of the Land Department, but it merely shows receipts from sales of lands.

In conclusion, the stockholder has not found in this annual report of the Northwestern all the information that is necessary to enable him to judge as to the efficiency of management of the company or the value behind his stock. The general magnitude of earnings makes it seem probable that the present high market price of his stock is justified; but an idea of general probability is not what is wanted. If a single condensed balance sheet be admitted as sufficient, it should at least be comparative; the information in explanation of important changes in the balance sheet from one year to the next is not forthcoming. The income account is not presented in the most useful form, and not all the statistics necessary to verify it and to judge of the efficiency of traffic management are printed. The statistics which are presented are not vouched for by a competent authority independent of the Northwestern's management. Finally, the stockholder has had to do a great deal of unnecessary " figuring " in order to extract the information which was obtained.

190

Reviews of Corporation Reports.

Conducted by THOMAS WARNER MITCHELL, Ph. D.

Corporate control is of three kinds, viz.: (1) the control exercised by the stockholder, (2) the control exercised by the board, (3) the control exercised by the officer. The purpose of accounts and reports is to make control intelligent. Do the reports rendered to stockholders contain such information as will enable them to exercise intelligent judgment with respect to the fidelity, efficiency and economy of corporate trustees and agents? This is the viewpoint of criticism and analysis appearing in this department of THE JOURNAL.

Reports of the International Paper Company.

With two exceptions, the corporation reports which have been dealt with in former articles have been those of railroad companies. Railway reports present fewer difficulties in the way of analysis than do those of industrial companies for two reasons, namely, the fact that in the analysis of the former the standards, though rough, are well established, and the further fact that in them the information is given in much greater detail. One of the best of industrial company reports is that published by the International Paper Company. But even this company's report proper consists of but four printed pages, the first a preface by the President, the last a certification by an accountant as to the correctness of the balance sheet and statement of earnings which constitute the second and third pages respectively.

The balance sheet and statement of earnings in each annual report are for the current year only, thus admitting of no ready comparison of the company's condition at different times. The tables following bring together the balance sheets and income statments for the years 1903 to 1906.

Beginning with the statement of earnings, probably the first thing that will be noticed is that although the "gross income" has steadily increased during the last four years, when we think of the large growth in railroad gross earnings during the same period and the general condition of great "prosperity" which has affected business, this increase of less than 8 per cent seems small. Further, the expenses have not only increased, more than proportionately but more absolutely; and with the increase in fixed charges, the net income available for dividends on the preferred and common stock has shown a decided tendency to decline in absolute amount.

After paying 6 per cent. dividends on the preferred stock the company has had surplus earnings which, for the four years included in this analysis have averaged 4.78 per cent. of the par value of the common stock. The yearly percentages, however, have varied considerably from this average: they were 6.8 per cent. in 1903, 4.1 per cent. in 1904, 4.55 per cent. in 1905 and only 3.6 per cent. in 1906. Manifestly the company's management was justified in not paying dividends on the common stock during this period.

192

BALANCE SHEETS OF INTERNATIONAL PAPER COMPANY.

Assets.

	1906.	1905.	1904.	1903.
Mill Assets	$43,291,874	$42,624,180	$42,014,400	$41,925,446
Woodlands	4,126,523	4,191,158	4,165,145	4,015,044
Securities	8,088,426	7,670,295	6,024,693	5,261,487
Sinking Fund 1st Consol. Bonds	308,476	150,000	101,201	104,727
Patents	6,000	8,000	10,000	12,000
Furniture and Fixtures	33,653	33,732	35,449	37,003
Cash	1,244,455	861,725	780,565	848,605
Accts. and Notes Receivable	6,169,625	5,225,959	5,235,802	4,492,611
Inventories	4,741,253	4,770,011	3,067,381	3,696,955
	$68,010,285	$65,535,060	$61,434,636	$60,753,878

Liabilities.

	1906.	1905.	1904.	1903.
Common Stock	$17,442,800	$17,442,800	$17,442,800	$17,442,800
Preferred Stock	22,406,700	22,406,700	22,406,700	22,406,700
First Consol. Mtg. Bonds	10,000,000	10,000,000	9,866,000	9,866,000
Divisional Mtg. Bonds	2,811,000	2,866,000	2,956,500	3,023,000
5% Consol. Conv. Bonds	5,000,000	5,000,000		
Accounts and Notes Payable	3,405,247	1,446,609	2,460,215	2,405,637
Accrued Interest, Taxes, Rentals	283,253	352,804	325,900	350,568
Surplus	6,661,285	6,020,147	5,976,431	5,259,173
	$68,010,285	$65,535,060	$61,434,636	$60,753,878

Statement of Earnings for Four Years.

	1906.	1905.	1904.	1903.
Gross Income	$21,837,815	$20,908,665	$20,304,514	$20,142,771
Raw Materials, Manufacturing, Selling, and Adminstrative Expenses	18,679,296	17,640,198	17,150,531	16,529,310
Taxes, Insurance and Interest	1,172,978	1,130,350	1,092,323	1,082,927
Net Income	1,985,541	2,138,117	2,061,660	2,530,534
Surplus After Paying 6% on Preferred Stock	641,139	793,715	717,258	1,186,132

Corporation Reports.

These surplus earnings should be put back into improvements and additions to the plant, and working capital for a few years, until, if possible, the company's earning power can be permanently increased and the common stock be placed on an investment basis.

An important point in dealing with trading or manufacturing is the profit on the turnover of the working capital, and the rapidity of turnover. A concern with a working capital of $100,000 consisting entirely of cash may lay this cash out in the purchase of materials. labor, repairs and replacements to machinery, selling expenses, etc., and as a result sell a finished product for $110.000. At one moment the working capital consists altogether of cash; at another it consists partly of labor purchased. half finished products; later it takes the form of finished products. which in turn are sold. partly for cash, partly on account, partly for commercial paper. It is evident that at any given moment the working capital will be embodied in all these forms—it will consist partly of cash, partly of raw materials, half-finished and finished goods. "accounts receivable" and "bills receivable."

193

In this way the three items of "cash," "accounts and bills receivable" and "inventories," which are found in the balance sheets for 1903, 1904 and 1905 indicate that the years 1904 and 1905 were begun with a working capital of approximately $9.000.000 each. while that of 1906 was about $10,800,000. This assumes that the inventories and accounts and bills receivable were stated at their real worth in the balance sheets; of course if the inventories could be duplicated at much less cost or if the "accounts and bills receivable" included an accumulation of "dead wood" from past years, the working capital has been impaired and is really much less than the sums stated.

To resume the illustration started above, the profit on the turnover was $10,000 or 10 per cent. The original $100,000 represents expenses, the $110,000 represents receipts from sales or "gross income."* The $110,000 will again be laid out on materials. labor, etc., yielding finished products which may be sold for $121,000. If this constitute the year's business, the working capital has been turned over twice, the total expenses have been $100,000 plus $110,000, or $210,000. the gross income has been $110,000 plus $121,000, or $231,000, and the net earnings have been $21,000, or 10 per cent. on the outlay. This illustration shows that. leaving out of account sources of income other than that of manufacturing and selling, the average rate of profit on the turnover will be identical with the rate of profit on the entire outlay for "expenses."

Comparing our company's "gross income" with its expenses—manufacturing, selling and administrative—we find that, ignoring other sources of profit, its average profit on the turnover was 21.8. 18.4, 18.5 and 16.9 per cent. for the years 1903 to 1906 in order. Assuming that the figures given above for the working capital were approximately correct we see after a little calculation that the working capital was turned over about 1.8 times in each of the years 1904 and 1905 and about 1.6 times in 1906. If any of the company's four to eight millions of securities yielded any

* " Gross income " may also include " income from securities owned."

income (which was the case, but the amount of this income without being stated was deducted from the expenses) then not only would the rate of profit on the turnover be less than that stated above, but the number of turnovers would be slightly larger. We may feel sure, however, that the working capital of the International Paper Company has in no case been turned over twice during a year.

Two turnovers during a year, a turnover once in six months, seems a rather small number even for a manufacturing concern. It suggests turning attention to the items which constitute working capital. Cash we may pass over. We have no means of testing the valuations placed on the inventories. The "accounts and notes receivable" may be investigated to some extent, however, even though nothing specific has been said about them in the company's report.

This item, which constitutes about 9 per cent. of the total assets and 60 per cent. of the working capital, represents about 27 per cent. of the gross income for the year. Naturally all the accounts and bills receivable which arose during the earlier parts of the year were converted into cash long before the close, provided they were collectible. If the business were distributed uniformly over the year and all sales were made on three months' credit, then all the sales of the last quarter, i. e., about 25 per cent. of the "gross income," would be represented in these accounts and bills receivable, but no other sales would be represented unless the debts proved uncollectible. This large item in the company's balance sheet might indicate, therefore, that the company was in the habit of giving its customers about three months' credit.

If the productive process and subsequent sale occupied an average period of three months' time, and the sale were made on three months' credit, it will readily be seen that the company would need a working capital about twice as that which would be needed if sales were made for cash, and that this working capital could be turned over only twice a year. Some such consideration might explain the size of the working capital and the infrequency of its turnover.

On the other hand a large portion of the "accounts and bills receivable" may consist of uncollectible accounts and bills carried over in the company's accounts from year to year. In this case the real working capital would be much smaller than the amounts stated above, and the number of turnovers during the year proportionately greater. For the further illustration of this point among others the table of changes in the company's balance sheet on the page following may be introduced.

A word in explanation of this table. Since the two sides of a balance sheet are equal in amount, the net change in the assets from year to year, whether this change is an increase or decrease, must exactly equal the net change in the liabilities (including the capital stock, reserves, and surplus). A little thought will convince us, therefore, that if the increases in individual assets and decreases in liabilities be grouped together in one schedule and the decreases in assets and increases in liabilities be thrown together in another, the totals of these two schedules must be the same This is what has been done in the table, the former group representing

Corporation Reports.

TABULATION OF CHANGES IN THE BALANCE SHEET OF INTERNATIONAL PAPER CO.

PURPOSES OF EXPENDITURES.	1905–6.	1904–5.	1903–4.
Increase in Mill Plants	$667,694	$609,780	$88,954
" " Woodlands	. . . .	26,013	150,101
" " Securities	418,131	1,645,602	403,206
" " Sinking Fund	158,476	48,799	. . . .
" " Cash	382,730	81,160	. . . .
" " Accounts and Notes Receivable	943,666	. . . .	743,191
" " Inventories	. . . .	1,702,630	. . . .
Decrease in Divisional Mortgages	55,000	90,500	66,500
" " Accrued Interest, Taxes etc	69,551	. . . .	24,578
" " Accounts and Bills Payable	. . . .	1,013,606	. . . .
	$2,695,248	$5,218,090	$1,476,530
SOURCES OF FUNDS.			
Decrease in Woodlands	$64,635	. . . .	. . . .
" " Patents	2,000	$2,000	$2,000
" " Furniture and Fixtures	79	1,717	1,554
" " Sinking Funds	. . . .	. . . .	3,526
" " Accounts and Notes Receivable	. . . .	9,843	. . . .
" " Cash	. . . .	. . . .	68,040
" " Inventories	28,758	. . . .	629,574
Increase in First Consolidated Mortgage Bonds	. . . .	134,000	. . . .
" " 5% Consolidated Convertible Bonds	. . . .	5,000,000	. . . .
" " Accounts and Notes, Payable	1,958,638	. . . .	54,578
" " Accrued Interest, etc	. . . .	26,814	. . . .
" " Surplus	641,138	43,716	717,258
	$2,695,248	$5,218,090	$1,476,530

195

purposes for which expenditures of funds have been made. the latter representing the sources from which these funds have been obtained. Now to recur to the "accounts and notes receivable."

This item has increased by nearly 38 per cent. since 1903; it showed a decrease in 1905, but this was insignificant. During the same time the total assets increased only 12 per cent. while the gross income increased less than 8 per cent. (see balance sheets and statements of earnings). These comparisons strengthen the suggestion that the item of "accounts and bills receivable" may contain a lot of "dead wood." They at least indicate that the company is maintaining its volume of sales either by granting its customers longer and longer credit, or, and this is the last explanation which will be suggested, by resorting to a large volume of credit sales just before the close of its fiscal year. If either suggested explanation corresponds to the facts our former judgment as to the weakness of the company's earning power is reinforced. This item of accounts and bills receivable will be referred to again later in another connection.

Let us make use of the table of changes in the company's balance sheet. In 1905 there appeared a new issue of "Five Per Cent Consolidated Mortgage Convertible" bonds amounting to $5,000,000. The financial papers allege that the proceeds from the sale of these bonds were to be used to reimburse the company's treasury for past outlays upon new plants, and for future new construction. What light will this table of changes shed upon this point? The scedule of changes for 1903-4 shows an increase in three capital assets, namely, "mill plants," "woodlands" and "securities," amounting altogether to $642,261; it also shows an increase in "accounts and bills receivable" of $743,191. The former amount represents the "past outlays" just mentioned. The principal sources of funds expended in this way are indicated in the decreases in cash and inventories, i. e., materials on hand, amounting to $697,614, and in the increase of $717,258, in the surplus account. The latter is more than taken up in the "accounts and bills receivable," which arise largely from the same source as the surplus itself, namely, the "gross income." Setting these two over against one another, we have left the major portion of the decreases in cash and inventories to account for the increases in the capital assets. That is, the expenditures upon the capital assets have been made out of working capital.

Now let us see what disposition has been made of the proceeds of the bond sales; the sale of the $5,000,000 of new consolidated convertible bonds and of $134,000 of old First Consols constitute the all important sources of funds for expenditure during the year 1905. The increases in cash and inventories together, i. e., of working capital, amounting to $1,783,790 constitutes one large item. Deducting from this the increase of $43,716 in the surplus account as accounting for a part of it, we observe that the working capital has been replenished nearly two and one-half times. If the principal item of this replenishment were cash we might say that this was only temporary and that the cash would eventually be expended upon capital assets. But the greatly preponderating item is that of inventories. Hence we may say that the company has bonded itself in part to get more working capital. Nevertheless, over two and one-half millions of dollars have been spent on capital assets, the same three as before, namely, "mill plants," "woodlands" and "securities." Unfortunately no information has been vouchsafed as to the precise character of these assets which have been built or purchased, so that the stockholder cannot learn from the reports whether their worth is commensurate with their cost. One very important use to which the proceeds of these bond sales has been put has been the reduction of the amount of the company's "accounts and bills payable" outstanding; that is, the company has funded a floating debt of over $1,000,000.

A small discrepancy between this table of changes in the balance sheet and the statement of earnings may attract the reader's notice. The increase in the surplus account during the year 1905 was $43,716 according to the balance sheet and $793,715 according to the statement of earnings. The discrepancy is $750,000. This was the amount of the discount on the new bond issue, which, because of the company's poor credit, was sold at a discount of 15 per cent. It speaks well for the company's management that they have deducted the amount of this discount from the stated surplus instead of adding it to the cost of the property, as is often done.

To pursue these changes into the year 1906, we find the "accounts and notes payable" reappearing in great force, having been increased by nearly $2,000,000. These together with the $641,138 of surplus earnings for the year furnished the bulk of the funds which were expended during the year. First, to dispose of the surplus earnings. Those ever recurring "accounts and notes receivable," which have increased by $943,666, will account for all of these and $300,000 more. Shall we say that to pay the 6 per cent. dividend on the preferred stock the company has had to borrow money in anticipation of the collection of a part of these "accounts and notes receivable"? There is nothing wrong in doing so, provided that after the most conservative judgment has been passed upon them these debts due from customers are considered perfectly good. Having disposed of the surplus, this leaves the continued large outlays on mill plants, the considerably smaller outlays for securities, the increase of nearly $400,000 in cash, etc., to be paid for in "accounts and notes payable" and the reduction of woodlands and inventories together of about $93,000.

197

Let us retrace this history of these "accounts and notes payable." During 1904, as we have seen, the working capital was turned into fixed capital to the extent of about $670,000. During the following year bonds were sold and not only was this $670,000 restored to working capital, but about $1,068,000 more. Thus, during the year 1906, the shortage of funds with which to carry forward the improvements and additions to the company's property, caused by this diversion of capital funds into working capital whence they could not readily be extracted again (the decrease in "inventories" during 1906 was only $28,758) together with the extension of credit in sales as evidenced by the large increase in "accounts and notes receivable," is very largely responsible for this extensive increase in "accounts and notes payable." Thus the end of the fiscal year 1906 finds the company with a gross floating debt, including accruals of taxes, water rentals, and interest, of $3,688,500.

We wonder how this floating debt will be met eventually. If the "accounts and notes receivable" are really good, the current assets, consisting of these and the cash as shown in the balance sheet will be doubly sufficient. Otherwise this floating indebtedness may lead to more bond sales, or, in the face of weakness in earnings and credit, especially should J. J. Hill's prophesied industrial depression set in in 1908, to financial embarrassment. There is no intention to prophesy the last named contingency; but unless the line of inquiry followed above is altogether wrong, there may come a time when the company will find it advisable to discontinue the preferred dividends and apply all its surplus earnings to strengthening its property.

In conclusion, the reader may think that a considerable amount of speculation and conjecture has been obtained from the two printed pages of financial data referred to at the outset. The amount of it is indicative of what the company could accomplish if it should take its stockholders into its confidence and show this analysis in the reports themselves and supplement it by the information necessary to take away all its indefiniteness. The usual reply to such a suggestion is that the company cannot afford to publish valuable trade secrets. Possibly we cannot expect a company to announce to the world that its financial strength is waning, because that might encourage competition and certainly would impair its credit. But there are two sides even to this. It would seem that the stockholders, especially those that represent any considerable interest in the stock, ought to be informed concerning the true condition of their company. Aside from this it is not at all certain that valuable trade secrets need be divulged in order to give the stockholder all the information needed by him to form an intelligent judgment concerning the condition and management of his company. Certainly the experience of British companies does not indicate that any vital trade secrets need be divulged; and there the company's accounts are audited by an accountant who is chosen directly by the stockholding body and who makes his report directly to that body instead of to the board of directors or president as in this country.

Reviews of Corporation Reports.

Conducted by THOMAS WARNER MITCHELL, Ph. D.

Corporate control is of three kinds, viz.: (1) the control exercised by the stockholder, (2) the control exercised by the board, (3) the control exercised by the officer. The purpose of accounts and reports is to make control intelligent. Do the reports rendered to stockholders contain such information as will enable them to exercise in telligent judgment with respect to the fidelity, efficiency and economy of corporate trustees and agents? This is the viewpoint of criticism and analysis appearing in this department of THE JOURNAL.

Reports of the Tennessee Coal, Iron and Railroad Company.

To one who has labored with the inadequate data contained in the ordinary industrial company report, it is refreshing to peruse that of the Tennessee Coal, Iron and Railroad Company for the year ended December 31, 1906. This company has recognized recently the advantages and advisability of submitting their accounts to an audit by an independent accountant, a prominent New York firm of certified public accountants having been called in to conduct this audit. It is probable that the changes in accounting methods referred to in the following quotation are due in some part to this fact. "The Income Account for the year 1906, you will observe," says the report to the stockholders, "reflects a radical change in accounting policy, both in respect to providing more liberally than heretofore for Provisional Funds, the necessary Replacements and Depreciation to Plant and Machinery, Depletion of Mineral Lands, and by Direct Charges to Costs for Repairs and Maintenance." The income account, balance sheet, surplus account, and inventories are certified by the accounting firm referred to, and this certificate states, not merely that the first two of these are correctly drawn from the company's accounts, but that, in the auditor's opinion, the balance sheet is " properly drawn up so as to show the *true* financial position of the company on December 31, 1906, and that the relative income account is a fair and correct statement of the net earnings for the fiscal year ending that date." It is needless to say that the part quoted is the part of the certificate which is of most importance to the stockholder, and it is this part which is frequently omitted from the auditor's certificate as drawn up in this country.

Although the Tennessee Coal, Iron and Railroad Company's report is not arranged in altogether the best order for the presentation of its condition to the stockholder, yet it represents a long step toward what a company's report ought to be. The statement of earnings for the last three years, as presented in the report for 1906, is as follows:

Corporation Reports.

	1904	1905	1906
Gross Sales and Earnings.........	$9,607,579	10,951,979	13,265,971
Operating Labor, Material, etc.....	6,300,287	6,764,700	8,439,505
Repairs and Maintenance.........	984,010	1,275,096	1,541,217
General Expense, Insurance, etc..	460,650	428,044	532,088
Total Cost of Operation..........	7,744,948	8,467,840	10,512,811
Earnings from Operation.........	1,862,631	2,484,139	2,753,160
LESS.			
Depreciation, Renewals and Replacements	534,789	625,090	770,678
Miscellaneous Interest and Fixed charges	831,583	830,765	895,145
Net Income for the year.........	496,259	1,028,284	1,087,337

The amounts of the various items for 1904 and 1905 are not quite the same as shown in the reports for those years. The change in accounting policy, alluded to above, which affected the items in the Income Account for 1906, necessitated, for purposes of comparison, a reclassification of the items of that account for earlier years. In so far as this change of policy meant smaller or larger charges against the earlier income accounts than those actually made, as shown in the reports of the previous years, certain assets in the balance sheets for those years, as well as the net surpluses, would also be affected. To enable the stockholder to complete his comparison of the last year's operations with those of the preceding years, those earlier balance sheets, adjusted to correspond to the alterations in the income accounts, should have been reproduced also. But the report for 1906 contains only the balance sheet as of the close of that year. Consequently the following comparative balance sheet for the last three years does not correspond strictly to the statement of earnings given above.

201

ASSETS.	1906	1905	1904
Cost of Properties.	$38,719,242	37,363,610	36,122,436
Capital Assets of Birmingham Southern R. R. Co. and Investments and Advances to Allied Companies	1,869,872	289,833	297,306
Trustees of Sinking Funds	40,455	38,459	54,104
CURRENT ASSETS:			
Inventories of materials, finished product...................	2,106,154	1,486,188	1,442,789
Accounts Receivable..........	1,552,513	1,476,590	1,151,278
Bills Receivable, less discounted	585,575		
Miscellaneous Investments......	3,792		
Working Capital in hands of Agents.....................	22,298	....	....
Cash in banks and on hand.....	690,557	574,189	463,108
Deferred charges to operations— Prepaid Insurance Premium....	11,502		
	45,601,960	41,228,869	39,531,021

LIABILITIES.	1906	1905	1904
Common Stock.................	$25,931,017	22,553,060	22,552,800
Preferred stock—cumulative......	124,500	228,300	228,300
Alabama Steel & Shipbuilding Co......	193,000	193,000	193,000
BONDED DEBT:			
Tenn. Coal, Iron & R. R. Co....	9,568,000	13,213,000	12,335,000
Subsidiary Companies..........	4,351,000	730,000	730,000
Potter Ore Co.—$700,000 1st m. 5% bonds guaranteed jointly with the Republic Iron & Steel Co......	350,000	....	....
DEFERRED PURCHASE MONEY NOTES			
Birmingham Southern R. R. Co. secured by collateral.........	1,101,849	....	....
CURRENT LIABILITIES:			
Accounts & Bills Payable.......	1,289,623	1,121,960	732,571
Interest Due and Accrued......	390,391	364,673	329,185
Dividends due and accrued.....	276,395	233,993	3,044
SPECIAL FUNDS:			
Replacement and Improvement.	946,199	152,797	....
Relining and Rebuilding Furnaces	50,000	1,970	42,725
Exhaustion of minerals.........	84,760		
Accidents, fire insurance, and contingencies	155,829	32,414	80,967
Reserve for Bad Debts........	....	126,745	132,364
SURPLUS:			
Sinking fund on general mortgage	....	48,240	48,730
Free Surplus.	789,397	2,228,717	2,122,335
	45,601,960	41,228,869	39,531,021

Several items in this balance sheet are worthy of special mention. The second among the assets, namely, Capital Assets of Birmingham Southern R. R. Co.," etc.. is given in some detail in the balance sheet of 1906, showing the extent of the Tennessee Coal, Iron & R. R. Co. in six other railroad, ore, iron, and land companies; since these details were not given in earlier balance sheets, only their total for 1906 has been included in the text. Also in the last report the accounts receivable and bills receivable have been shown separately; and, what is most worthy of notice, not merely the bills receivable on hand have been shown, but also those which have been discounted by the company and have not yet matured; thus the company's balance sheet shows " Bills Receivable, $1,906,658.38, *less* discounted $1,321,083.32," leaving to be carried out the $585,575 stated in the text. Needless to say, the advantage of this method is that it shows the amount of the company's contingent liability for such discounted bills.

Among the liabilities, the common stock is classified by the company's report into " fully paid," " 75% paid." " 25% paid," and " Avdance Installments." The occasion for this classification was a new issue of common stock, subscription payable in installments, some of which had not yet been paid, a short time before the close of the fiscal year. It will be noticed that the reserve for bad debts has disappeared in the last balance sheet; yet a company with over two millions of accounts and bills receivable will probably have some uncollectible items. The probable explanation of this disappearance is that the reserve has been deducted from the accounts and bills receivable on the other side. In 1905 the reserve amounted to about 9% of the total accounts and bills receivable on hand at the date of the balance sheet. Finally, the inclusion in the surplus of the " Sinking fund on the general mortgage " is the writer's classification; it is believed that the sinking fund reserves are properly to be included in the surplus, since their effect is, by reducing the bonded debt and at the same time keeping the total capital intact, to increase the net proprietorship of the stock-holding body.

Let us revert to the statement of earnings. The company is to be commended for showing its "gross sales and earnings," which have increased to a noteworthy extent; the title is somewhat ambiguous, however, and the "earnings" possibly represent income on securities of other corporations; if so, the shareholder would like to have them stated separately. Costs of production have been given in general classes. We are not altogether sure, however, that the item of "Depreciation, Renewals, and Replacements" should not have been included in the "Total Cost of Operation"; if the character of this charge is as its name would indicate, it is truly as much a part of the cost of operation or production as is labor. In the remainder of the discussion it is assumed that this item *is* a part of cost, and the net earnings are correspondingly reduced.

Making this change the total costs of operation for the three years, 1904 to 1906, were $9,607,579, $10,951,979, and $13,265,971 respectively, and the net earnings were $1,327,842, $1,859,049, and $2,982,492 in order. On this basis the profits or the turnover were 16.04%, 20.44%, and 26.41% for the three years in order. These percentages have increased at a remarkable rate and show that the net earnings have increased not only absolutely but relatively to the costs.

Comparing the total costs of operation in 1905 and 1906 with the working capital, which is represented by the "Current Assets," namely, $3,057,273 and $3,536,967, on hand at the close of the preceding fiscal years (1904 and 1905), we find that the working capital has been turned over slightly more than two and one-half times during each of these years. For a manufacturing concern of this character this probably represents fairly good management.

Comparing the accounts and bills receivable on hand at the close of the fiscal years, namely, $1,151,278, $1,146,590, and $2,138,088 respectively, with the "gross sales and earnings," we find that the former amounted to but 10.9% of the latter in 1904, 13.5% in 1905, and 16.1% in 1906. If the accounts and bills were held until maturity, these percentages would represent an excellent showing, although they are rapidly increasing, indicating that the company was not giving excessively long credit, about 60 days

203

in 1906 and considerably less in the previous years. This conclusion as to
the length of the credit period must be modified somewhat, however, because of the fact that the company, in 1906 at least, has discounted a large
quantity ($1,321.083) of its bills receivable before their maturity. If these
discounted bills were added to those still on hand, the combined item of
accounts and bills receivable for 1906 would amount to more than 26% of
the gross sales. This would indicate a much longer credit period. Unfortunately the bills discounted of previous years are not given, so that
no comparison can be made. If we consider that such customers' notes are
probably all good, since the banks are willing to deal in them, and that the
much smaller amount ($585.575) of notes on hand at the close of the year
probably represented recent sales, the first percentages stated above may
still be held to make a good showing.

Computing the changes in the balance sheet from year to year and
classifying them as explained in previous articles, we obtain the following
table:

SUMMARY OF CHANGES IN THE BALANCE SHEET

Purposes of Expenditures.	1905–6	1904–5
Increase in cost of properties...............	$1,355,632	1,241.174
" " capital assets B. S. R. R. Co., etc.	1,580,039	......
" " sinking funds....................	1,906	......
" " inventories.....................	610,966	43.399
" " accounts and bills receivable	661.498	325,312
" " miscellaneous investments.........	3,792	
" " working capital in hands of agents..	22,298	...
" " cash.	110,368	111,081
" " prepaid insurance premium.......	11,502	
Decrease in preferred stock..............	103,800	
" " bonded debt Tenn. C. I. & R. R. Co.	3.645,000	....
" " sinking fund on general mortgage..	48,240	400
" " surplus..	1,430,320	......
	9,609,451	1,721,456

Sources of Funds:		
Decrease in capital assets of B. S. R. R. Co....		7,473
" " sinking funds.		15,645
Increase in common stock....................	3,377,957	260
" " bonded debt Tenn. C. I. & R. R. Co..	....	878,000
" " bonded debt Subsidiary Companies.	3,621,000	....
" " Potter Ore Co., guaranteed bonds..	350,000	....
" " deferred purchase money notes ..	1,101,849	....
" " accounts and bills payable........	167,663	389,389
" " interest due and accrued..........	25,718	. 35,488
" " dividends due and accrued........	42,402	230,949
" " reserves......................	922,862	.. 57,870
" " surplus...	......	106,382
	9,609,451	1,721,456

Corporation Reports.

The principal purposes for which expenditures were made in 1905 are represented in the four items, cost of properties, accounts and bills receivable, cash, and inventories. As explained in a former number, an increase in the second named item is naturally associated with an increase in the surplus, since both are the results of the same cause, namely, the successful prosecution of the business for the conduct of which the corporation was organized; a sale, if made on credit, results in an account receivable or a bill receivable, and, if profitable, in an increase of the surplus, unless this profit is appropriated in some other way as by increased dividends, fixed charges, improvements charged against income, *et cetera.* We notice that the increase in accounts and bills receivable in 1905 was three times that of the surplus. In this case the difference is partly explained by an increase of $145,056 in taxes and interest on loans and about $18,000 in interest on bonds. It will be noticed that this difference is fully covered by an increase of $230,949 in "Dividends due and accrued"; the latter does not explain the former, however, since there has been no increase in dividends, but, on the contrary, a small decrease due to the retirement of some of the preferred stock.

The principal sources of the funds expended are represented in the increases in the bonded debt, accounts and bills payable, dividends due and accrued and the surplus. The last two have been sufficiently discussed. The company issued $970,000 of new general mortgage bonds during the year and redeemed $71,000 of general and "divisional" mortgage bonds. The increase of $1,241,174 in the cost of the properties absorbed the proceeds of the bond sales and of the $389,389 of notes (accounts and bills payable) as well. The report gives a description, in considerable detail, of the company's activities in the way of new construction and improvements, showing total capital expenditures of $1,313,516.

During 1906 the company's activities were more extensive. The chief purposes of expenditure were, in order, a decrease of $3,645,000 in the bonded debt, of $1,439,320 in the surplus account, and of $103,800 in the preferred stock, an increase of $1,580,039 in capital assets of the Birmingham Southern R. R. Co. and others, of $1,355,632 in the cost of properties, of $661,498 in accounts and bills receivable, and $619,966 in inventories. The decrease in the surplus account will attract attention. There was a surplus for the year's operations of $126,881; but the company charged off $1,313,516, the amount added to properties during the preceding year; it also deducted the premiums on bonds and preferred stock purchased during the year, and claims for arrears of taxes, etc., altogether $252,684.

The company's report offers no explanation of the decrease in the bonded debt. It contains an excellent table enumerating the changes in the working capital, enumerating the sources of working capital and the objects of its expenditure; but bond redemptions except for the sinking funds are not mentioned therein. Stock sales are not mentioned as a source of working capital funds, either, and one is thus led to believe that the funds thus obtained were used for the payment of these bonds. The increase in cost of properties is represented by the construction of a number of new furnaces, and the development of coal and ore mines; that of

205

the capital assets of the B. S. R. R. Co., *et cetera,* by acquisition of the control of, or by advances to several new coal, ore, or railroad companies.

The principal sources of funds have been the increase in common stock, which has been alluded to, in the bonded debt of subsidiary companies and purchase money notes, which the report does not explain, in the Reserves, which, probably, should have been deducted from the stated values of certain assets since they largely represent depreciation of those assets, and the Potter Ore Company's bonds which have been guaranteed jointly with another company, by the Tennessee Coal. Iron and Railroad Company.

The company's report contains much other matter in tabular and other forms which will be found of interest and profit to the reading stockholder, but which cannot be reproduced or summarized here on account of space considerations. The last report contains more information than do earlier ones, a fact which may be due to the influence of the accounting firm which was called in or to the spirit which actuated the company when it decided to have an independent audit. The company expressly states that $329,871 of the depreciation which it charged off during 1906 was due to the recommendation of the accountants. As before stated. the company has taken a long step toward making an industrial company's report what it should be. Its example is worthy of emulation by other companies.

206

Reviews of Corporation Reports.

Conducted by THOMAS WARNER MITCHELL, Ph. D.

Corporate control is of three kinds, viz. : (1) the control exercised by the stock-holder, (2) the control exercised by the board, (3) the control exercised by the officer. The purpose of accounts and reports is to make control intelligent. Do the reports rendered to stockholders contain such information as will enable them to exercise intelligent judgment with respect to the fidelity, efficiency and economy of corporate trustees and agents? This is the viewpoint of criticism and analysis appearing in this department of THE JOURNAL.

Reports of the Chicago & Alton.

The reports which have been received in former numbers of THE JOURNAL have been chosen mostly from among those which, considered from the standpoint of the information contained in their pages, are the best of their kind. In this number, we deal with a report which leaves much to be desired, but which for other reasons will be of considerable interest. The Chicago & Alton certainly does not emulate the copiousness of information found in the reports of the two companies, namely, the Union Pacific and the Rock Island, which control it.

The first matter to receive attention is the Income Account. No criticism is offered against this account as found in the Alton's report for the fiscal year ended June 30, 1906. In form and content this account is that ordinarily found in a railway report; further, the Income Account for this particular year reflects the operations of only one company, namely, the present Chicago & Alton Railroad Company. The Income Accounts of former years, however, are not so fortunate. Prior to March, 1906, as is well known to every reader, there were two Alton companies, namely, the Chicago & Alton Railroad Company, which owned certain railway lines extending between Chicago, St. Louis, and Kansas City, and the Chicago & Alton Railway Company, which owned a small amount of branch mileage and leased the properties of the former. It also owned most of the stock of the Railroad Company. Now, the reports which were given to the general public prior to 1906 were drawn up solely from the standpoint of the Chicago & Alton Railway Company, which is represented, therefore, as having relations with the Railroad Company; but the latter company's operations are nowhere portrayed.

To illustrate: In the Railway Company's report for 1905, that company is represented as paying to the Railroad Company a rental, according to the terms of the lease, of $4,020,989, consisting of interest on the latter's bonds, guaranteed dividends on the stock of its leased subsidiaries, taxes, and the balance of net earnings made from the operation of its line. But $1,525,622 of this is paid back to the Railway Company in the form of dividends on the Railroad Company's stock which it owns. Finally, the Railway Company carries each year a small remainder of its income to its surplus account. This surplus account, it must be impressed upon the reader, is merely that of the Railway Company. Out of the rental received by it, the Chicago & Alton Railroad Company might build up a large surplus or an equally large deficiency year by year, and in neither case would the stock or bond holders of either company, except those who were officers, have the faintest suspicion of its existence. The deficiency is, perhaps, improbable, but a surplus is not, and it is sufficiently important for consideration.

The portrayal of the operations of the one company is all right in itself. But for completeness of information, the other company's operations should also be presented. Otherwise a report drawn up, not from the standpoint of the business of either company alone, but from that of the entire system, eliminating all relationships which exist merely between the companies, should be presented.

The following income statement has been compiled from the income accounts presented in the successive reports from 1901 to 1906 inclusive. It will be seen that the gross earnings have increased over the whole period by about 29 per cent., but have fallen off during the last year. Operating expenses, however, have shown no tendency toward diminution, with the result that the net receipts for 1906 were less even than those of 1904.

The item "Income from Investments for 1906" as compared with that of 1905 reflects the effect upon the accounts produced by the consolidation. The latter item contains $1,525,622 of "dividends on stock owned," which was first paid by the Chicago & Alton Railway Company to the Railroad Company as a part of the rental for the latter's property, and then paid back to the former company as a dividend on its stock. With the consolidation in March, 1906, the identities of these two companies were merged, and this paying of the left hand by the right hand pocket, and vice versa, ceased. The net earnings of the formerly leased line are no longer a fixed charge to the company making the report; this reduces the stated fixed charges nearly $2,000,000. At the same time the stated income from investments and gross income are reduced a million and a half. "Net Income" now means the entire net income of the system; and the dividends paid include those on the "prior lien" stock, which represents the few thousands of old Railroad shares which were never exchanged by their owners for stock of the Railway Company. The surplus also represents, for the first time, the entire surplus earnings, for the year, of the system.

The next step in a review would naturally be an examination of the maintenance allowances to see whether they were adequate. But here the investigator strikes a snag. The only average figures obtainable are those for repairs of locomotives per mile run and the average expenditure for maintenance of way per mile. It is true that the report for 1906, for instance, shows average repairs per locomotive of $3,234 for the year, and similar repairs to passenger and freight cars of $671 and $47.56 respectively; but stated in this form the data do not have much meaning—the yearly average for the unit of equipment would depend largely upon the extent of its usage. Such data as can be found are presented in the following table:

	Locomotive repairs per mile	Repairs per locomotive per annum	Repairs per passenger car per annum	Repairs per freight car per annum	Average maintenance of way per mile
1901	4.56	2,072	1,216	25.24	1,206
1902	6.21	2,952	881	28.08	1,043
1903	6.35	2,758	881	43.40	1,325
1904	6.50	2,808	669	40.45	1,580
1905	6.99	3,199	632	45.94	1,599
1906	7.04	3,234	671	47.56	1,472

The expenditure per mile for maintenance of way is, on the whole, as high as or higher than similar expenditures made on other roads in the same section of the United States. When we reflect, however, that this expenditure is made almost altogether on a main line, for the Alton does not have much branch mileage, they at least do not seem too large. Since 1902 the expense per mile run of repairing and renewing locomotives has been about normal; six to seven cents is the range usually found on roads in that part of the country. It is to be remarked that this cost has been steadily increasing, a fact which might call for explanation. This might be due to many causes: higher cost of labor, materials, and new locomotives, heavier train load, higher speed, and betterments of this branch of the equipment at the expense of the operating department may be mentioned as possible causes. The increase in the cost per mile run is reflected in the increase in the average cost of repairs and renewals per locomotive for the year.

The figures for maintenance of passenger cars seem high for the first three years included in the table; that for 1901 is certainly an excessive, or perhaps we should say an extraordinary, amount. The figures for 1904 to 1906 inclusive are about the same as those found in the reports of other companies operating lines in the Middle West.

The expenditures for maintenance of freight cars seem low throughout the table, and especially so during 1901 and 1902. While some companies expend an average of only $45 a year on this branch of the equipment, the usual expenditure is $60 or above. With this possible exception, it may be conceded that the Chicago & Alton properties have been properly maintained.

Sometimes one has occasion to compile a history of what may be termed the capital finances (as distinguished from the operating finances) of a company, and the question arises, Where should the investigator begin his work of collecting information, and how should he build it up in order that, when he has finished, he can be reasonably certain that he has given a faithful account of his company's financial activities? It is

210

CHICAGO & ALTON RAILWAY COMPANY INCOME STATEMENT.

	1901	1902	1903	1904	1905	1906
Gross Receipts	9,036,056	8,225,739	10,071,092	11,425,853	11,797,314	11,586,095
Operating Expenses	5,595,068	6,023,919	6,625,196	7,524,600	7,602,663	7,818,904
Net Receipts	3,440,988	3,206,820	3,445,896	3,901,253	4,194,651	3,767,191
Income from Investments	1,531,381	1,528,139	1,770,071	1,766,273	1,794,139	259,146
Gross Income	4,972,309	4,720,959	5,215,967	5,667,520	5,988,790	4,026,335
Fixed Charges	4,123,461	3,904,618	4,335,199	4,550,050	5,013,709	3,016,356
Net Income	848,908	825,341	880,708	1,111,470	975,081	1,009,979
Dividends	781,760	781,760	781,760	781,760	781,760	$ 815,000
Surplus for Year	67,148	43,581	90,008	329,710	193,321	194,973
Adjustments	......	......	29,728	205,800	41,914	66,417
Total	67,148	43,581	60,280	123,907	151,407	261,390

purposed in the remainder of this review to illustrate one method which, it is believed, will give satisfactory results. To this end the next thing to be presented is a comparative balance sheet of the Chicago & Alton.

ASSETS, CHICAGO & ALTON.

	1906	1905	1904
Cost of Road, Franchise. and Secu's	117,303,976	66,794,631	66,759,317
Betterments,Additions,New Equipment	1,095,873	....	1,300,182
Cash	1,441,264	1,213,838	703,246
Other Current Assets	2,170,275	2,142,953	1,921,535
Deferred Assets	836,934	....	....
Contingent Assets	24,006	178,140	266,924
	128,287,328	70,329,562	70,961,204

LIABILITIES, CHICAGO & ALTON.

	1906	1905	1904
Capital Stock	39,986,100	39,086,800	39,086,800
Guaranteed Stocks	3,693,200	....	....
Funded Debt	72,350,000	27,000,000	27,000,000
Equipment Notes	3,106,918	....	....
Interest Accrued or Matured	860,822	774,821	760,013
Bills Payable	580,244	....	1,140,000
Vouchers and Pay-Rolls	1,282,766	926,291	1,187,422
Other Current Liabilities	560,109	845,538	455,843
Deferred Liabilities	225,597	....	....
Contingent Liabilities	55,180	852,348	637,779
Surplus	261,392	844,754	693,347
	122,872,328	70,329,562	70,961,204

211

This balance sheet is presented mainly to show the reader the source of materials out of which the next table is constructed. Attention may be called in passing to the large cost of road, franchises, and equipment in 1906 as compared with 1905, and also to the growth in the funded debt. These will receive detailed attention later. From these balance sheets and that of 1903 is drawn the summary of changes shown on another page, which puts the materials in much better form for use. As in former reviews, the changes are classified, grouping together the increases in assets and decreases in liabilities as representing purposes for which expenditures of funds have been made, and the decreases in assets and increases in liabilities as representing the sources of the funds expended.

To continue the illustration: Consider the changes which are represented as taking place between 1905 and 1906. According to the table, the principal purposes of expenditures were represented in an increase in the "cost of road, equipment, and franchises," and in "betterments, new

---

SUMMARY OF CHANGES IN THE BALANCE SHEET.

PURPOSES OF EXPENDITURES	1905–6	1904–5	1903–4
Increase in Cost of Road, Franchises. Securities, etc....	50,509,345	35,314	2,528,800
" " Betterments, New Equipment........	1,095,873	....	683,510
" " Cash...............	227,426	510,592	....
" " Other Current Assets...	27,322	211,418	....
" " Deferred Assets.......	836,934	0	0
" " Contingent Assets.....	....	....	35,074
Decrease in Bills Payable...........	....	1,140,000	1,370,000
" " Vouchers & Pay-Rolls	....	201,131	120,473
" " Other Cur. Liabilities..	284,429	....	50,577
" " Deferred Liabilities...	....	....	11,674
" " Contingent Liabilities.	797,168	....	....
" " Surplus.............	583,362	....	....
	54,361,859	2,158,455	4,800,108

SOURCES OF FUNDS.			
Decrease in Betterments, New Equipment.......	....	1,300,182	....
" " Cash.............	....	....	269,600
" " Other Current Assets..	....	....	1,986,216
" " Contingent Assets.....	154,134	88,784	....
Increase in Capital Stock.........	899,300	0	0
" " Guaranteed Stock.....	3,693,200	0	0
" " Funded Debt.........	45,350,000	0	2,365,000
" " Equipment Notes......	3,016,918	0	0
" " Interest, Accrued or Matured..........	85,991	14,818	32,852
" " Bills Payable.........	580,244	....	....
" " Vouchers & Pay-Rolls.	356,475	....	....
" " Other Cur. Liabilities..	....	388,695	....
" " Deferred Liabilities....	225,597	....	....
" " Contingent Liabilities...	....	214,569	22,531
" " Surplus.	....	151,407	123,909
	54,361,859	2,158,455	4,800,108

---

equipment, etc.," the one to the extent of $50,509,345, the other $1,095,873. What have been the principal sources of these funds? The funded debt has been increased $45,350,000. "Guaranteed Stocks" appear for the first time and to the extent of $3,693,200, as also does an item of equipment notes of the amount, $3,016,918. Finally, there is an increase of $899,300 in capital stock. The appearance of $580,244 of "bills payable" might be mentioned, but let that pass; the others are sufficient for present purposes.

Apparently the company has made enormous expenditures upon its property and equipment, raising the funds by means of bond, equipment bond, and stock sales. But all of this is merely on the surface. The Chicago & Alton reports furnish an excellent example of the errors into which an investor might fall if he depended solely upon an analysis of the statements contained therein as a source of information. The investigator will find that such an analysis furnishes an excellent starting-point for further investigation, because it gives him a bird's-eye view, as it were, of the whole of a company's financial operations for each year. But he must then get closer to the scene. In other words, he must seek further explanation of the changes which he has tabulated. This explanation he will find in other parts of the company's reports, in the announcements found from time to time in the financial newspapers, in official circulars sent out to stock or bond holders, in advertisements, and in the investors' manuals.

The story of the Alton's financial operations for 1906 will furnish a good example. As before stated, the present Chicago & Alton Railroad Company is the result of the consolidation or legal merger in March, 1906, of the identities of two formerly distinct corporations or legal entities, namely, the Chicago & Alton Railroad Company and the Chicago & Alton Railway Company. After this consolidation they were no longer twain, but were one flesh, both legally and in fact.

Let us describe once more the situation which existed at the time of and prior to this consolidation. In the first place, there was the Chicago & Alton Railway Company. Its principal assets consisted of some railway mileage owned directly, nearly all the capital stock of the older *Railroad* Company, and a ninety-nine-year leasehold interest in the railroad properties and equipment of the latter company. These various properties, stocks, and leasehold interests it carried on its books at a valuation of $66,794,631 (see balance sheet for 1905). This valuation, as will readily be seen, represented not a money but a securities cost; for the company had outstanding $39,086,800 of its common and preferred stock and $27,000,000 of bonds and collateral trust notes—altogether $66,086,800.

The Chicago & Alton Railroad Company, on the other hand, was the company which *owned* the railway mileage and equipment which had been leased to the Railway Company. It had its own accounts, and carried those properties and equipment at valuations of its own; unfortunately, reports of this company are not at hand, so that the precise amount of the valuation is not known. This valuation, whatever it may be, also represented largely a securities cost, the securities consisting at this time of bonds to the extent of about $45,356,000 and capital stock to the amount of about $22,360,000. Of the latter all but a few thousand

213

shares were owned by the Railway Company: say, $899,300 par value of this stock was in the hands of the general public.

What happened when the consolidation took place? For two systems of accounts one system is substituted. The stock of the Railroad Company which was owned by the Railway Company is no longer an asset, as it had been from the standpoint of the latter, or a capital liability, as it had been from that of the former; it ceased to be an asset or a liability to the extent of its par value at least, for now there is only one legal person, which, of course, cannot owe itself or hold its own obligations as more than a nominal asset.

But the influence of that stock of the old Railroad Company upon the valuations and capitalization of the new company was not entirely obliterated. While its par value was only about $21,460,000. it had cost the Chicago & Alton Railway Company about $61,000,000. This cost was in securities consisting of the latter company's preferred and common stock and $22,000,000 of bonds. When the consolidation of the two companies came, the $21,460,000 of par value could be eliminated because it figured among the assets of one company and the liabilities of the other. But the remaining thirty-nine millions had to be carried over into the accounts of the consolidated company, and. since there was no stock left upon which to put this valuation. there was nothing to do, practically, but to add this to the old Railroad Company's valuation of its properties, resulting in the figure given in the balance sheet for 1906, namely, $117,303,979.

Thus we account for the one great change in the Alton's schedule of assets. It came about through the consolidation of the properties accounts of the too formerly distinct companies and the elimination of the par value of the securities which were common to the two balance sheets. On the other hand, that part of the old Railroad Company's stock which was held by the public would naturally be represented in the consolidated balance sheet; its place was taken by an equal amount of "prior lien" stock; this accounts for the apparent stock increase of $899,300. Similarly its outstanding bonds, which amounted to $45,350,000, would appear in the consolidated balance sheet, as also would the stocks of subsidiary companies whose dividends were guaranteed by the old Railroad Company and which stocks were carried by it in its own balance sheet.

The above account illustrates a method by which a corporation could inflate its capitalization, even if stock watering were absolutely forbidden by the laws of every State and of the nation; that is, the capitalization could be inflated without the appearance of stock watering, and be done legally so long as consolidations or the merging of the identities of two or more corporations was legal. The first step, whenever the inflation of a certain company's capitalization was desired, would be the formation of another corporation to buy its stock, paying for it by means of its own stock or bonds issued at rates of exchange based upon the par value of the latter as compared with the market value of the former. This step effects the inflation at once, but it is completed by means of the second

214

step, which is to consolidate the two companies into one, substituting one stock issue for the two existing before and of the same amount, par value. This leaves the way clear for similar activities in the future, if they be found desirable.

The above example has given the story of only one year's financial operations of this railway system; a similar procedure could be applied to those of other years. But this will suffice to illustrate a method of procedure in compiling financial history which, though laborious, will give the investigator the satisfaction of feeling, when he has finished, that his interpretation of the company's financial operations has been substantially accurate and exhaustive.

We may conclude this review by presenting the following table showing the growth of the Chicago & Alton's traffic and earnings since 1901:

Year	Passenger-miles per mile of road opera'd	Ten-miles per mile of road operated	Gross earnings per mile $	Operating expenses per mile $	Operating ratio %	Net earnings per mile $
1901	144,500	804,991	9,826	6,084	61.9	3,742
1902	150,702	981,620	10,032	6,550	65.3	3,482
1903	160,424	1,204,698	11,002	7,614	69.2	3,387
1904	188,012	1,201,854	12,484	8,593	66.2	3,891
1905	264,337	1,103,000	12,890	8,684	67.4	4,206
1906	171,061	1,210,611	11,940	8,423	70.5	3,517

From this we see that the volume of traffic carried by the Alton has increased considerably since 1901, namely, about 18 per cent. for the passenger, and 35 per cent. for the freight traffic. The gross earnings have not increased correspondingly, namely, only 21.5 per cent., and have declined at least during the last year. The operating expenses, however, have progressed steadily during all except the last year, taking up a greater and greater proportion of the gross earnings. As a result the net earnings, though increasing at times, have also fallen at times, and were lower in 1906 than they were in 1901. Possibly the Alton is "drying up" again.

The explanation offered by the management for this weakness in earning power is that, although the traffic has increased, the traffic rates have fallen off largely, thus depriving the company of the benefit of its increased business. This is correct, as is shown by the fact that the average receipts per ton-mile from the freight traffic were 7.23 mills in 1901 and only 6.39 mills in 1906. But whatever the explanation, the fact remains that the company's earning power is weak as compared with the requirements upon it. A system which, after paying interest charges and dividends on only its preferred stock, has only $194,973 to carry to its surplus account is not in condition to receive congratulations.

The New England Railroads.

A Review of the Accountants' Analysis of the Reports of the New York, New Haven and Hartford and the Boston and Maine Railroad Systems.

By Thomas Warner Mitchell, Ph.D.
University of Pennsylvania.

Late in July, 1907, there was appointed by the Commonwealth of Massachusetts a commission on commerce and industry. Its duties were to " investigate the present condition and future possibilities of investment in the commonwealth, the present condition and future possibilities of transportation and facilities connected with it, of manufactures, of industries " and to consider legislative, executive or other measures for the exploitation and development of the industries of that commonwealth. Having only until January, 1908, in which to complete its deliberations and make a report to the general court, the commission evidently was compelled to direct its activities along one or two important lines of investigation. The most burning topic of the time was that of the future relations between the New York, New Haven and Hartford and the Boston and Maine Railroad systems—the two great systems of New England. Accordingly this topic was chosen.

A year or so ago the investment world was startled by the news that the New Haven was purchasing the control of the Boston and Maine. In fact the former had purchased 109,948 out of the 302,928 shares of the latter's stock before the General Assembly of Massachusetts stepped in early in 1907, and not only forbade it from acquiring any additional shares, but from voting, prior to July 1, 1908, the shares it already owned. It was recognized, however, that the management of the Boston and Maine was not progressive, that the development of that system was practically at a standstill, and that after all it might be advantageous to consolidate the two great New England railroad systems under a more progressive management. Accordingly this question of consolidation was left open, the New Haven management having the authority to bring it before the Massachusetts

217

Board of Railroad Commissioners at any time prior to July 1, 1908. The New Haven management, however, announced that it did not desire to consolidate with the Boston and Maine outright, although it did desire to retain the stock it already held, this giving it practical, even if not technical control of that system.

It was the desirability of this relationship which the Massachusetts commission chose to investigate. With its recommendations in connection with that subject we are not concerned in this article. However, in the furtherance of its investigations the commission called in two accountants to examine and report upon the financial condition and results of operation of these two railroad systems. One of these. Stephen Little, is an accountant of national reputation. having been prominent in many railroad investigations: it was he, it will be remembered, who startled the investing public with the account of the Atchison's enormous rebates during the three years prior to the receivership of 1893.

The report of these accountants, which is appended to that of the commission itself, is an interesting document. It is an illustration of what every investor who is imbued with a little common sense might do for himself by carefully analyzing the reports which the various railroad companies make to their stockholders, for the accountants drew all of their data from the annual reports of the two companies to their stockholders, to the Interstate Commerce Commission, and to the Railroad Commissioners of Massachusetts and Connecticut, all of which are available to the investor.

This report is also a good illustration of the limitations under which an accountant works. The method of investigation is primarily the statistical method of the accountant. The principal exhibits consist of a condensed general balance sheet of each system and a statement of earnings and expenses. Each is comparative in form, comparing the data for 1907 with that of 1900 or 1901. Each is accompanied by schedules, either tabulating the changes which have occurred during the six years or explaining in detail some item which has been presented in summary form in the balance sheet or income account. But all of these schedules represent information to obtain which one need not go outside of the books of account themselves and the auxiliary statistical records which accompany them. The accountants can say nothing about the actual physical condition of the two properties, whether it is such as to lend itself to economical operation; for they have neither inspected these properties themselves, nor (since they could not be expected to form a valid judgment concerning the condition of the properties even if they did have the requisite time to inspect them personally) have they obtained the certificates of competent engineers concerning their condition. Indeed, since the accountants have not themselves made an audit of the books of the two systems but have drawn their data almost wholly from the three sources mentioned above, the nearest they come to this is in the certificate of the accountants who audited the New Haven accounts for the annual report of 1907, to the effect that that company's "balance sheet and relative exhibits are properly drawn up, so as to show the true financial condition of the combined companies, and that the statements of income and profit and loss are correct."

219

Let us go into the accountants' analysis in some detail. One of the principal points to which the inquiring investor will turn his attention, especially when trying to decide whether or not the policy of the existing management is progressive, consists of the changes in the balance sheet from one point of time to another. For, when these are properly explained, they reveal the activities of this management in the line of expansion and improvement of its lines and equipment, the sources of funds with which these activities are carried on, and the company's policy in regard to the expansion of its capital stock and funded debt. The following summary of changes in the balance sheet of the New Haven system between the years 1900 and 1907 is reproduced:

RESOURCES TO BE ACCOUNTED FOR.

Decrease in Assets.

H. R. & P. C. R. R. Co.	$5,646,212
N. Y., P. & B. and O. C. R. R. Term Co.	1,531,587
Terminal lands at Providence	756,117
Dedham and Hyde Park improvements	99,623
Due from companies and individuals	1,423,096
Stock of leased lines (not merged) exchanged for stock of N. Y., N. H. & H. R. R.	14,399,291
Stocks owned	6,860.353
Bonds owned	2,291,033
Advances on acct., Dartmouth St. Station, etc.	3,987,265
Property, South St., N. Y.	90,000
Prepaid insurance, taxes, etc.	51,827
	$37,136,404

Increases in Liabilities.

Capital Stock	$42,395,000
Outstanding stock subsidiary companies	280,400
N. Y., N. H. and H. Debentures, including debentures assumed of merged roads	146,965,400
Debentures of subsidiary companies	24,173,000
N. Y., N. H. & H. bonded debt, including debt assumed of merged roads	32,399,000
Bonded debt of subsidiary companies	25,232,000
Reserve for equipment and personal property taken over with leases	8,630,462
Traffic balances	1,811,440
Audited vouchers	1,137,787
Bills payable	3,077,700
Miscellaneous accounts payable	887,479
Unpaid wages	208,755
Reserve for insurance and accident claims	751,043
Interest due or accrued	3,093,562
Dividends due or accrued	2,461,028
Taxes accrued	16,461
Insurance fund	1,077,847
Accident and casualty fund	148,146
N. H. & Northampton Sinking Fund	884,779
Ct. Vy. Ry. & Lightg. Co., sinking fund, etc.	260,982
Providence Securities Co., guaranty fund	490,327

$296,322,598

Increase in profit and loss ... 5,215,907

Grand Total ... $338,674,909

Accounted for as Follows:

Increase in assets.

Cost of properties	$137,695,833
Equipment	47,752,967
Investments of stocks of leased companies (not controlled)	9,192,362
Other investments	38,653,335
Real estate in Boston and New York, held for sale	5,210,000
Expenditures for additions and betterments to properties leased	7,835,867
Materials, fuel, and other supplies	2,547,847
Agents' and conductors' balances	1,945,735
Traffic balances	264,794
Miscellaneous accounts	3,611,025
Bills receivable	14,034,589
Marketable bonds and stocks	5,273,791
Deferred payments on subscriptions to debentures	22,327,619
Cash	11,286,996
Insurance fund (at cost)	704,415
N. H. & Northampton, sinking fund, at cost	884,779
H. R. & P. C. R. R., first mortgage, special deposit	736,600
Maine Steamship Co., sinking fund	95,824
New London Steamboat Co., first mtg., bonds, etc	166,440
Ct. Ry. & Lighting Co., sinking fund	186,640
Woonsocket St. Ry. Co., bond redemption fund	10,000
Prepaid Insurance, pier rentals, etc	232,697
Betterments to piers	180,671

$310,931,806

Decrease in Liabilities.

Convertible debenture certificates, due 1908.....	$16,397,200
Debentures (non-convertible 50-year, 4%)	3,000,000
First mtg. 4% bonds, N. Y., N. H. & H., due 1903	2,000,000
First mtg. 4% bonds, N. Y., P. & B. R. R., due 1901	300,000
Genl. mtg. 4% bonds, N. Y., P. & B. R. R., due 1942	1,000,000
First mtg. 4½% bonds, Housatonic R. R........	100,000
Consol mtg. 5% bonds, Housatonic R. R., due 1937	3,839,000
Rentals, leased lines accrued	7,767
Matured interest coupons unpaid	1,260
Loans account of B. & P. R. R................	1,625,625
Dividends not called for	2,068
Rentals leased lines due July 1, 1900...........	3,000
Accrued interest, not due....................	267,183
	$27,743,103

Grand Total accounted for $338,674,909

The above tabulation is preparatory to the real investigation of the changes in the balance sheet. The first schedule with its total of $338,674,609 represents in a bookkeeping way the sources of funds which were expended upon the items deailed in the second schedule. Apparently all the funds are accounted for, since the totals of the two schedules are the same. But this is to be expected and is merely formal, since we are dealing with double entry bookkeeping; the two schedules constitute merely a condensed trial balance of the intervening years' operations and adjustments of accounts. The real investigation comes in the explanation of the important changes depicted in these two schedules.

To begin with, a point not clearly brought out by the accountants, many of these changes represent merely bookkeeping adjustments. In 1900 a large portion of the New Haven's lines were leased, but since that company did not own all their stock, they were not merged with the lines of the New Haven proper. For this reason their assets and their obligations in the hands of the general public were omitted from the balance sheet of that year. Between 1900 and 1907 some of these lines were merged. Again, in 1907, it was decided, for purpose of giving information to the stockholders, to include the assets and liabilities not only of the leased roads not merged, but of railroads, street railways, and the like, not leased but controlled through stock ownership and operated as a part of the New Haven system. These changes expand the items in the balance sheet and necessitate many bookkeeping adjustments without representing any real additions or improvements to the New Haven's properties.

These bookkeeping adjustments account for the greater portion of the decrease, amounting to $37,136,404, in certain assets. Supplementary explanatory schedules given by the accountants show that the "cost of properties" of the New Haven proper was increased, through the purchase of real estate, already constructed road, and new construction, to the extent of $24,203,457. And a further examination of these schedules reveals the fact that the remainder of the one hundred and thirty-eight million dollar increase in "cost of properties" is due to bringing into the balance sheet the following items: (1) steam railroads controlled by stock ownership and operated as a part of the New Haven system, but not merged, $46,031,988; (2) steam railroads leased to New Haven, but not controlled, $300,489; (3) wharf and freight terminals in Boston, $3,033,742; (4) street railways merged with New Haven, $26,807,485; (5) street railways controlled and operated as a part of the system, but not merged, $17,906,088; (6) steamship properties owned or controlled and operated as part of the system, $6,193,006; (7) lighting and power companies controlled and operated as a part of the system, but not merged, $2,163,049; (8) investment in Millbrook Co. (N. Y. and Port Chester and N. Y., West Chester and Boston railway companies), $10,995,000; miscellaneous properties, $101,600—Total, $113,492,376.

So far so good. The above shows that only a minor portion of the balance sheet changes is due to expansion and improvement of the New Haven properties proper. But what portion, if any, of the above detailed adjustments represent improvements to those subsidiary properties or what portion of those properties themselves have been brought into the system since 1901 we are unable to ascertain Presumably most of the steam roads were in the system in 1901, since the total of this mileage inclusive of trackage rights increased only 22 miles during these six years, while exclusive of trackage rights, this mileage actually decreased by two miles. What portion of the street railway and other properties was included in the system in 1900 or 1901 we are not told.

Now, for the increase in the "cost of properties" of the New Haven proper, namely, $24,203,457. The accountants' analysis of this shows that $19,012,671 represents the purchase of road already constructed, $7,696,055 represents new construction, $7,806,089 represents the purchase of real estate and $733,476

represents personal property of leased roads "taken up as a liability and charged to cost of properties." The first item represents in large part, probably, the merger with the New Haven of
lines which formerly were included in the system by means of
leases, but were not then controlled through stock ownership,
subsequent purchase of stock enabling the merger to be made.
To the extent to which this is true, this addition to the cost of
properties would not represent added mileage. Against these we
find credits of $11,044,834. Most of the latter consists of an item
of $8,880,137 which was credited to "cost of properties" and
added to the equipment account: the purpose of this adjustment
was to make the book value of the equipment agree with its
appraised value as ascertained in a re-valuation made in 1903-4
and again in 1906-7. Making allowance for this adjustment, the
net increase in the "cost of properties" was $33,083,594.

The accountants do not analyze the expenditures for new construction. As shown above, the total main track mileage of steam
roads of the system decreased by two miles between 1901 and
1907. This includes the leased and controlled mileage as well
as that of the New Haven Company proper. However, the mileage of second, third and fourth main track increased by 87 miles,
while that of sidings and yard tracks increased by 149 miles,
making a total net increase of 121 miles of main track and 270
miles of all track. Assuming that this is all new construction, it
represents an average cost per mile of single main track of
$51,560. Just where the new mileage is located, what it repre-
sents, what it really cost and the like, the accountants do not tell
us: for, as before stated, the accountants confine their attention
to the books, which deal with book values and not the physical
facts.

The cost of equipment increased $47,752,967. It has already
been shown that $8,880,137 of this consists of a book adjustment.
We are led to infer that the New Haven has been improving
and increasing its equipment, charging a large part of the cost
thereof to maintenance. Thus, when the equipment was re-valued,
the above discrepancy appeared between the appraised and the
book value. The management chose to credit that amount to
"cost of properties," however, rather than add it to the surplus.

During the seven-year period the management bought new
equipment to the value of about $9,845,800. The management

also adjusted this account by adding to it $8,852,366, representing the value of the " equipment of leased roads at the time of the leases and for which the New Haven was liable to the lessors, thus being taken into the books of the New Haven in the years 1906 and 1907, both as an asset and a liability." With minor differences these account for $27,531,146 of the total increase in equipment. According to another explanatory schedule, to represent this there is an increase between the years 1901 and 1907, of 254 locomotives, 6,861 freight cars and 377 passenger cars. At an average cost of $10,000 per locomotive, $1,000 per freight car and $5,000 per passenger car, this would represent an expenditure of $10,286,000, as compared with the $9,845,800 mentioned a few lines back. Of course, a large part of the latter amount may represent equipment, not of steam lines, but of street railway lines merged with the New Haven properties; the expenditures are not analyzed for us. Naturally the equipment of leased lines was already included in the equipment statistics, even if its cost was not on the books in 1900. The inclusion in the 1907 balance sheet of the equipment of street railways and steamships amounting to $6,458,237 and $13,763,583, respectively, accounts for the remainder of the total increase stated at the outset of the preceding paragraph. Again we have no means of knowing how much of this was in the system in 1900 and how much has been added since.

224

While we are discussing these changes in cost of properties, we should mention the fact that, as will be shown latter in the income account, the New Haven appropriated for betterments in 1906 the sum of $3,326,998, charging the same against surplus earnings of that year. Further, during the period 1901 to 1907, both inclusive, the management expended for betterments, improvements and new equipment the sum of $16,861,439, charging the cost of the same against the profit and loss (surplus) account. Of this $11,038,513 was spent in 1904 and 1906, according to the reports for new equipment. Unless either our estimate of the added equipment, made in the preceding paragraph is grossly understated, or the expenditures were almost wholly for street railway equipment, it is difficult to see where there is room for these charges to profit and loss for new equipment. The reader will also recall the adjustments made in the same two years by which a total of $8,880,137 was added to the equipment account, though credited not to profit and loss, but to cost of properties.

The next important change in the assets of the New Haven is the increase of $38,653,335 in " other investments." This is composed principally of the following items: (1) $29,102,200 par value of N. Y., Ontario and Western stock carried at a book valuation of $13, 108,398; (2) about $15,000,000 par value of the shares and income bonds of the Central New England Railway, carried at a book value of $6,500,366; and (3) $10,994,800 par value of Boston and Maine common stock, valued on the books at $12,855,984. It is for the purpose of deciding whether it is advisable to permit the New Haven to retain the last named stock that the the commission's investigation was made. Possession of the New York, Ontario and Western stock insures the New Haven a certain amount of the traffic which otherwise might go by way of the Boston and Albany, a New York Central line or even through the port of New York rather than Boston. We need not dwell on these any longer than did the accountants except to say that the prices paid for these stocks do not seem to be excessive.

225

The large increase in cash and the item " Deferred payments on subscriptions to debentures " represent recent sales of debenture bonds and of stock.

How were these activities financed? As already shown, about $5,000,000 represent reclassifications of accounts already in the balance sheet of 1901. Other than this, the principal sources of funds seem to have been the increases in: (1) capital stock, $42,395,000; (2) N. Y., N. H. & H. debentures, $146,965,400; (3) debentures of subsidiary companies, $24,173,-000; (4) N. Y., N. H. & H. bonded debt, $32,399,000; (5) bonded debt of subsidiaries, $25,232,000; (6) reserve for equipment and personal property of leased lines, $8,630,462; (7) and profit and loss (surplus), $5,215,907. The item of $16,861,439 charged to profit and loss representing betterments, improvements and new equipment, has already been mentioned. The third, fifth and sixth items are included in the book adjustments whereby the assets and liabilities of subsidiary controlled and leased lines were incorporated in the balance sheet.

It seems that a very large portion of the second and fourth items is to be explained in the same way. For instance, in 1905 as in 1900, the bonded debt of certain subsidiaries shown in the balance sheet was $4,139,000. That of the New Haven proper was $7,865,000 in 1905, this having grown up in two years. In 1906 none of these appears separately, having been combined in the one item " N. Y., N. H. & H. bonded debt, including bonded debt assumed of merged roads," which, however, is stated at $20,043,000. How much of this represents new bonds issued in 1906 and how much the bonds of additional roads merged with the New Haven we are not told. The same item reaches in 1907 the figures named in the preceding paragraph. Again the New Haven debentures in 1905 amounted to $25,185,300, no debentures being stated for subsidiaries; in 1906 these are replaced by the item " N. Y.. N. H. & H. debentures, including debentures of merged roads." which has jumped to $70,315,725 and attains the figure $146.965,000 by 1907. It is altogether probable that a considerable portion of this increase reperesents these adjustments; but just what portion we are unable to ascertain.

The accountants furnish us with a detailed statement of the uses to which the new stock has been put. The total new stock issued was $42,395,000. while $1,293,600 of stock held in the treasury in 1900 had also been sold, making a total of $43,688,600. Of this, $10,994,800 was issued in exchange for an equal amount par value of Boston and Maine stock, $16,211,900 for an equal amount of N. Y., N. H. & H. convertible debenture certificates, $5,546,000 in exchange for other securities and terminal lands, while $9,935,900 was sold for cash to finance the acquisition of other stocks and bonds, pay off temporary loans and maturing first mortgage bonds. pay for additional rolling stock, floating equipment, etc.

So much for the changes in the balance sheet of the New Haven. We need not dwell long upon the corresponding activities of the Boston and Maine. That company's balance sheet in no case includes the assets or liabilities of its leased properties, although the income account includes the results of the entire system. Making allowance even for the adjustments on the New Haven's books, the exhibit for the Boston and Maine show nothing like the activities which have been carried on by the former. The latter has increased its stock only $5,969,440 since 1900, its funded debt by only $9,156,166 and its profit and loss (surplus) by $6,977,286. To represent these its cost of road has been in-

226

The New England Railroads.

	New Haven 1907	New Haven 1901	Boston & Maine 1907	Boston & Maine 1901	Increase 1907 over 1908 N. H.	Increase 1907 over 1908 B. & M.
Passenger earnings	26,758,029	19,853,093	15,623,495	12,526,160	6,905,836	3,097,335
Freight	28,386,704	19,864,701	25,212,843	18,210,599	8,522,003	7,002,244
Miscellaneous	456,303	414,517	288,918	70,078	41,786	218,840
Total earnings, steam roads	55,601,936	40,132,311	41,125,256	30,806,837	15,469,625	10,318,419
Operating expenses, steam roads	37,850,082	28,048,479	30,968,397	21,518,785	9,801,603	9,449,612
Net earnings, steam roads	17,751,854	12,083,832	10,156,859	9,288,052	5,668,022	868,807
Net earnings, street railways and steamships, and income from other investment	6,328,901	562,560	704,359	568,783	5,766,341	135,576
Total income	4,080,755	12,640,392	10,861,218	9,856,835	11,434,363	1,004,383
Taxes, steam railroads	2,025,548	2,367,035	1 674,836	1,547,315	557,913	127,521
Taxes, street railways and steamships	666,688				666,688	......
Interest, rentals, sinking funds and other charges	11,595,478	5,620,460	6,587,187	6,619,107	5,975,009	31,920
Total fixed charges and taxes	15,187,714	7,988,104	8,262,023	8,166,422	7,199,610	95,601
Net divisible income	8,893,041	4,658,288	2,599,195	1,690,413	4,234,753	908,782
Preferred dividends			2,188,988	188,988		
Common dividends	6,904,988	4,204,738	1,784,344	1,456,012	2,610,250	328,331
Surplus income	1,988,053	363,550	625,863	45,413	1,624,503	508,450
Additions and betterments charged to income			493,49			493,249
Remaining surplus income for year	1,988,053	363,550	132,614	45,413	1,624,503	87,201

227

313

creased to $8,316,388, its cost of equipment, $7,849,191 and its stocks and bonds owned, $3,973,976. The Boston and Maine has charged only $493,249 against surplus income to represent betterments and additions, and nothing to profit and loss (surplus) for betterments and new equipment. In other words the cost of any improvements or additions to properties which may have been made during these seven years has been religiously capitalized; and, even at that, the company's activities in this direction are so slight as to indicate that the development of its system is practically at a standstill.

Let us now direct our attention to the income accounts of the two systems and follow the interesting comparison made by the accountants. The comparative statement for the two systems shown on the preceding page is reproduced, with slight abridgment, from the accountants' report.

This is accompanied by a supplemental table showing the totals of the main items of the foregoing table for each road for each of the years 1901 to 1907, inclusive. In another connection the accountants show that in 1907 the New Haven's fixed charges amounted to 63.1% of the total income from all sources, leaving only 36.9% of this income as a margin of safety. For the Boston and Maine the percentages are even less favorable, being 76% and 24%, respectively. The accountants make no comment upon these figures. It is generally held, however, that for the fixed charges to exceed 50% or at most 55% of total income is an unfavorable sign unless the company's volume of traffic and earnings are very steady. In another exhibit the accountants do reproduce some data concerning the traffic. They show that for each mile of road operated the New Haven carried 637,475 tons of freight one mile in 1901 and 835,693 tons in 1907; the Boston and Maine carried during the same year, 681,585 tons and 1,024,473 tons, respectively. For each mile of road operated the New Haven carried 468,140 passengers one mile in 1901 and 665,729 passengers in 1907; the Boston and Maine carried 280,233 and 340,091 passengers, respectively, during the same years. Thus, considering the whole period, the traffic of each system has greatly increased in density. The density of New Haven's freight traffic has increased 46.9%, while that of its passenger traffic has increased 42.2%; the corresponding percentages for the Boston and Maine are 50.2 and 21.4, respectively.

Three criticisms are to be placed upon these, however: First, the data for intervening years is not furnished although this was available to the accountants; second, the period covered is too short, covering merely a period of general prosperity, similar data for years of depression should be examined, to see how the volume and density of traffic have varied; third, this data is not brought into organic connection with the subject upon which it bears, namely, the steadiness of earnings and the margin above fixed charges.

To complete the accountants' analysis we give the following information concerning the proportion of each system's income which is required to meet fixed charges. For the New Haven the average proportion of fixed charges to total income for the period of 1901 to 1907, inclusive, was 58.9%; the percentages for the years in order were 63.2; 62.8; 62.6; 56.6; 56.4; 48.9 and 63.1. Thus we see a rapid decline in the proportion until 1906 when it was below 50%, while all this ground was lost in just the last year, 1907. The system's balance sheet for 1906 shows a net increase in the funded debt amounting to $77,052,235 while that for 1907 shows a still further increase of $117,242,891. These increases are due, as already shown, partly to consolidations with merged roads, partly to the fact that the New Haven has taken onto its books the liabilities of subsidiary companies which it controls through stock ownership. Thus the company's reports show fixed charges which existed before but which had not been reported formerly. To a large extent, however, these were represented in the earlier reports by rentals which would disappear, as such, in the later report the interest on the bonds of subsidiaries being substituted for them.

For the Boston and Maine, the average proportion of fixed charges to total income for the same seven-year period was 80.9%; the percentages for the individual years 1901 to 1907 in order were 82.6; 82.1; 81.8; 81.5 ;80.4 and 76.0. Thus the Boston and Maine uses nearly 81% of its total income to pay fixed charges; the decline to 76% occurred practically in the one year 1907.

On a very important point the accountants do not touch, although they furnish the necessary data. That is the proportion of net divisible income which is left as a margin to assure the payment of dividends. In 1901 the New Haven had only

229

$363.550 of its earnings left after paying dividends. This is only 7.8% of the net divisible income, 2.9% of the total income and 9/10% of the gross earnings; had the gross earnings been 1.3% less the dividend would not have been earned. During the entire seven-year period the New Haven accumulated a surplus of $7,057,073, which is 15.3% of the net divisible income, 6.3% of the total income, and 2.1% of the gross earnings. From this it is seen that a very small reduction in gross earnings due to the business depression or other causes would have left the New Haven's 8% dividend not earned.

The above assumes both that the New Haven has adequately maintained its property and that it has not actually improved its property charging the cost thereof to maintenance. The accountants draw a comparison which is intended to show that the latter is precisely what the company has been doing. Of this more anon.

The Boston and Maine's showing on this point is even worse. In 1901 after paying 7% dividends only $45,413 remained out of the year's income; that is but 2.7% of the net divisible income, 46/100% of the total income and 15/100% of the gross earnings. Had the gross earnings been 1/5% smaller the dividend would not have been earned; a very small difference in the expenditures for maintenance even would have made the difference between an earned and unearned dividend. Taking the period as a whole we find that the Boston and Maine has accumulated a surplus of $1,080,484 which is 8% of the net divisible income, 1.5% of the total income or 4/10% of the gross earnings. While this average showing is better than that of the single year just mentioned, yet it still shows that a very small reduction in gross earnings would leave the 7% dividend unearned and possibly necessitate its reduction. Assuming that the Boston and Maine's properties have been adequately maintained and kept up to date, of which we are by no means sure, the company would need a traffic as strong and steady as the Rock of Gibraltar to enable it to continue its present rate of dividends during a period of depression.

Let us deal now with the very important item of maintenance. The accountants do not tell us whether either system has been adequately maintained. An interesting comparison is drawn, however, between the New Haven's expenditures for this purpose and those of the Boston and Maine. Assuming that the character of roadbed, bridges, gradients, curves, *et cetera,* of the two systems were substantially alike, tables of average expenses are shown of which the following are the essential fragments:

	Average Maintenance Expenses per mile of main track owned and leased.		Average Maintenance Expenses per mile of all track owned and leased.	
YEAR	NEW HAVEN	BOSTON&MAINE	NEW HAVEN	BOSTON&MAINE
1901	$1,947	$1,238	$1,378	$866
1902	2,187	2,439	1,537	1,005
1903	2,214	1,317	1,549	918
1904	1,940	1,370	1,350	954
1905	1,795	1,614	1,244	1,125
1906	1,952	1,029	1,353	1,333
1907	1,891	1,759	1,302	1,207
Ave...	$1,988	$1,525	$1,386	$1,059

It appears that the New Haven's maintenance of way expenses are uniformly much greater than those of the Boston and Maine. On the basis of main trackage it averages $463 per mile more per annum or over 30%. Now, argue the accountants, assuming that the Boston and Maine properties have been adequately maintained, this difference is equivalent to an excess expenditure by the New Haven amounting to $9,221,000 for the eight-year period. Of this more anon.

In like manner we find the following statistics of maintenance of equipment:

	Average Expenses per Locomotive per Year.		Average Expenses per Freight Car per Year.		Average Expenses per Passenger Car.	
YEAR	NEW HAVEN	BOSTON & MAINE	NEW HAVEN	BOSTON & MAINE	NEW HAVEN	BOSTON & MAINE
1901	$1,512	$1,476	$77.70	$59.30	$715	$488
1902	1,868	1,251	122.30	59.60	613	470
1903	1,569	1,185	52.00	47.10	490	508
1904	1,827	1,379	58.60	60.20	413	495
1905	1,927	1,812	54.10	63.30	472	516
1906	2,116	1,942	60.30	58.90	527	564
1907	1,838	1,623	63.70	55.80	521	636
Ave...	$1,841	$1,531	$68.10	$58.40	$532	$527

231

Again it appears that the New Haven's maintenance expenses were, with the exception of the passenger equipment, uniformly much higher than those of the Boston and Maine. Summing up, the accountants state that during these seven years: (1) the New Haven charged in operating expenses for repairs and renewals of locomotives an average of $310 per locomotive per year more than did the Boston and Maine, which is equivalnet to an excess expenditure of $2,249,050 on 7,255 locomotives in use; (2) the New Haven charged in operating expenses for repairs and renewals of freight cars an average of $9.70 per car per year more than did the Boston and Maine, which is equivalent to an excess expenditure of $1,060,666 on the 109,347 cars in use; (3) the New Haven charged in operating expenses for repairs and renewals of passenger cars an average of $5 more per car per year than did the Boston and Maine, which is equivalent to an excess of $69,645 on the 13,929 cars in use; (4) the New Haven charged in operating expenses for maintenance of way an average of $463 per main track per year more than did the Boston and Maine, which is equivalent to an excess expenditure of $9,221,000.

Thus the New Haven's total excess expenditure for maintenance of its properties is estimated at $12,600,000. As the accountants put it, if the New Haven had taken the Boston and Maine's expenditures as standard, they would have added $12,600,000 to their net income during these seven years, making the surplus $19,657,000 instead of $7,057,074.

We may well agree that if the accountants' premise is true, then all these statements are true of the New Haven. But are we warranted in assuming that the Boston and Maine has adequately maintained its properties? We have shown in the above analysis that in paying its seven per cent. dividends the Boston and Maine has had left each year but a thin margin of income—so thin that a reduction of the gross earning to the extent of a fractional part of one per cent. would have left the dividend unearned. Can we feel assured that the dividend was earned? Is it not likely that, had the company found its earnings insufficient in any year, it would have charged to "cost of properties" every item of expenditure which could possibly be construed to be a capital expenditure, even though it would not clearly increase the economy of operation? Indeed we have already seen that the company has not made a single betterment at the expense of its surplus account, that it has charged but a paltry sum in a single year against surplus earnings to represent betterments, that it has religiously added the cost of all improvements and extensions to its capital accounts. What assurance have we that the last named costs really represent improvements and extensions in their entirety? Is it not reasonable to suppose that in its finely drawn classification of expenditures as capital or maintenance the company would show a small surplus of earnings after the dividend was paid, even though a conservative classification would result in a deficit instead? When a company habitually skates on such thin ice, the rational man thinks it probable that it breaks through in places. In other words, we can not believe that the Boston and Maine properties are in first class operating condition, and have been maintained at their former standard at the expense of earnings, without a certificate to that effect from competent engineers who have inspected them.

233

This being the case, the accountants' strong statements concerning the over maintenance of the New Haven's properties should be very much modified. If they really have been improved. this should show in economy of operation in the company's ability to carry the same volume of traffic at a less cost per unit than before, or a greater volume at a greater decrease in cost per unit than would have occurred without the improvements. The last is impossible of measurement, of course. Up to a certain point— the point of full utilization of existing properties and equipment every increase in the volume of traffic means a decreased cost per unit of handling. Hence, where there has been an increase of traffic, as happened with every important railroad in the United States between 1901 and 1907. it is impossible to separate that economy of operation which is due to the larger traffic from that which is due to improvements in the facilities.

Unfortunately, most companies do not publish statistics of ton mile and passenger mile cost. But the income statement reproduced above shows that while the New Haven's gross earnings increased $15,469,625 or 37.6 per cent. from 1901 to 1907, the operating expenses increased only $9,801,603 or 31.6 per cent., leaving an increase in the net earnings at $5,668,022 or 55.8 per cent. This is a good showing although, as stated above, it is impossible to say how much is due to the larger traffic and how much to improvements. It is possible that considerable improvements have been made. The charges of nearly $17,000,000 to profit and loss for alleged betterments and purchases of new equipment are a possible argument to that effect, although, as before stated, it is difficult to find sufficient added equipment to account for the sum claimed to have been spent. We can not arrive at any definite conclusion on this point.

In conclusion, the accountants' report will well repay the investor's perusal, because it shows how much valuable information an intelligent analysis can extract from railway reports. Barring a few instances in which the accountants did not make as full use of their data as they might, their work has been as well done as is possible where the investigation is limited to the data found in the financial and statistical books or annual reports. Whether or not we can agree with the accountants in assuming that the Boston and Maine's maintenance expenditures can be taken as a standard for New England roads, their comparison does show that the management of the New Haven is the much more progressive and much to be preferred.

For Product Safety Concerns and Information please contact our
EU representative GPSR@taylorandfrancis.com Taylor & Francis
Verlag GmbH, Kaufingerstraße 24, 80331 München, Germany